Inside *Bluebeard's Castle*

Inside *Bluebeard's Castle*

∾ *Music and Drama in*
Béla Bartók's Opera

Carl S. Leafstedt

New York   Oxford

Oxford University Press

1999

Oxford University Press

Oxford   New York

Athens   Auckland   Bangkok   Bogotá   Buenos Aires   Calcutta
Cape Town   Chennai   Dar es Salaam   Delhi   Florence   Hong Kong   Istanbul
Karachi   Kuala Lumpur   Madrid   Melbourne   Mexico City   Mumbai
Nairobi   Paris   São Paulo   Singapore   Taipei   Tokyo   Toronto   Warsaw

and associated companies in
Berlin   Ibadan

Library of Congress Cataloging-in-Publication Data
Leafstedt, Carl Stuart.
    Inside Bluebeard's castle : music and drama in
Bartók's opera / Carl S. Leafstedt.
        p. cm.
    Revision of the author's thesis (Ph.D.)
—Harvard University, 1994.
    Includes bibliographical references and index.
    ISBN 0-19-510999-6
    1. Bartók, Béla, 1881-1945.   Kékszakállú herceg vára.
    I. Title.
ML410.B26L43   1999
782.1'092 — dc21   98-40668
                    MN

9 8 7 6 5 4 3 2 1

Printed in the United States of America
on acid-free paper

ACKNOWLEDGMENTS

Among the many who have helped in the preparation of this book, Reinhold Brinkmann and Elliott Antokoletz deserve special recognition for the support and guidance they have offered from the very beginning. It is to Elliott and his enthusiasm for Bartók's music that I owe my interest in *Bluebeard's Castle*, and he has remained a valued sounding board for ideas ever since. Reinhold supervised with patience, wisdom, and discernment the initial completion of these thoughts in doctoral dissertation form. The following pages, now thoroughly revised, owe much to his example as a musicologist, and to his abiding interest in music's broader cultural context. Thanks also are due to Judit Frigyesi, Malcolm Gillies, and László Somfai, who pointed me to important documentary information and whose comments on the book's general scope helped shape its final form. To Judit I am particularly grateful for her close reading of the entire manuscript.

The process of gathering together the source material necessary for this study of Bartók's opera was facilitated by grant from the International Research and Exchange Board for research in Hungary. At the Budapest Bartók Archive Adrienne Gombocz and László Vikárius helped me locate unpublished letters from Balázs to Bartók in the collections. Their courtesy and helpfulness during this and other visits to the Archive made my time in Hungary unfailingly pleasant. Peter Laki reviewed many pages of my translations with a sharp eye for detail and deep understanding of the difficulties involved in rendering Balázs's richly imagined, stylized prose into English. Additional help was provided by Adrienne Vikárius, Gábor Kiss, Laurie Shulman, and Thomas Kozachek. Special thanks go also to Faye and Bill Montgomery of San Antonio, Texas, for the countless hours of child care they offered to my son Wendell as the book was being written; they stepped in as only grandparents can.

Musicologists who work with Bartók's autograph scores today inevitably turn to Peter Bartók, the composer's son, for help obtaining primary source material. His collection in Homosassa, Florida, includes all of what used to be known as Bartók's American estate. Unfailingly prompt in his replies, and generous in ways too numerous to mention here, Peter Bartók has made available to me the many letters and *Bluebeard* scores in his possession, without which my study of the opera's revisions would not have been possible. He furnished, and gave permission to reproduce, the two facsimiles included in this book. I gratefully acknowledge his support.

When *Bluebeard's Castle* was published in 1921 it appeared with a dedication from Bartók to his wife Márta. This gesture, I believe, was not intended as a wry comment on the state of their marriage, as it usually is taken, but instead as a sincere expression of gratitude for her help and support during the long period before the opera saw the light of day. In a similar spirit I would like to dedicate this book to my wife Ann, who read countless drafts of individual chapters as they moved toward completion and who gave me the type of support and understanding every writer should enjoy when working on a project of this magnitude.

An earlier version of Chapter 2 was published under the title "*Bluebeard* as Theater: The Influence of Maeterlinck and Hebbel on Balázs's Bluebeard Drama" in a volume of essays produced in association with Bard College's 1995 Bartók and His World festival (Peter Laki, ed., *Bartók and His World* [Princeton, N.J.: Princeton University Press, 1995]). Chapter 7 appeared, in condensed form, in the proceedings of the 1995 International Bartók Colloquium held in Szombathely, Hungary ("Judith in *Bluebeard's Castle*: The Significance of a Name," in *Studia Musicologica* 36, nos. 3–4 [1995]: 429–47).

CONTENTS

⎯ PART III. CONTEXTUAL STUDIES

Inside *Bluebeard's Castle*

INTRODUCTION

The two decades prior to World War I embraced a period of tremendous vitality in the creative arts in Hungary. As in the rest of Europe, a brilliant array of minds blossomed during this period, challenging accepted modes of expression in literature, music, drama, and the visual arts, and creating a multitude of strongly defined, individual styles. Figures like the poet Endre Ady, the painters Róbert Berény and Károly Kernstock, musicians Béla Bartók, Ernő Dohnányi, and Zoltán Kodály, author Ferenc Molnár, and writer/philosopher Georg Lukács all experienced their formative years in the first decade of the twentieth century, lending their voices to the early modernist strivings of that era. The members of this "generation of 1900," as they have sometimes been called, reacted in various complex ways to the society that surrounded them, often revealing dissatisfaction with the cultural values held by the bourgeois, industrial society of which they were a part. In many respects, the issues that engaged them paralleled the issues that engaged creative artists all over Europe: the relationship between the sexes, the role of the artist in society, and the creation of a unique personal style.

Interwoven in the fabric of works from this period, we find evidence of the increasingly strong sense of Hungarian national identity that began to emerge at the end of the nineteenth century as a result of sociopolitical tensions within Hungary. In 1900, Hungary was still a part of the Habsburg Austro-Hungarian Empire. Though not fully independent, the Hungarian nation possessed its own system of parliamentary government and had earned, following the 1867 Compro-

3

mise, a considerable measure of political autonomy from Vienna. What formal ties remained between Hungary and Austria by the turn of the century, however, were showing signs of strain. The emergence of nationalism in Hungarian society took shape in response to Hungary's close historical relationship with Austria; complicating matters was the fact that approximately 50 percent of Hungary's inhabitants belonged to other ethnic groups such as Croatians, Ruthenians, and Slovakians, people who themselves wished for some degree of independence or recognition. All strata of society were affected by the increasingly nationalist stance. For the creative artists of the generation of 1900, the result was that where their predecessors had looked primarily to the West for inspiration, gradually during the decades from 1890 to 1910 these younger creative artists began to turn their attention inward, to their own people and culture. Simón Hollósy moved his celebrated painting school from Munich to the rural Hungarian town of Nagybánya in 1896. Endre Ady moved back to Budapest from Paris to write his poetry. The great millenial celebrations held in Budapest in 1896 refocused the attention of many Hungarians on an element they had previously undervalued: the indigenous peasant culture of their own land. As a result, some began to incorporate peasant or folk motifs into their own artistic work. Ödön Lechner designed his famous Postal Savings Bank and Geological Institute buildings, mingling decorative floral motifs from Hungarian folk art into his secessionist style. Bartók and Kodály began to collect folk song material in rural areas at this time.

The notion that they were contributing to the birth of a new, uniquely Hungarian art style animated these young writers, musicians, and artists. They aided each other's efforts, actively supporting each other's modernist leanings. Organized groups existed, such as the group of postimpressionist painters who called themselves "The Eight," and the short-lived "New Hungarian Music Society," founded by Bartók and Kodály in 1911. Informal levels of support were more typical, however. At exhibitions of new art, Ady would read poetry, Bartók would play the piano, and the event would receive coverage by sympathetic journalists; a few months later, Lukács, in his role of generational voice, would write an extensive analysis of the whole affair, to be published in the leading literary journals of the day. A palpable sense of community and support existed among these young Hungarian modernists.

One of the more enduring artistic creations to emerge from this period is Béla Bartók's one-act opera *Duke Bluebeard's Castle*, the creation of two Hungarians whose close acquaintance blossomed with unexpected vigor to produce a work that explores a theme deeply personal to both: the loneliness of the human spirit. Temporally and musically, *Bluebeard's Castle* occupies a central position in Bartók's early career. As the first of the three stage works that would consume much of his compositional energy in the years before and during World War I, *Bluebeard* initiated a trend in Bartók's music in which the composer branched out to the more public genres of ballet and opera in an effort both to gain a wider audience for his works and to demonstrate the viability of the new style of Hungarian music he and Kodály, each in his own way, had begun to champion. *Bluebeard* was composed in 1911. It was followed by *The Wooden Prince* in 1914–17 and *The*

Miraculous Mandarin in 1918–19. After composing these works Bartók never returned to the world of musical theater, a decision no doubt facilitated by the frustrations and indifference he encountered in securing staged performances for his opera and pantomime.

Though later in life Bartók encountered relatively little few obstacles to the timely premiere of major compositions, his three stage works all came up against —and, in the case of the *Mandarin*, nearly foundered upon—the reluctant inertia of Budapest's leading musical stage. The Royal Opera House, which since its construction in 1884 had been a grand symbol of Hungarian musical life, initially proved unreceptive to Bartók's stage works, the *Wooden Prince* excepted, and many hurdles had to be overcome before performances could take place. The *Wooden Prince* was produced for the first time on May 12, 1917, to great critical acclaim. Encouraged by its reception, the Opera House entered into production Bartók's other existing stage work, *Bluebeard's Castle*, and on May 24, 1918, the opera received its belated premiere.

For *Bluebeard* the path from creation to first performance was strewn with disappointments of the sort Bartók regularly endured in the mid-1910s. The opera's labored route to the stage actually began at the time of its creation, when Bartók entered it in two separate opera competitions in Budapest. On both occasions it failed to win, a fact made more humiliating by the number of entries for each competition: two. Compounding this disappointment, a stage performance of the play alone, on April 20, 1913, directed by its creator Béla Balázs, with Bartók playing selections from his piano music at intermission, was a complete failure. This latter performance actually marked the public stage debut of *A kékszakállú herceg vára* (literally, *The Bluebearded Duke's Castle*), even though Bartók's music, already written, was not heard. It thus makes a logical entry point into the study of the opera.

In a small Budapest theater rented for the occasion, Balázs cobbled together basic sets, what rudimentary lighting he could find and press into use, and several actors to present *Bluebeard's Castle* in a performance sponsored by *Nyugat* (West), the prominent Hungarian literary journal dedicated to enriching the spirit and style of Hungarian culture through contact with West European models. *Bluebeard* was presented as a strictly theatrical production, on a double bill with another one-act play by Balázs, *A Szent Szűz vére* (The blood of the Blessed Virgin). Bartók, whose operatic version had suffered defeat only the previous summer and fall, introduced some of his new piano compositions during the pause between plays.[1] Balázs later wrote in his diary that

> the performance, especially of *Bluebeard*, was awful. None of the actors understood a word of what they were saying. . . . I was afraid that the set would collapse during the performance like a house of cards. It had been fastened together with safety pins and thumbtacks. *Bluebeard* was downright comical. The lights did not go on, or they did at the wrong time and in the wrong place. The only reason there was no scandal was that the public did not understand what was happening anyway.[2]

Bluebeard's Castle was never again staged as a theater piece. The poor performance and bad reviews stung Balázs. What Bartók thought is unknown. Balázs quickly moved on to other literary projects, abandoning further attempts to bring the *Bluebeard* play to the stage. Five years would pass before Bartók's operatic version was introduced to the Budapest public. Had he not created one of the twentieth century's great operatic scores based on it, *Bluebeard* might have rapidly fallen into the same oblivion that has received the other drama performed that evening.

This single stage performance of *Bluebeard's Castle* in 1913 stands as an important reminder that Balázs viewed his drama as an entirely self-sufficient work in its own right, capable of functioning as an independent work for theater. This status is often forgotten or overlooked by writers exploring the historical background of the *Bluebeard* opera. In general, the reception history of Bartók's opera has not been kind to its libretto. Since its premiere in 1918, the music has been recognized for its greatness, while the play that inspired Bartók to this creation has languished unappreciated in the music's shadow. The greatness of Bartók's music has effectively relegated Balázs's libretto to the status of the music's "handmaiden," to borrow a familiar formulation for the relationship of an operatic text to its music. It provided the springboard for the imagination of a supremely talented composer, the prevailing opinion has run, but was itself not a very good play, an attitude that can still be encountered today. Zoltán Kodály, who knew both Bartók and Balázs intimately, argued in his 1918 review of the opera that such criticism was unwarranted:

> The almost unanimous disapproval [Balázs's libretto] has met with—for which, as a matter of fact, no reasons were given—is apt to create the impression as if the exigencies regarding operatic librettos were in these parts rather high. Yet, our writers do not take the libretto seriously, forgetting that in the golden ages of the opera the words, too, had always been the work of a competent hand. This is why it makes a sensation when a libretto is written by a genuine writer, and even more so in the sense of a dramatic author. So Béla Balázs deserves particular credit for having worked up one of his finest and most poetical conceptions into an opera book, contributing thus to the birth of a genuine *chef d'oeuvre*.[3]

Balázs's libretto, he implies, deserves greater credit for the quality of the opera than it has received. The sureness of its dramatic art and its eloquent treatment of what he goes on to describe as "the eternal insolubility of the man/woman problem" form a vital contribution to the overall work.[4] Unfortunately, such words of praise for Balázs's text have rarely been echoed by other writers. The sense of balance in Kodály's review, where text and music are each evaluated for their part in the creation of a successful opera, has found few counterparts in the flow of criticism and analysis since 1918.[5]

To appreciate Bartók's opera it is necessary to examine closely the text on which it is based. Analysis of music-text relationships, or of the drama's message, cannot take place until a firm understanding of the *Bluebeard* play's structural organization, dialogue style, and theatrical context has been achieved. In the pages of this book, therefore, I will draw freely upon the events of Balázs's career, and his artistic beliefs, in order to cement a foundation for further music and dramatic analysis. By doing so, I am attempting to adopt a broader perspective in opera analysis by considering the work of the dramatist as a subject worthy of attention in and of itself. *Bluebeard's Castle* is the collective work of two young modernists. Balázs's contribution to the opera merits our sustained interest.

In his writings Balázs alternately referred to *Bluebeard's Castle* as a "libretto," an "opera text" (*operaszöveg*), a "drama," a "dramatic scene" (*drámai jelenet*), and a "poem" (*költemény*). He took pains at one point, around 1915, to state specifically, "I did not write the Hungarian original of *Bluebeard's Castle* as a libretto, but simply as poetry, as one is accustomed to writing verse in general."[6] His approach to the *Bluebeard* play exhibited the ambivalence we might expect of a dramatist who sees his work adapted and transformed into a libretto, thereby incurring all the attendant implications of reduced status. He periodically reasserted the play's integrity and self-sufficiency, as if to regain credit for the work and thereby return it to the context of his own dramatic output.

In the following pages, the *Bluebeard* play generally will be referred to as a "play" or "drama" instead of a "libretto." This distinction is intended to restore, in a subtle way, the sense of the drama's integrity as a work for theater. The *Bluebeard* play possesses its own relationship to the time and place in which it was created. The particular nature of its unusual dramatic aesthetic—the static action, frequent pauses, and portentous atmosphere—can be understood only in light of Balázs's interest in the new dramatic trends spreading across Europe in the early twentieth century, about which relatively little has been absorbed into the existing Bartók literature apart from general observations. To some extent, criticism of Bartók's *Bluebeard* opera has been molded by the language barrier that quickly arises for non-Hungarian speakers in search of deeper background material on the opera. Many of Bartók's letters, including some that shed light on the murky chronology of the opera's first years of existence, remain unpublished. Balázs's letters to Bartók, preserved in the Budapest Bartók Archive, suffer a similar fate, to mention nothing of the author's numerous dramas, poems, and other writings dating from the time of *Bluebeard*, almost none of which have been translated into languages other than Hungarian. Lack of accessible information has effectively channeled non-Hungarian speakers into the discussion of Bartók's musical score, rather than into the cultural or historical context in which the score and the play lie enmeshed. This book, it is hoped, will present a broader view.

Carl Dahlhaus has described a category for early-twentieth-century opera called "literature opera," in which a composer adopts "a spoken play unchanged, if abbreviated, as an opera text."[7] In this operatic genre, the literary quality of the play and its ability to provide cohesive dramatic language served to counterbalance what was perceived as the increasing unintelligibility of musical language. For many composers at the turn of the century, the accelerating dissolution of the tonal system made more difficult the organization of musical form using traditional tonal relations, a tendency that in turn led to greater emphasis on the libretto as an agent of music-dramatic coherence. In setting such a drama to music, a composer preserved intact its language, poetry, and structure—that is, those elements that made it work in purely theatrical terms. Prominent examples of literature operas include *Pelléas et Mélisande, Salome,* and *Elektra. Bluebeard's Castle* epitomizes the literature opera genre, though it has not been examined in that light. Bartók takes over Balázs's play in its entirety, making many small changes but leaving the overall dramatic structure and dialogue patterns essentially intact. The action on stage flows logically from beginning to end, uninterrupted by the insertion of purely musical forms such as arias or duets. The very term "literature opera" suggests that analysis of such works might entail the investigation of the "literary," or dramatic, aspects of an opera in addition to its music.

Under the umbrella of the literature opera concept, then, this book draws together a variety of subjects from the larger constellation of dramatic and musical issues that intersect in *Bluebeard's Castle.* The first chapter traces the history of Bartók's relationship with Balázs and the chronology of the opera's composition and eventual performance. In this and later chapters, supplemental information drawn from Balázs's own writings is made available in English for the first time, together with new information gleaned from sources preserved in the Budapest Bartók Archive. In chapter 2 the unusual dramatic aesthetic pursued by Balázs in his *Bluebeard* drama is examined. Essays by Balázs on Maeterlinck and other dramatists reveal how clearly he modeled certain aspects of his own dramatic technique on the work of non-Hungarian authors. A new influence on *Bluebeard* is suggested: the theories of tragedy set forth by the mid-nineteenth-century German dramatist Friedrich Hebbel. The book's third chapter offers an investigation into the music's motivic and tonal features and their impact on the work's overall music-dramatic symbolism. Discussion of individual scenes in chapter 4 brings out the details of Bartók's compositional technique.

It is not generally realized how extensively Bartók revised *Bluebeard's Castle* after its initial composition in 1911 and prior to its first performances seven years later. In the fifth chapter, Bartók's revisions to the score from 1911 to 1918 are examined for the impact this activity had on the opera's conclusion. Both the musical style and dramatic impact of its final moments were affected. Chapters 6 and 7 focus on aspects of *Bluebeard* that have either been overlooked thus far in the literature on the opera (the symbolism of the name Judith and its impact on the drama) or have attracted little previous scholarly attention (how the fairytale character of Bluebeard was transformed from villain to improbable object of compassion in turn-of-the-century literature). Both chapters attempt to shed additional light on the opera's enigmatic meaning, as it was likely to have been understood by its creators and their contemporaries. Readers interested in what the opera is trying to express about human love—and its underlying message about the inevitability of spiritual loneliness—will find the discussion in these two chapters the most informative.

My own interest in the opera's deeper background—in all its historical and contextual richness—has led me to engage topics not often treated at length by previous writers on the opera. I have been motivated to pursue these topics by a deep love of the music to *Bluebeard's Castle* and by my belief that, at this stage in the development of Bartók studies and in the historiography of this opera in particular, what is needed is not another review of the opera's general characteristics but a book that, while not neglecting the analytical and historical features of the opera described by previous writers, also opens up new avenues of scholarly inquiry. In part, too, the book was written to bring new information to light for Bartók enthusiasts unfamiliar with the Hungarian language. For these singers, conductors, scholars, and listeners, I have attempted to include as much primary source material as is reasonable within the limits of the study, in order to make available in English translation a portion of the previously unpublished letters and writings that bear upon the opera and its two creators. Regrettably, not everything could be included. The finished product will, it is hoped, consolidate in one volume much of the accepted knowledge about the opera while also suggesting new interpretive angles and offering essays that illuminate its place in the broader flow of twentieth-century cultural history. In my approach to the music I acknowledge a deep debt to those scholars who have turned their attention to *Bluebeard* before me, notably Elliott Antokoletz, Judit Frigyesi, György Kroó, and Sándor Veress. Their insights inform my attempt to shed further light on the history and meaning of Bartók's only opera. It is a work that sustains, and will continue to sustain, the collective intellectual fascination of all who encounter it.

Part I

*Bartók, Balázs, and the Creation
of a Modern Hungarian Opera*

BARTÓK, BALÁZS, AND THE CREATION OF *BLUEBEARD'S CASTLE*

> I would most willingly have printed on my calling card — Béla Bartók's librettist.
>
> — Béla Balázs

Despite its importance to Bartók's career, and to the history of twentieth-century opera, *Bluebeard's Castle* remains a piece of closed doors to many musicians interested in its deeper background. The basic facts of its composition are well known and, while still open to minor refinements in chronology, faithfully transmitted in most studies of the composer's life and works. Bartók himself, in response to a request from the Budapest journal *Magyar Színpad*, traced the outlines of the opera's creation in a statement made at the time of its premiere in 1918:

> I composed the music for the mystery play *Duke Bluebeard's Castle* from March to September, 1911. It was simultaneously my first stage and my first vocal work. At that time conditions were not suitable for its performance, so that I showed it to Count Miklós Bánffy and to conductor Egisto Tango only after the performance of *The Wooden Prince*. I am most grateful to them for sparing neither trouble nor pains in producing such a first-rate performance. Olga Haselbeck and Oszkár Kálmán sang their parts so perfectly that the performance completely came up to my expectations.[1]

The circumstances of this statement's publication—a casual public forum for "artists' thoughts"—would certainly offer little encouragement to greater exertion or reminiscence on behalf of a composer so averse to public scrutiny as Bartók, and it is entirely characteristic that he supplied here only the briefest of remarks, devoid of all significant detail and muted in emotion. What a world of frustration and bitterness are concealed, however, behind the phrase "at that time conditions were not suitable for its performance," and how gracefully Bartók then proceeds to compliment Bánffy, director of the Opera House, even though this same man had shown little interest in *Bluebeard* when it was first written and within his power to produce. Bartók also refers to "a competition"—in the singular —when we know the opera was entered in two competitions. The early history of *Bluebeard's Castle* is consistently intriguing in ways like this. Yet only a handful of comments in the composer's own words survive with which to fill in the picture of the work's creation, most of them equally terse in expression.

Bartók, a deeply private man, rarely spoke openly about his works in public. When he did, it was usually to offer a dry review of a work's formal construction, as in his analyses of the *Fourth Quartet* or *Music for Strings, Percussion and Celesta*.[2] Personal motivations or secrets from the composer's workshop were closely guarded, a natural consequence of his habitual reserve. Scholars are familiar with this situation, and have learned to sift further insights from Bartók's letters to family members and acquaintances, where he revealed the pattern of his interests most clearly.[3] About Béla Balázs, one learns quickly, he rarely had anything to say, either publicly or privately; perhaps he felt words were unnecessary, that the act of selecting Balázs's play to set to music constituted the highest form of endorsement, unworthy of further justification to the outside world. When in 1917 he offered some thoughts on *The Wooden Prince* to *Magyar Színpad*, he mentions Balázs only in passing, then turns with warm appreciation to the subject of Egisto Tango's conducting and Bánffy's sets and costume designs. Balázs's reputation as a librettist among Budapest's artistic and intellectual elite, moreover, could scarcely have been bolstered by Bartók's quiet ruminations on the reasons for the opera's poor reception five years earlier at the hands of competition juries:

> It may sound peculiar but I must admit that the preterition of my one-act opera *Bluebeard's Castle* prompted me to write *The Wooden Prince*. It is common knowledge that this opera of mine failed at a competition; the greatest hindrance to its stage production is that the plot offers only the spiritual conflict of two persons and the music is confined to the depiction of that circumstance in abstract simplicity. Nothing else happens on stage. I am so fond of my opera that when I received the libretto of [*The Wooden Prince*] from Béla Balázs, my first idea was that the ballet—with its spectacular, picturesque, richly variegated actions—would make it possible to perform these two works the same evening. I believe it is unnecessary to stress that the ballet is just as close to me as my opera.[4]

Only in a few instances did he commit to paper any words about the talented writer and dramatist whose work made such an impact on him as a young man. His reticence on the subject grew more pronounced in the 1930s and 40s, after he and Balázs drifted apart. Peter Bartók, the composer's younger son, does not recall ever hearing his father talk about Balázs.[5]

Surviving documents that concern *Bluebeard*, written either at the time of composition or years later, reinforce two constant themes: Bartók's high regard for his opera, usually measured against the less-favored *Wooden Prince*, and his almost complete silence on the subject of the librettist. In a 1925 letter to Ernst Latzko, the Weimar music director who led performances of both *The Wooden Prince* and *Bluebeard*, he offered a candid appraisal of these two works: "I was very pleased to receive your news about the performance. But especially to note that you, as well as the audience, appreciated "Bluebeard" more than the "Wooden Prince." To tell the truth, I am not very fond of this latter work; I consider "Bluebeard," as regards its music as well as words, an incomparably better work."[6]

To flesh out the history of the opera's creation, and its subsequent hardships prior to the first performances, one must turn not to statements like these, but to the writings of Balázs, with their characteristic blend of penetrating observation, erudition, dry humor, and intensely personal emotion. Balázs, fortunately, was anything but laconic. He recorded his impressions of Bartók at numerous times during his life, beginning at their first meeting in 1906, when they collected folk songs together in rural Hungary, and continuing into the 1920s and later. In the 1940s he penned several short memoirs of Bartók. A compulsive diarist, he left volume after volume of detailed personal observations on the lives of those around him. His diaries, published reminiscences, and surviving correspondence offer rare insight into Bartók's personality and the nature of their relationship at the time *Bluebeard's Castle* was written.[7] The intervening decades have failed to keep Balázs's many books and other publications in circulation, however, even in Hungary, with the result that he, too, is something of an unfamiliar figure to most admirers of Bartók's opera. It seems appropriate, then, to begin with Balázs, and then turn to his accounts of working with Bartók.

Composer and Librettist at the Time of the Opera's Creation

In the pantheon of twentieth-century Hungarian literature, Béla Balázs occupies a marginal position among the literary talents that blossomed in the decades before World War I, a golden age in the Hungarian arts. Born in Szeged to German immigrant parents, Balázs (1884–1948) began writing poetry at an early age, even publishing selected poems in a local newspaper under the pseudonym "Béla Balázs," a name he adopted while still in his teens to conceal from the public his germanic heritage, a potential liability in the chauvinistic sociopolitical climate in Hungary at the time. His birth name was Herbert Bauer, and he encouraged closer acquaintances, including Bartók, to call him by that name.[8] Balázs moved to Budapest in 1902 to begin studies at the University of Budapest. During his university he combined studies in German and Hungarian literature, philology, and philosophy with a variety of his own literary projects. His roommate at the Eötvös Kollégium, a building housing an elite subgroup of students destined for careers in teaching and the arts, was Kodály, two years his senior. Kodály and

Balázs became close friends. Out of this relationship Balázs eventually was introduced to Bartók, whom he met for the first time in 1906. (Kodály himself had met Bartók only one year previously.)[9] A common goal of creating new art forms based on authentic Hungarian folk idioms drew these men together. Bartók and Balázs were never truly close, however, despite their encouragement and support for each other's work. "Apart from his music," Balázs once wrote of the composer in his diary, "I am able to enjoy little about him."[10] Sentiments like this would continue to surface periodically in Balázs's writings up to the early 1920s, mixed with a profound admiration for Bartók's musical gifts.

Balázs's precipitous entry into Hungarian literary life took place in the years 1907 and 1908, while he was a doctoral student. He began to publish poems, drama reviews, and other short works in Budapest's literary journals, and in 1908 he contributed a number of essays to the inaugural issues of *Nyugat*. That same year he received his doctorate in German philology from the University of Budapest for a dissertation entitled *Friedrich Hebbel's PanTragicness, As a Result of the Romantic World View*, which was subsequently published serially and in book form in Budapest from 1908 to 1909 under his real name, Herbert Bauer. Over the next four to five years, he wrote steadily for Budapest's leading literary journals. His first play, *Dr. Szélpál Margit* (1906), a three-act drama about a woman biologist who must choose between her career and marriage, was performed in Budapest's National Theater on April 30, 1909. *Bluebeard's Castle*, his third completed play, was sketched out in the summer of 1908, shortly after he completed his formal studies; the bulk of the writing was done in 1909 and early 1910. Throughout this time he continued to write poetry. An interest in dance led to the writing of *The Wooden Prince* in 1912, which Bartók began to set to music in 1914.

Though prolific, thoughtful, and blessed with an undeniable gift for writing, Balázs was never able to establish himself as a major writer or poet in Hungary. Almost from the beginning he was viewed as something of an outsider to the main literary establishment in Hungary. Though deeply interested in folk lore, he matched this affinity with an proclivity for German literature and culture too pronounced for a nation then enduring an uncomfortable political relationship with Austria. His writing often was perceived as too intellectual, or too unrelenting in its pursuit of deeper questions about life. Balázs on his part did little to discourage this perception: the volume with which he introduced himself to the Hungarian public in 1907, after all, had been graced with the singularly uninviting title *Death Aesthetics*. A copy of this book is preserved in Bartók's personal library. The *Bluebeard* play itself is a good example of his sober, intense writing style, which he would leaven on occasion with sardonic wit, as seen in the three-part essay *Dialogue about Dialogue* (1909–11). He enlisted in the Hungarian army in 1916 and afterward wrote a book about his experiences, *Soul in War: Diary of Béla Balázs, Army Corporal*. His alienation from the literary establishment intensified through the war years as his political leanings moved further left. "The entire Hungarian literary world has become a unified, solidarized camp against me," he lamented in his diary in 1918.[11] He joined the Communist Party in 1918 and, together with Lukács, played an active role in the overthrow of the ruling monarchist government in October 1918 and the subsequent Communist takeover in March of 1919. He held minor administrative roles in the new government, where he strove to put into effect his utopian beliefs in the education of the masses through literature and the arts. In the White Terror that followed in the summer of 1919, Balázs barely escaped the violent backlash against the short-lived Communist government. Along with many other leftist Hungarians, he escaped abroad, slipping into Austria disguised as his brother.

Balázs lived the life of an exile for the next twenty-five years, returning to Hungary only in 1945, where he died three years later. He was a persona non grata in Hungary throughout the 1920s and early 30s, a situation that caused him to lose contact with many former friends and colleagues, including Bartók and Kodály. In Vienna his career took a new turn when he began to write about film. His influential 1924 book on film aesthetics, *Der sichtbare Mensch, oder die Kultur des Films*, is considered by film historians today as one of the seminal books on film theory. He participated in the production and writing of dozens of films, including *Die Abenteuer eines Zehnmarkscheines* (1926), *Das blaue Licht* (1930), starring Leni Riefenstahl, and the film version of Kurt Weill's *Die Dreigroschenoper* (1930). Another book, *Der Geist des Films* (1930) further established Balázs as a leading figure in film theory. Many Hungarians worked in the Austrian and German film industry in the 20s and 30s; among them, Balázs stood out as one of the more prominent emigré writers and scenarists. In 1931 he departed for Russia to work in the film industry there, eventually ending up in Alma Ata, Kazakhstan, an important Russian film center in the 1930s. Balázs's life was based on a personal quest for fulfillment through writing and other artistic activity. Like many intellectuals of his generation, in Hungary and elsewhere, his modernist inclinations led naturally to a leftist political orientation. At the root of his genuine concern for the plight of the lower class, however, rested a nineteenth-century faith in the power of art and literature to elevate the human spirit to higher modes of thought or awareness. A Zarathustra-like impulse to lead his contemporaries forward to uncharted spiritual territory can be seen underlying his accomplishments in drama, film, and even politics.

The first documented contact between Bartók and Balázs took place in September 1906, when Bartók visited Balázs's family home in Szeged while on a folk-song collecting trip to that region. Balázs accompanied him on the expedition, and wrote down his recollections of Bartók in his diary. "Béla Bartók was here," he began.

> We spent a week collecting folksongs together. He is naive and awkward. A twenty-five-or-odd-year-old *Wunderkind*. And yet there exists in him an incredibly quiet tenacity. He is a weak, puny, sickly little man, and yet I was already more than exhausted when he was still urging us on, to collect some more. He plays splendidly, and writes beautiful works. . . . He is inquisitive, impatient, unable to keep still, but he seems to be searching for something whose *reality* he already senses. . . . He is modest like a little girl—but also vain. And outside of his music, I am able to enjoy nothing about him. His

naivete is not fresh enough, and his irony (for that exists too) is without
force. And yet his face is sometimes very beautiful. Perhaps he is, after all,
more than a grown up Wunderkind-composer.[12] (Balázs's emphasis)

The year 1906 was a landmark time in Bartók's career as an ethnomusicologist.
Since 1904 he had been investigating, with increasingly passionate devotion, the
rural folk music of his native land. As a composer he had been seeking to develop
an authentically Hungarian musical style, and he soon recognized the potential
for artistic growth offered by this previously overlooked body of peasant music.
It was in 1906 that he was first able to devote significant time to collecting folk
songs. Summers and holidays in this and subsequent years would find him traveling through Hungary, Slovakia, and Rumania in pursuit of this material, which
he recorded on wax cylinders and brought back to Budapest for transcription
and study. Its unusual modal and rhythmic properties intrigued him, not just as
an authentic expression of Hungarian or other East European cultures, but also
as a vital source of new ideas for his original compositions. In December 1906 he
and Kodály established themselves at the forefront of folk music studies in Hungary with the publication of their *Hungarian Folksongs* [Magyar népdalok], a
group of twenty songs set to a simple piano accompaniment and prefaced by a
short introduction explaining the songs' authentic Hungarian qualities. Balázs
thus captures at a propitious moment in his new acquaintance's career the seemingly inexhaustible energy Bartók could draw upon—now and throughout his
life—when pursuing folk material, a "quiet tenacity" all the more noteworthy, as
Balázs suggests, for emanating from a man whose external appearance was otherwise unremarkable, even childlike.

In his mid-twenties was already beginning to withdraw into the loneliness that he sensed to be his lot in life, devoting himself with singleminded intensity to his work and despairing of finding close companionship. Writing to his
mother in 1905, he confessed that, even when among friends and fellow musicians, "there are times when I suddenly become aware of the fact that I am absolutely alone!" "And I prophesy," he continued, ". . . that this spiritual loneliness
is to be my destiny. I look about me in search of the ideal companion, and yet I
am fully aware that it is a vain quest. Even if I should ever succeed in finding
someone, I am sure that I would soon be disappointed."[13] In Kodály he soon
found a male friend with whom he could share his growing folk music interests
and pessimism over contemporary Hungarian musical life. Five years later, however, and recently married, he could still write to Frederick Delius, "I am so
alone here, have no-one to talk to, apart from my only friend Kodály, and have
never met anyone anywhere to whom, right from the start, I have felt so close as
to you."[14] What drew Bartók to Balázs, in addition to his interest in creating art
forms based on Hungarian folk culture, seems to have been the writer's equally
fateful sense of his own predestined loneliness. Themes of painful love and solitude suffused Balázs's early poetry, striking a sympathetic chord in Bartók, who
we know was deeply moved by Balázs's writing.

In the same 1906 diary entry, Balázs noted that "Bartók took my last noc-
turne with him—he wants to set it to music."[15] This work, if ever composed, has

FIGURE 1.1   *Béla Bartók in 1916*

not survived. In January 1908, Bartók appended a Balázs poem to the manuscript score of the violin concerto he had composed for Stefi Geyer. At the very end of this score, given to Geyer as a token of his broken love, Bartók wrote "In vain! In vain this poem too fell into my hands," and proceeded to copy out an untitled poem that reads in part: "My heart is bleeding, my soul is ill / I walked among humans / I loved with torment, with flame-love / In vain, in vain! // No two stars are as far apart / As two human souls!"[16] As he disentangled himself from his infatuation with Geyer that year, Bartók turned not only to music but also to Balázs's poetry in order to express his sorrow. Geyer later remembered that she originally

TABLE 1.1 Chronology of *Bluebeard's Castle*, 1907–1921

1907	December 18	Balázs mentions in his diary that he has begun a new play involving the figures of Bluebeard and Don Juan.
1908	August 4	Balázs sketches out the play in his diary.
1908–10		Balázs writes the *Bluebeard* play. Most work is probably accomplished after December 1909.
1910	April 20	"Prologue of the Bard" appears as a separate poem in the theater journal *Színjáték*.
	June 13	*Bluebeard's Castle* play is published in *Színjáték*, dedicated to Bartók and Kodály
1911	Early	"Prologue of the Bard" reprinted in Balázs's first poetry collection, *The Wanderer Sings*. The entire volume is dedicated to Kodály.
	Feb.–Sept. 20	Bartók composes the opera.
	July	First German translation of the play, by Henrik Horváth, is published in *Jung Ungarn* (Leipzig).
	Summer	Emma Kodály begins a separate German translation
	October	Bartók enters the opera in the Erkel Competition sponsored by the Lipótvárosi Kaszinó.
1912	February?	Bartók revises the opera's ending
	March	The opera is entered in the Rózsavölgyi Competition.
	Spring	*Bluebeard's Castle* drama is published as the first of Balázs's three *Mysteries*.
	July	Results of Lipótvárosi Kaszinó competition are announced. *Bluebeard* does not win.
	November	Results of Rózsavölgyi competition are announced. *Bluebeard* does not win.
1913	April 20	*Bluebeard's Castle* play is performed in Budapest; Bartók plays some piano pieces at intermission.
1917	Summer	Bartók throughly revises the *Bluebeard* score in preparation for its upcoming premiere.
1918	May 24	Bartók's opera is premiered at the Royal Opera House in Budapest.
1921	Spring	Universal Edition publishes the piano-vocal reduction, the opera's first edition.

thought the poem had been written by Bartók himself.[17] Bartók was favorably disposed to Balázs's work at this time in his life, from the early poetry through *Bluebeard* to *The Wooden Prince*. The poet gave voice to emotions Bartók could not express in words—what Judit Frigyesi has described as the "existential loneliness" felt, in varying degrees and with differing artistic results, by a number of their contemporaries in Hungarian intellectual circles. Balázs was more inclined, and, as a writer, more able, to explore in words the longing to be understood and failure to communicate they had both experienced in love.[18]

The Writing of the *Bluebeard* Play

Balázs began to sketch the *Bluebeard* play in Paris in mid-December 1907, at a time when Bartók, back in Budapest, was composing the Bagatelles and the first

FIGURE 1.2   *Béla Balázs. Undated photograph, 1910s*

Violin Concerto. Work proceeded sporadically over the next few years until the drama as we know it was published in June 1910. During these years Balázs's diaries mention the new project repeatedly, affording us glimpses of its creation. As originally conceived, the play centered around the interaction of not one, but two legendary womanizers, Bluebeard and Don Juan. With time, the latter figure dropped out of the scenario completely. A diary entry of December 18, 1907, notes that "I have begun 'Don Juan and Bluebeard.' For two days before I roamed about, not venturing to begin, as I had done at the time of *Szélpál Margit*.

FIGURE 1.3   *The Royal Opera House in Budapest, where* Duke Bluebeard's Castle *received its premiere performances.*

I was fearful, and afraid, as if I were assuming a great responsibility."[19] Nine months later, however, in August 1908, the play apparently was still more idea than reality. "Don Juan and Barbebleu—will be the short play. They meet in the pub. Barbebleu speaks, and thereby leads Don Juan away to his place. Don Juan is afraid of his mother. Even the thought of her is horrible to him."[20] Apart from the name Bluebeard, this sketch holds nothing in common with the finished Bluebeard drama as we know it. The only female character mentioned is Don Juan's mother, of all people, while the setting itself—a pub—removes Bluebeard from the story's traditional context. Balázs, who identified with the figure of Don Juan at this time in his life, soon dropped that angle and returned Bluebeard to a castle setting. He would go on to explore the Don Juan legend in other creative works, while the Bluebeard story began to assume a new form.[21]

Exactly when during the next year-and-a-half he completed the play is uncertain, though evidence points to the winter of 1909–10. In December 1909 his companion Edith Hajós wrote to Lukács, "Balázs is in Szeged writing his *Bluebeard*. Just received his prologue and will send it to you."[22] Shortly thereafter the prologue was published, in the April 20, 1910, issue of the theater journal *Szín-játék* [Stageplay], and the rest of the play followed two months later, in the June 13 issue of the same journal, where it bore a dedication to Bartók and Kodály.[23] In a curious anticipation of later performance practice, whereby the prologue is frequently omitted in staged performances of Bartók's opera, Balázs evidently

FIGURE 1.4   *Bartók and Balázs on a country road in Hungary. Undated photograph, ca. 1915*

felt the prologue to be a poem in its own right, and consistently asserted its semi-autonomous status at various points in his career. Under the title "Regős Prologusa" it was included in his first poetry collection, *A vándor énekel* [The wanderer sings], published in Budapest in 1911. There, however, the last three lines, with their topical reference to the "ancient castle" in the Bluebeard tale, were eliminated to make the poem's imagery less specific. A second edition of *The Wanderer Sings* appeared in print in 1918, at approximately the same time Bartók's opera was receiving its premiere performances. In 1945, three years before his death, Balázs retitled it "A közönségnek" [To the public] in a volume of his collected poetry, *Az én utam* [My path], again making no reference to its connection with the *Bluebeard's Castle* play.[24]

Many years later, in 1922, from his exile in Vienna, Balázs looked back on the writing of the Bluebeard play and his relationship with Bartók in the years around 1910. He described the bonds that arose between them as they pursued, in drama and in music, their goal of creating recognizably Hungarian art forms. Balázs had written his play in a style he knew would appeal to Bartók and Kodály. It was modern, drawing on the latest symbolist style for its dramatic technique, but it was also thoroughly Hungarian in its dialogue style. With some fondness Balázs recalled the spirit in which he had created the work:

> I was seeking a Hungarian dramatic style. I wanted to enlarge the dramatic
> vein of Székely folk ballads for the stage. I wanted to delineate modern

FIGURE 1.5   *At the opera's premiere, May 24, 1918. Olga Haselbeck (Judith), Oszkár Kálmán (Bluebeard), Dezső Zádor (stage director), and Béla Bartók*

souls with the plain primitive colors of folk song. I wanted the same as Bartók. We wanted it together in our youth. In our belief, complete novelty could be derived only from what was ancient, since only primeval material could be expected to stand our spiritualization without evaporating from under our fingers. Because only that which was simple was true, and only that which was simple could be truly new. (Because all that is complicated already existed as merely complicated.) My mystery was born of the common faith of common youth. It wasn't prepared as a libretto. It was given without music at one of the Nyugat matinees. This poetry was addressed to Bartók in the same way as when a weary, parched wanderer strikes up a tune to induce his still more exhausted companion to sing. Because a melody will carry you along for a while when your legs are at the point of giving way. And I contrived to trick him into music. Bartók intoned and broke into such singing as has not been heard in Europe since Beethoven.[25]

Written more than ten years after Bartók composed the opera, these words eloquently recapture the sense of common purpose that drew Bartók and Balázs together at this time in their lives. Balázs's description of the artistic chemistry that yielded the *Bluebeard* drama could just as easily apply to Bartók's music, also based upon the plain, primitive colors of folk songs. Balázs felt he was responsible for inducing Bartók to set his play. "I contrived to trick him into music." His version of events is valuable for its information about the influence of Székely ballads and because it is Balázs himself speaking. It unquestionably romanticizes the creation of *Bluebeard's Castle*, however, and should not necessarily be taken as wholly accurate.

The metaphor about parched wanderers urging each other to sing, and the words about the "common faith of common youth," for example, imply that *Bluebeard's Castle* was in some way a joint venture, conceived out of the union of their interests. There is no reason to doubt that at least in part, this may have been true; we will have to trust Balázs's recollection. But we know that Balázs played at best a passive role in the opera's creation. He contributed little to its final form through consultations or advice sought by the composer (see below and chapter 5). Bartók apparently began writing the music without informing Balázs, who tacitly acknowledges that fact when he writes not that he collaborated with Bartók, which he undoubtedly would have remembered, but instead that he "tricked him into music." Balázs's 1922 recollection emphasizes what happened *before* Bartók composed the opera. After that point he has little to say: he wasn't there for its creation.

Bartók left for Paris on July 8, 1911, leaving the almost completed draft with Márta for her to begin preparing a clean copy. (The history of the opera's composition in 1911 is discussed in detail in chapter 5.) Balázs learned of his Paris address and wrote to him on July 13, expressing pleasure that Bartók had decided to set the *Bluebeard* play to music. His letter, reproduced here in full, suggests that the two men had had little personal contact during the early summer. Beneath Balázs's eager retelling of the news, moreover, can be detected a slightly deferential tone toward the composer, as if he does not wish to jeopardize his friendship with Bartók by acting presumptiously regarding the storage of some of Bartók's personal effects.

July 13

Dear Béla

At last I know your address! It's certainly too late for me to say farewell in person, but at least I can write to tell you I wanted to come out but didn't know where to go. I asked once at the Academy, and also once at Emma's, but they weren't able to tell me. So it would have been left for the last week, but by then you were unlocatable at the Academy, and besides,

I was so insanely worked up I couldn't even climb the Rózsadomb once to say goodbye, which also chagrins me. I really hurried. For hundreds of reasons. Forgive me then. It wasn't my fault. Your things: thick woolen blankets, embroidery, a flower pot, and scores—I would have sent them if I had known where. So all of these things are at the Hajós's, in Edith's room, packed in naphthalin and sealed; they have been brought to Mrs. Hajós's attention, and she pays them close mind. They're available anytime, if you write a letter to Frau Dr. Zsigmond Hajós or if you discuss the matter in person with her. With the exception of two small pieces of embroidery. These I brought with me. That's not a problem, is it? I can send them in the mail if you need them. Please write and tell me truthfully your opinion on all of this.—You, too, would only pack these things in naphthalin now, and sometime in the fall I will arrange for them to be returned to you. It's all there and nothing will be spoiled by dampness.—I write on account of Emma's Bluebeard translation. You'll receive it as soon as possible. With regard to the money—(the Devil take all that exists in the world)—I'll be content with whatever you give. After all, I didn't write the piece for the competition. Write me only this: whether Rózsavölgyi's proprietary rights mean I can no longer offer the text without music to theaters.[26] If this were the case, things would be more unfortunate. By the way, I am terribly pleased you have worked on it after all. For many reasons: 1) because it shows that you are feeling better— 2) because I will hear it sooner— 3) because only with this do I feel my own work as finished. I have just begun my 1-year leave of absence with much restlessness and ten times as many plans as are technically feasible. This wears me out a little. I work all day. We've only been in the mountains twice. We're waiting to see if Zoltán and Emma are coming to Zürich. I asked Zoltán to send me his favorite folk tales or their titles at least—so that before I turn to my fairy-tale piece [*mesedarab*] I also know something of his sympathies. Because I want to write a text for him, too. I have a strong desire to do this. I'd finish it by the fall. It would be a large two- or three-acter. Written directly as a libretto—Don't you think this would be good for him, too? But he answers my letter with not a single word. As I say, I'm working and struggling quite a lot. The outcome of my sabbatical for the time being is only that I see all of what should be done. I think much of you and Zoltán. Why did you go to Paris now? When are you coming back? Won't you come by here and stay for 1–2 days?—If you will answer, I'll write you now and then.

Good work, good success.

Edith sends greetings to Márta, too.[27]

Herbert

His reference to money in this letter indicates his knowledge of the substantial prize to be awarded by the Rózsavölgyi competition and the terms governing its dispensation: according to the competition announcement (see chapter 5), composer and librettist were to decide between themselves the appropriate division of money. His letter also confirms that Emma Kodály's German translation of *Bluebeard* was well under way, or already completed, by July, which meant that she had undertaken the task before the music was completed. The words about *Bluebeard* and the competitions in the middle of the letter are interesting, too, in that they appear to suggest that Balázs had only recently learned that Bartók was composing the opera. He expresses genuine pleasure that Bartók was writing music to his play.

In August the Kodálys did meet Balázs in Zürich, together with Bartók, who began to orchestrate the opera in July while vacationing near Zermatt. Balázs was joined by Edith Hajós for a two-week stay with the composers and Emma at Waidberg, a resort in the mountains near Zürich that specialized in open-air bathing (Márta Bartók remained in Budapest). He wrote an account of their time together in his diary:

> I am becoming all the more fond of Béla Bartók. He is the most moving and most marvellous man. He, too, undressed to the skin. His frail, weak, delicate little body, even when he ran after the ball, seemed as if it moved in robes in front of an altar. He has unbelievably magical dignity and nobility. You could peel his skin off him, but not his unconscious dignity. The genius, in the most rational, most romantic sense. And how much childishness, how much charm exists within him. He travels with a knapsack and ten cigar boxes, filled with insects and flies, which he gathers with scrupulous care and constant wonder. He will sit for hours on the edge of a dirty pond and fish for water insects with Edith. . . . Meanwhile he worked six to eight hours a day on the orchestration of Bluebeard.[28]

Balázs's early descriptions of Bartók all have the stylish, well-turned phrases of a skilled writer unconsciously practicing his craft. The elegance and evocative power of his words attest to the effect Bartók's personality had on those around him. Balázs slips readily into exalted, grandiose modes of expression as he paints his verbal images of the composer. Bartók appears alternately as the "Rococo prince," the "genius," the "wunderkind," or, above, as a sort of dignified priest moving about "in robes in front of an altar." By 1911, Balázs was clearly developing more of an affection for Bartók as an individual. The reserve that characterized his diary entry in 1906 had given way to a tone of bemused fascination with the habits and characteristics of a composer he had already marked as a genius.

Table 1.1 presents a chronology of *Bluebeard's Castle* for the years 1907–21, encompassing the time when Balázs began to contemplate writing a play based on the Bluebeard story, up to the year of the opera's publication in piano-vocal format. In the spring of 1912, *Bluebeard* and the two other one-act plays Balázs had written between 1909 and 1911 were included in a volume entitled *Misztériumok: Három egyfelvonásos* (Mysteries: Three one-acters).[29] Both prologue and play, then, were republished within two years of their first appearance, as Balázs continued to consolidate his literary work. Like *The Wanderer Sings* the year before, *Mysteries* represented a compilation of previously unrelated writings brought together from various sources. Both publications bore opus numbers: *The Wanderer Sings* was Balázs's opus 2; the three *Mysteries*, opus 4. Balázs imitated the opus numbering system used by composers, a trait—unusual among nonmusicians—that almost certainly springs from his friendship with Kodály and Bartók. He continued to use opus numbers for several more years, assigning them only to his creative writings, not to his literary or aesthetic studies, which suggests a conscious attempt to shape his public image by identifying poetry, drama, and fiction as his true contributions.[30]

The fact that Bartók had written music to *Bluebeard* did not prevent Balázs from attempting to secure a premiere for the play in Budapest theaters, a situation he alludes to in the letter cited earlier. In early 1912, he confided to his diary that "the National [Theater] accepted my mysteries, and they seriously want to give Bluebeard." Mindful of an earlier failure at that theater with *Dr. Szélpál Margit*, however, Balázs remained skeptical. "We'll wait and see," he concluded.[31] A year later, the National Theater's interest had evaporated, and Balázs chose to stage two of his mysteries himself, which led to the fiasco described in the introduction to this book.

Balázs's Reminiscences of Working with Bartók

In his writings about Bartók, Balázs repeatedly emphasizes how passionately he believed in the new Hungarian art forms he, Bartók, Kodály, and other young Hungarian artists were championing. That they encountered little public support for their endeavors proved to be a constant source of frustration. A picture of Bartók and Balázs, the only known photograph of the two men together, was taken on a country road in the mid-1910s. They are shown from the rear, moving away from the camera. Balázs later remembered, only half-jokingly, that the caption under the photo read "Béla Bartók and Béla Balázs leave the country"—one response to the difficult climate they each endured in their native land.[32] Bartók at least briefly entertained the idea of emigrating to another country in the mid-1910s. He and Balázs must have shared this desire, though neither of them acted on it until necessity drove them away, Bartók in 1939, Balázs in 1919.

Balázs felt he played an important role in encouraging Bartók to maintain faith in the ultimate value of their goals, and he took pains to point out in his diary, and occasionally in public, how his ardent support often went underappreciated by its recipients, including Bartók. Elsewhere in his 1922 article he reminisced that Bartók "was convinced of the futility of his life work. . . . And it was I, then, the emigrant revolutionary, who revived his faith. It was I who spoke to him about the great Hungarian cultural renaissance, the Hungarian people's mission in the advancement of European culture; I encouraged him, I talked—I the homeless vagrant—until blood gushed from my mouth. . . . Then I wrote 'Duke Bluebeard's Castle.'"[33] He clearly felt that the *Bluebeard* drama must be understood in the broader context of his and Bartók's interest in creating new modes of expression that would advance the state of Hungarian art. Here, as above, he perhaps overstates his own importance to Bartók, but we must measure this statement against the silence emanating from the composer and at least appreciate the playwright's statements as an honest reflection of how he felt in 1922. His words evince the slightly bitter, injured tone of one who felt he had been unjustly neglected for his achievements. This feeling became exacerbated following his exile.

Balázs's support for Bartók could take pugilistic form if needed. At the 1910 Waldbauer-Kerpely Quartet concerts devoted to Bartók and Kodály's music, Balázs brought a pair of brass knuckles to the first concert in case a fight broke out. His sister and Edith had to forcibly restrain him from attacking those who jeered.[34] The battle theme also resounds throughout his recollections of the premiere of *The Wooden Prince* in 1917. Balázs played a significant and multifaceted role in getting this piece produced at the Opera House, serving at different times as writer, agent, and stage director. On several occasions he told the story of how Miklós Bánffy, the Opera House's director, stopped him outside the National Theater the day after his *Wooden Prince* ballet scenario appeared in the Christmas 1912 issue of *Nyugat*:

> "I read your ballet. Interesting . . .," he said, rolling his r's. "I like it. One could paint beautiful backdrops for it, in the style of the Hungarian folk story. Do tell, who are you going to commission to compose it?"
>
> "The music is already finished," I lied. "Béla Bartók did it."
>
> "Too bad, too bad," he said, as he tugged at his walrus mustache, "seeing as the public doesn't like him. Because I've conceived some very pretty scenery. I've even got sketches already. Come up and see me anyway, and we'll talk about it."
>
> In a nutshell, the count became so enthusiastic about painting the scenery for the ballet that he agreed to do *The Wooden Prince*, along with its unheard, unwritten score by Bartók. . . . Then, in the fall [of 1916], the battle of *The Wooden Prince* began at the Opera. Because a count is an important man in Hungary, and if he feels a noble desire to paint the scenery for a pantomime, then nothing will daunt his intentions, not even the protestations of ten conductors, two stage managers, and a ballet master.[35]

Though Bartók's music represented a principal attraction, it is evident that other factors, including Balázs's determined advocacy, were equally responsible for the Opera House's decision to produce *The Wooden Prince*.[36] When the scheduled director quit in protest, Balázs assumed the directorship himself. "There was no other way to save your music, Béla Bartók," he later recalled. "I had to take it in hand. That's how I became a director."[37] He worked for months rehearsing the dancers, assisting in the choreography, and performing miscellaneous small tasks needed to ensure a smooth production. "For two entire months I worked, fought, so that I became ill—because I had to have Bartók break through the front of Hungarian indifference," he wrote in his diary following the ballet's successful premiere on May 12, 1917.[38] At the premiere he had been called to the stage "at least thirty times. . . . They raved for more than half an hour. The next day the papers gave Bartók full recognition, but me mostly abuse."[39]

In 1917 Balázs dedicated a newly written children's play, *The Fisherman and the Silver Moon*, to Bartók's six-year-old son, Béla Jr., in further indication of his esteem for the composer. The play was printed that year with the text to *The Wooden Prince* in a handsome volume featuring Bánffy's costume designs for the ballet and Róbert Berény's illustrations for *The Fisherman and the Silver Moon.*[40] On the same day the ballet premiered, the Bartók family attended a matinee of the children's play. Bartók later sent his personal copy—a gift from Balázs—to Ion Buşiţia, drawing his attention to Berény's fine illustrations while commenting, "I don't like the text itself very much (I find it rather commonplace, like so many of the verses in picture-books for children.)."[41]

The *Bluebeard* Premiere

The success of *The Wooden Prince* revived the Opera House's dormant interest in Bartók's unperformed opera, and in mid-1917 Bartók was requested to submit his score to the director of the Opera House to enable preparations for performances the following season to begin. Balázs took a passive role in the production of *Bluebeard's Castle*, merely attending the rehearsals, which began in May 1918. "The Bluebeard rehearsals have begun," he noted in his diary on May 16.

> The premiere is on the 24th. A man named Dezső Zádor directs, with truly conscientious work, but with today's typical Pest fictional approach. He would make Judith a hysterical little beast if the text would permit it. He hasn't the least idea what the work is about. And then he impudently and detestably rejects my comments; I never go to the rehearsals anymore. When I introduced myself I could already see on his face that they had informed him, and he knew, that it would look better with the critics if he were to appear to hate me. If I am there together with Bartók, then they are overtly polite to Béla and they do not even notice me. Well, at least Béla is in. I'll still wait.[42]

After the premiere, on May 24, 1918, he entered in his diary a lengthy description of the *Bluebeard* rehearsals and first performances. Ever sensitive to others' opinions, he was deeply hurt by Bartók's lack of public support for his libretto, as evinced in the composer's published statement about the opera, quoted at the beginning of this chapter. "Again a great assault on me by the critics. Again they are sorry for Bartók. I am a drag on his wheels." That Bartók could thank everyone but him for their contributions to the performance stung Balázs.

> He did not even mention my name. It did not occur to him that he was the only one who could have repudiated these attacks. . . . My heart aches over Bartók. He is a great musician, and as long as he does not compromise in his music, it is all the same how he behaves as a person. But my heart aches. Because it turns out that he joined forces with me quite accidentally, without any inner necessity, and in doing so he sensed no kind of predestined meaning in it at all. He did not choose me as a standard to live up to, as I did him.[43]

Balázs felt that despite his years of support for Bartók and Kodály, the two composers were now throwing him out, like "a sandbag from a rising balloon." "They try to do it very tenderly, gently," he wrote, "so that no bitterness remains."[44] These feelings evidently had been developing for some time. At a private gathering eight months earlier where Ernő Dohnányi and Jenő Kerpely played Kodály's Cello Sonata, Balázs noted in his diary that "afterward the Bartóks, Kodálys and Reinitz came over to our place for dinner. Even in this mostly 'friends' company I still feel like I'm on uncertain ground, and that I'm an insignificant figure."[45]

Balázs was correct in perceiving a widening split between him and his longtime friends. From this point forward they would grow farther apart. We can only conjecture as to why the dissolution appears to have accelerated at a time of mutual artistic success and public recognition for both him and Bartók. At the very least, it seems clear from his writings that Balázs desired more from the relationship than Bartók was willing, or able, to give. Bartók, for his part, certainly could have done more to deflect the criticisms his librettist was enduring. But to speak out publicly was not his style, except on rare occasions, and, for better or worse, his friendship with Balázs suffered accordingly. My own sense is that this was one of those friendships that grew too burdensome emotionally for one of the parties, who then, without any sense of malice and without conscious effort, simply began to find the company of other people preferable. In an elliptical manner Bartók gave some indication—privately—of how highly he valued the *Bluebeard* text when he sent a copy of the *Mysteries* to Buşiţia in Rumania to read in advance of the opera's performance. "The other two mystery plays," he wrote in the accompanying letter, "are also worth reading."[46] He may not have felt it necessary to publicly reiterate his belief in the libretto's quality.

In the early 1920s, after Balázs had escaped into political exile in Austria, his association with Bartók developed into a liability for the composer. *The Wooden Prince* and *Bluebeard's Castle* were effectively blocked from production in Hungary because their texts were written by a writer who had participated in the former Communist government. Political reasons, therefore, were in large part responsible for the lack of revivals in Hungary. The climate was so bad that in 1923, the director of the Opera House in Budapest wrote to Bartók suggesting that they try to "break the ice with a performance of *The Miraculous Mandarin*"—surely the only time this work has been thought of as an icebreaker.[47] Staging the *Mandarin*, it was thought, would smooth the path toward reviving Bartók's other stage works by helping to silence all opposition to the librettist. Unfortunately, the projected performances of these works never took place. Partly on account of this official reluctance to stage *Bluebeard*, the opera would not be performed again in Hungary until over a decade later, in 1936.

Balázs publicly broke his friendship with the composer in 1922, hurt that Bartók had neglected to visit him in Vienna on several occasions, including after the opera's first foreign premiere. "Béla Bartók's opera had its premiere in Frankfurt the evening of May 13th," he wrote at the opening of the *Bécsi Magyar Újság* article whose contents were cited earlier.

On this occasion I want to write about Béla Bartók for the last time. I wrote about him—and for him—first. I wrote much on his behalf, and for a long time I was almost alone. Today Béla Bartók's victorious ship sails out onto the waters of the world, flags aflutter. Of my dilettantish promotion the music no longer has any need. When ships descend on the waters they break on their prows, to bring luck, a champagne bottle. Today, with a clean heart, with proud and best wishes, I too . . . break something.[48] (Ellipses in original)

Composer and dramatist communicated occasionally in the 1920s and 1930s and met once after a concert Bartók gave in Berlin in 1928, but their careers now proceeded in different countries and under different circumstances.[49] Balázs went on to work with other composers. He wrote the ballet scenario for Ernst Krenek's *Mammon*, first performed in Münich in 1927. In 1929, with Franz Schreker, he contemplated writing a film opera, a project that never came to fruition.[50] An earlier work based on one of his ideas, Egon Wellesz's ballet *Das Wunder der Diana* (1914–17), received its first performance at Mannheim's National Theater in 1924. Wellesz, an old friend, had known Balázs since 1909, when he dedicated to him his first song cycle, *Wie ein Bild*, based on texts by Peter Altenberg. Through Bartók's intervention this work had been published by Rózsavölgyi as Wellesz's opus 3. Wellesz recalled Balázs as "a wonderful storyteller: there was something of the ancient folk poet in him."[51] After Balázs returned to Hungary, Kodály composed an opera based on a new libretto, *The Ballad of Panna Cinka* (1948), to commemorate the hundredth anniversary of Hungary's 1848 revolution. An unusual, dramatized interpretation of Bartók's *Dance Suite*, to a libretto by Balázs and choreographed by Gyula Harangozó, received seven performances in Budapest in 1948.[52]

Toward the end of his life, Balázs wrote several long open letters to Bartók that were published in émigré journals.[53] In these letters, he looks back upon his years of involvement with Bartók as some of the most artistically fulfilling years of his life. He lingers over the details of their relationship, recalling the spirit with which they battled to gain recognition for their work. Nostalgia for that earlier time pervades his words. The wanderer, speaking from new outposts in the world, seems resigned to the fact that his relationship with Bartók now belonged mostly to the past, and that it was unlikely their paths would cross again.

✑ 2

BLUEBEARD AS THEATER
The Dramatic Heritage of Balázs's Symbolist Play

W hile we know a great deal about the types of music that interested Bartók in the years prior to *Bluebeard*, our understanding
of the factors that contributed to the unusual dramatic style Béla Balázs
adopted for his *Bluebeard* play is fairly one-dimensional and may be summarized
as follows: French symbolism, and specifically the work of Maurice Maeterlinck,
formed the predominant influence on the young Hungarian writer. Balázs's
dark, atmospheric play about the folk character of Bluebeard shares with Bartók's music the fundamental attribute of looking east and west at the same time.
By virtue of its language and of certain textual features, the *Bluebeard's Castle*
drama displays a strongly national character that Hungarians have long recognized as deriving from the ancient folk heritage of the Transylvanian magyars
(see chapter 3). In other respects, though, the play's essential spirit holds much
in common with broad trends in early-twentieth-century European theater,
particularly with French and German drama. The *Bluebeard* drama's roots in the
Western intellectual tradition are deep. While often acknowledged, this aspect
of Balázs's play is at once more complex and more revealing than has generally
been recognized.

During the late nineteenth and early twentieth centuries, young Hungarians
seeking the latest artistic or literary trends were drawn to Paris to absorb, and be
inspired by, the French capital's vibrant intellectual life. The great poetic voice
of Hungary at this time, Endre Ady, spent many years in Paris before publishing
his sensational *New Poems* in 1906; these poems drew heavily on the work of

Baudelaire, Verlaine, and other French symbolists. Ödön Márffy, Bertalan Pór, and Róbert Berény all studied art in Paris before returning to Budapest, drawing personal inspiration from the works of Cézanne, Matisse, Gauguin, and the impressionists—a pattern followed to some extent by virtually all painters of their generation. "In the decade before the War," wrote novelist Aladár Kuncz, "it became almost a passion with us Hungarians to investigate French literature and things French in general."[1] France, however, was not the only destination for acquisitive Hungarians bent on gaining exposure to new, progressive trends in the arts. Vienna and Berlin, too, beckoned with an established cultural life whose equal could not be found in their native land.

Hungary's cultural and economic ties with Germany were historically strong. Many people of either German or Austrian origin, and predominantly middle-class, emigrated to Hungary in the nineteenth century; most voluntarily took steps toward assimilation.[2] The rapid magyarization of the Budapest population contributed to many social and political changes after 1900, among them the rejection of German language and all things German by the increasingly outspoken nationalists during the 1900–1903 period (it was at this time that Bartók stopped signing his compositions "Béla von Bartók" and began dressing in native costume).[3] German arts and literature maintained an appeal among Hungary's intellectual circles, though some of the luster inevitably had worn off. In 1906 Balázs and Kodály, venturing in directions characteristic of their generation, together began a year-long tour of the west by spending a winter in Berlin attending concerts and plays, where Balázs took classes with the renowned philosopher Georg Simmel. The following spring and summer they moved on to Paris, where Kodály's interest was piqued by the music of Debussy.[4] Their commitment to art refreshed through personal contact with the latest western European trends, these Hungarian writers, artists, and musicians returned to their homeland seeking to create modes of expression that were at once genuinely Hungarian and, by international standards, modern.

When Balázs wrote *Bluebeard's Castle*, he was still a young man in his midtwenties just beginning his literary career. He was extremely well versed in the work of other late-nineteenth- and early-twentieth-century European playwrights such as Ibsen, Strindberg, d'Annunzio, Hofmannsthal, and Maeterlinck. It is quite natural that traces of the work of prominent figures such as these should filter into the expressive voice of the aspiring Hungarian writer. The symbolist technique of Maurice Maeterlinck's dramas forms the most recognizable influence on the style of Balázs's play. Additional literary and aesthetic connections may be detected, however. No turn-of-the-century dramatist could ignore the important new developments in theater represented by the work of August Strindberg, the Swedish playwright whose fantastic dream plays drew theater into the world of the subconscious, or Henrik Ibsen, the eminent Norwegian author whose *Ghosts* and *A Doll's House* gave the burgeoning nineteenth-century women's movement a theatrical voice. In subtle ways, each of these playwrights shaped Balázs's artistic conscience.[5] Theories of tragedy propounded by the mid-nineteenth-century German playwright Friedrich Hebbel, though chronologically more distant, had a noticeable impact on the *Blue-beard's Castle* drama. On a purely theatrical level, the imaginative use of stage lighting in *Bluebeard* owes much to the example of stage directors like Germany's Max Reinhardt, whose innovative lighting techniques profoundly altered the theatrical experience for early-twentieth-century audiences. And at the core of the drama's message lies something akin to the philosophy of Friedrich Nietzsche: Bluebeard, a Zarathustra-like figure, is ultimately resigned to the loneliness that is his fate.

All of these influences, some more important than others, come together in the *Bluebeard* play. Two of the more powerful strands of influence are teased apart for discussion in the present chapter: the symbolist style of Maeterlinck's dramas and Friedrich Hebbel's theories of tragedy. The Maeterlinck influence, often acknowledged as a significant factor in the creation of Balázs's own dramatic style, has never been examined in detail. The Hebbel influence is proposed here for the first time. Examination of Balázs's own writings reveals that the intellectual disposition of this young Hungarian dramatist was conditioned as much by a deep-seated attraction for German romantic drama as by the more immediate, and passing, influence of French symbolism. *Bluebeard's* dramatic style flows from multiple sources in the literary world Balázs enveloped himself in during his student years in Budapest. Awareness of the writers engaging Balázs's attention at the time he worked on the *Bluebeard* play, it stands to reason, can shed additional light on the sources of its symbolist language. Even more important, new reasons come to light that help explain at least one of the drama's lingering unanswered questions: why Judith submits so willingly to the fate of entombment in Bluebeard's gloomy castle.

In its dramatic style and means of expression, *Bluebeard's Castle* shows strong connections to the late-nineteenth- and early-twentieth-century symbolist movement in European literature. Its reliance on atmosphere, portentous visual symbols, and lack of action is characteristic of the dramatic style pioneered by Maurice Maeterlinck in Paris in the 1890s and termed "symbolist" by later critics. Maeterlinck's dramas and their underlying philosophy had a profound impact on other dramatists of his day, many of whom, like Maeterlinck himself, sought meaningful expression of the perceived emptiness and tragedy of contemporary human existence through the technique of allusion. That *Bluebeard's Castle* is a drama that derives much of its effect from the use of visual symbols is immediately apparent to even the most casual observer. Perhaps the most striking symbol is the castle itself, with its seven large, forbidding doors, each of which opens to reveal another aspect of Bluebeard's life and identity. Colored light emanates from each of these doors. Red light pours forth from the torture chamber, golden light from the treasury, blue-green from the garden. As Judith advances farther into Bluebeard's gloomy domicile, bringing light to its darkened hallways, it becomes increasingly evident that the castle doors and their contents have a significance far greater than outward appearances would suggest and that the sequence of door openings has gradually been assuming another level of meaning. Judith's penetration into the castle, we realize, also represents the unfurling of

Bluebeard's soul before the firm but loving advances of his new wife. The doors, therefore, represent windows into his soul; the castle, the man himself.

Dramatic symbolism like this becomes more inscrutable as Judith progresses deeper into the castle. The silent lake of tears that rises, gray and lifeless, behind the sixth door is interpreted by Judith as the tears of Bluebeard's former wives, but it is just as likely that these tears are Bluebeard's own, wept in anguish over his lost loves. From behind the seventh and last door step the three former wives, splendidly adorned with jewels and rich fabrics, each associated by a kneeling Bluebeard with a time of day: morning, noon, and evening. By opening the seventh door, Judith has passed beyond the same mysterious, unspoken threshold that also claimed each of these women before her. To know that the former wives exist is to become one yourself: to move, in effect, from present into past, receding into the dreamscape of Bluebeard's memory. Bluebeard symbolically links Judith with night, thereby bringing about a completion of the twenty-four-hour day and, presumably, closure to his fruitless attempts to find love. The darkness that had been slowly creeping back into Bluebeard's castle after the sixth door was opened now becomes complete as Judith takes her place next to the former wives and the stage lights ebb to blackness.

In an unused introduction to the *Bluebeard* play dating from around 1915, Balázs partially explained the meaning behind symbols such as these: "Bluebeard's castle is not a realistic stone castle. The castle is his soul. It is lonely, dark and secretive: the castle of locked doors. . . . Into this castle, into his own soul, Bluebeard admits his beloved. And the castle (the stage) shudders, weeps and bleeds. When the woman walks in it, she walks in a living being."[6] Befitting its central role in Balázs's conception, the castle was included on the list of dramatis personae in the first published version of the play, just after the names Judith and Bluebeard, as if it, too, were a participant in the drama. (Bartók removed the castle from this list.) Dialogue between Judith and Bluebeard frequently alludes to the castle's human qualities. When Judith's hand strays against the castle's wet walls at the beginning, she remarks, "The castle is weeping." Following her declaration of love in the second door scene, Bluebeard speaks as if the castle itself were alive and responding to her:

> My castle's dark foundations tremble
> From within its gloomy rocks, pleasure shivers.
> Judith, Judith.—Cool and sweet
> Blood flows from open wounds.

The castle sighs when Judith turns the key in the first and sixth doors. Repeated references to the castle's "coldness" and "darkness" emphasize the icy loneliness of Bluebeard's solitude. Bluebeard's human attributes are thereby transferred to the castle, which becomes implicitly identified with its owner.

Withdrawal from the world of dramatic realism, as seen in *Bluebeard's Castle*, necessarily elevates the element of stage lighting to new importance as dramatic moments are now created and defined not by language but by atmosphere. Lighting effects themselves become significant symbols in *Bluebeard*, bearers of meaning that help shape the progression of events on stage. The play begins and ends in total darkness. In between, the stage slowly lightens with the opening of each successive door up to the fifth, after which the castle's gloom gradually returns. This arc from darkness through light and back to darkness mirrors the outward progression of Bluebeard and Judith's hope for love.[7] The glimmer of brightness occasioned by Judith's entry into the castle slowly increases in magnitude through the first five doors. The blinding white light streaming forth from the fifth door represents the conquering of darkness in Bluebeard's soul and the triumph, however fleeting, of optimism; it is Judith's compulsion to open the remaining two doors, and Bluebeard's acquiescence to her wishes, that causes darkness to return. As Judith steps toward the sixth door, the hall darkens slightly — "as if a shadow was cast over it," the text reads. Deepening shadows from here to the end parallel the extinction of hope in Bluebeard's soul.

A specific color of light is associated with each door. When Judith opens a door, the audience sees only a sudden shaft of colored light emanating from the opening in the wall. The actual contents themselves are not visible.[8] Judith describes them aloud, her words confirming the symbolic impression of the light's color. By replacing scenes of splendor and horror with appropriately colored shafts of light, Balázs reduces the stage to utmost simplicity. This helps focus the audience's attention on the two characters before them. The contents of the doors are not themselves important, Balázs seems to say; it is what each door represents to Bluebeard and Judith that determines its dramatic significance. To underline the psychological impact of the lighting, Balázs scripts some stage directions in animate terms. Thus, the red light of the first door cuts "like a wound" into the darkness. The yellow-red of the weapons hall appears "dark and frightening." Such emphasis on the symbolism of color is reminiscent of the elevated role Wassily Kandinsky assigned to colors in his experimental stage composition *Der gelbe Klang* (1912), a work published in the famous *Blaue Reiter Almanac*. Kandinsky numbered color among the three visual and aural elements that, in his words, serve the "inner value" of musical drama.[9] To that end, he specified in abundant detail the colors of the stage lighting and every object and character present. Strange yellow giants and vague red creatures move indistinctly across Kandinsky's often darkened stage, enveloped in a thick blue fog. It is in this respect that resemblances can be seen between *Bluebeard's Castle* and the expressionist movement in early-twentieth-century German theater, for German playwrights, taking a cue from works like *Der gelbe Klang*, began to rely on creative lighting effects to enhance the depiction of internal, dreamlike psychological states.

Balázs, Maeterlinck, and Symbolist Drama

Balázs's interest in the expressive possibilities of Maeterlinck's dramas has long been recognized as an important factor in the shaping of his own style. Emil Haraszti mentions Maeterlinck's influence in his 1930 description of the opera, and

Halsey Stevens elaborates on this angle in his 1953 study of the composer and his work.[10] Most discussions of *Bluebeard* in the secondary literature at least mention Maeterlinck as an influence on the young Hungarian playwright. Unfortunately, beginning with Haraszti, attention has focused almost exclusively on Maeterlinck's *Ariane et Barbe-bleue* as the primary source of inspiration for Balázs. *Ariane* was first performed, in an operatic setting by Paul Dukas, in Paris in 1907. "Béla Balázs was primarily influenced by Maeterlinck's *Ariane et Barbe-Bleue,*" writes Simon Broughton.[11] "Béla Balázs attempted to compress Maeterlinck's three-act tragedy into a one-act drama," asserts an unsympathetic Emil Haraszti.[12] In fact, stylistically very little in *Bluebeard* can be traced to this play, as I shall argue below. Far more important in their influence on Balázs's drama are Maeterlinck's symbolist plays from the early 1890s, works such as *L'Intruse*, *Les Aveugles*, and *Intérieur*. The one-act format of these plays, combined with their dreamlike atmosphere and virtual lack of action, shows them to be the true stylistic predecessors of *Bluebeard's Castle*, even though they claim no connection with the Bluebeard story.

Maurice Maeterlinck is far from a household name in the later twentieth century. His dozens of plays and volumes of thought-provoking essays, extremely popular and influential at the turn of the last century, have fallen into a near oblivion from which it does not appear they will be rescued anytime soon. Only *Pelléas et Mélisande* still keeps his name before the public, and that is due primarily to Debussy's music. In the 1890s, however, few dramatists generated more excitement in European literary circles or inspired as many followers as this Belgian playwright. Maeterlinck's career traced a meteoric path from the moment his first play, *La Princesse Maleine*, was published in Paris in 1889. Heralded exuberantly by Octave Mirbeau, a leading Parisian author and critic, as one of the most notable playwrights since Shakespeare, Maeterlinck rapidly emerged as a leading figure in late-nineteenth-century French drama. His plays addressed the mystic aspects of humans powerless to control their fate, of souls battling with universal forces they can neither understand nor alter. Pessimism and darkness pervade the works that established his reputation: *L'Intruse* (1890), *Les Aveugles* (1890), *Intérieur* (1894), and *Pelléas et Mélisande* (1892).

Maeterlinck's was an exciting new style of theater in fin-de-siècle Europe. In contrast to the naturalist style of theater championed in France by Emile Zola and his followers, where the emphasis was on the accurate, realistic portrayal of dramatic situations as they occurred in daily life, Maeterlinck moved the drama inward to portray the psychological states of humans captured in tragic situations not of their own making. Little action occurs in his plays, and pregnant pauses expand into silence as the characters haltingly address each other. In a book of essays published in 1896, Maeterlinck expressed an admiration for "tragedies without movement" in which "events are lacking," a quality he discerned in Greek drama and likened to his own theatrical style.[13] In his view, words function as external symbols of an inner dialogue between souls, a dialogue that transcends language. "It is idle to think that, by means of words, any real communication can ever pass from one man to another," he expressed in an essay entitled "Silence."[14] Maeterlinck's personal philosophy brightened through the 1890s and 1900s as his dramatic output became more optimistic in tone and less overtly symbolic, a shift that directly affected *Ariane et Barbe-bleue*. He won the Nobel Prize in literature in 1911 and toured the United States in the wake of his now worldwide celebrity.

Béla Balázs was an early apostle of Maurice Maeterlinck in Hungary. In 1908, at the time he was beginning to contemplate the play that eventually became *Bluebeard's Castle*, Balázs contributed a substantial article on Maeterlinck to the inaugural issue of *Nyugat*.[15] In this attractive, well-crafted essay, Balázs reviews Maeterlinck's dramatic and literary output in light of its ability to express the mysteries of human existence. All of the Belgian's work, in his opinion, is unified by its attempt to express life's profound, unknowable depths. Different dramas and essays are merely alternative ways of projecting the mystic forces that govern our actions. Thus, plays like *Aladine et Palomides, Pelléas et Mélisande, Les Aveugles*, and *L'Intruse* all exhibit a fundamental spiritual similarity to one another. Balázs describes them as

> fable names and fable scenarios. Somewhere nonexistent so that they may exist anywhere. For who knows? That silence, that motionlessness locked up in those sullen castles, does it not undulate around me here as well? That invisible, all-ruling great mystery. For *that* is the hero of Maeterlinck's plays. Within that protracted silence where nothing happens, the invisible force is active which holds back this life, the silence which depicts its movements. And as for the vast Unknowable, within whose breast we live as if in a dark forest: its most visible, most dramatic manifestation is death. Death is the hero of these dramas. But death here is not the terrible sad end, not burial pit and skeleton, but the dark secret, the lurker. *It is only a symbol of the great mystery*. It is the invisible, *living* figure which walks among us, caresses us and sits down at the table as an "uninvited guest." Nothing happens in these plays. Life happens.[16] (Emphasis in original)

The last two sentences in this quotation sum up Balázs's attraction to Maeterlinck's dramatic style. Balázs pursues this observation to the logical conclusion that, as Maeterlinck has written, action is but a surrogate. "Depiction of eventless motionlessness is the ideal," he asserts.[17]

Balázs was fascinated with the possibilities for dramatic expression Maeterlinck's plays offered. The liberal peppering of his article with phrases like "the Great Secret," "the Vast Unknowable," and "the Great Mystery" shows him to be primarily interested in the mystical side of Maeterlinck's philosophy, which manifests itself in Maeterlinck's choice of stories and settings for his dramas, the sketchy nature of his characters, and his attempt to express, through silence and a minimum of stage action, what cannot be seen or described. But as a dramatist himself, Balázs was also interested in how Maeterlinck successfully transferred this mystic philosophy to the stage. Literary historian Ivan Sanders, examining this same essay, concludes that it is "clear that its author has become an advocate of this new, plotless, often voiceless theatre of mood, nuance and effect."[18]

Balázs's observations about Maeterlinck resonate deeply with the dramatic style of *Bluebeard's Castle*. The heavy, mysterious atmosphere of Balázs's play, in which characters barely move in response to the portentous dramatic events enacted on stage, is clearly inspired by Maeterlinck's example. Bluebeard and Judith themselves seem modeled after Maeterlinck's dramatic characters. Maeterlinck had conferred the title "Marionettes" on the characters in his early plays, referring to the manner in which their actions were controlled by an external fate instead of their own internal thoughts or motivations. Balázs elaborates on this designation: "For indeed they are Marionettes. Because the true, principal, and only character is that force within each of them which pushes and pulls them, the 'force, which we do not see.'"[19] Bluebeard and Judith appear to exhibit somewhat greater internal complexity than Maeterlinck's Marionettes. Their thoughts evolve as they weigh the import of Judith's discoveries. Taints of blood behind each door force upon Judith an increased awareness of her situation, and her thoughts develop accordingly. She is not a "single immobile mood from beginning to end," as Balázs describes Maeterlinck's characters.[20] But Judith and Bluebeard do possess Marionette-like qualities: "forces which we cannot see" push and pull them, conditioning their actions and responses to each other.

Interestingly, Balázs was not nearly so attracted to the work of another contemporary dramatist, August Strindberg, whose plays might well have appealed to him. The Swedish playwright's characters and dramatic techniques elicited a mixed response from Balázs in another essay from that same year, 1908, where three one-act plays by Strindberg are reviewed: *Creditors* (1888), *The Stranger* (1888–89), and *Playing with Fire* (1892), all performed in Budapest by the Berlin Hebbeltheater.[21] Strindberg's mastery of theatrical forms of expression impressed Balázs, but his overly subjective and personal approach to drama emphatically did not. Balázs objects to the surfeit of definition he sees in these plays: "Everything is defined. One character highlights, crisply verbalizes the characteristic traits of another. Yet definition is the most antidramatic of all conceivable things." Strindberg's characters and their psychological problems become too realistic on stage. Balázs concludes, "Pity, he understands the profession of drama but uses it simply to express an opinion."[22] Had Balázs known at this time the later works such as the *Road to Damascus* trilogy, *A Dream Play*, or the chamber plays *The Pelican* and *The Ghost Sonata*, all of which draw heavily on symbolist techniques, one suspects he would have found the Swedish dramatist's outlook more akin to his own.

The nature of his Strindberg criticism reveals how thoroughly Balázs's dramatic ideals were molded at this time by the eventless theater of Maeterlinck. It is plain that the standards by which Balázs judges Strindberg's plays are the standards of a symbolist dramatist. His pronouncements about drama in this essay radiate the same passionate interest in inexpressible, mystic profundities of the human soul that we see in his more lengthy exposition of these principles in the Maeterlinck essay. Balázs is always interested in the dramatization of internal thoughts and emotional states. In his Strindberg essay, for example, he enthuses about "visible thought, visible feeling, atmosphere. Surely this is the dramatic ideal."[23] In these two 1908 essays, Balázs yearns for the expressive capabilities of music in true symbolist fashion:

> Yet why is the mystical music which is breathed toward us from Maeterlinck's dramas . . . so inconceivable? Perhaps because it's music? Perhaps because it's mystical? It is my eternal envy that musicians need not speak and my eternal love that in drama it is likewise possible not to. ("Maeterlinck," 450)

> Music and drama are the agents of expression of the undefinable areas of life. ("Strindberg paradoxes," 518)

Music, drama, and the mystic expression of human longings would later intersect in Bartók's opera based on the *Bluebeard* play. Balázs's choice of the subtitle "Mysteries" for his collection of three one-act plays written from 1909 to 1911 thus becomes more understandable, in light of his clearly expressed admiration for the mystical qualities of Maeterlinck's dramas.[24]

Bluebeard and Maeterlinck's Ariane: A Study in Contrasts

Ariane et Barbe-bleue, a work Maeterlinck described as a "simple libretto, a canvas for the musician," was written during the spring of 1899.[25] Along with *Soeur Beatrice*, completed later that year, *Ariane* represented a new direction for the Belgian playwright: it was specifically created as an opera libretto, for an as-yet-unnamed composer. (*Pelléas* had not been intended as a vehicle for music; Debussy adapted the existing play.) Unlike the plays that brought Maeterlinck acclaim earlier in the 1890s, *Ariane* features considerable dramatic interaction between the characters. It is less overtly symbolic than previous plays and is noticeably less gloomy. Oblique references to life's eternal mysteries are correspondingly few.

Maeterlinck gave this work a subtitle that captures the essence of his treatment of the Bluebeard story: *Ariane et Barbe-bleue, ou la délivrance inutile* (Ariadne and Bluebeard, or The useless rescue). *Ariane* is a rescue drama in which Ariane, Bluebeard's assertive, heroic new wife, liberates her predecessors from their entombment behind the seventh door and offers them a choice: to follow her and leave the castle or to remain. The five imprisoned wives choose to stay. Ariane boldly leaves, simply walking away from Bluebeard and his castle at the end. The plot unfolds through three acts, engaging a full cast of peasants; the two principal roles, Ariane and Bluebeard; Ariane's nurse; and the five former wives. Though ostensibly a retelling of the Bluebeard story, the drama actually centers on the strong leading figure of Ariane, whom one writer has described as "the prototype of the liberated woman."[26] She is a woman of heroic will and clear conscience whose decisions never cloud with uncertainty and whose actions alone impel the drama to its surprising conclusion. Bluebeard, in contrast, does little except glower helplessly when thwarted by Ariane or the peasants. Though he seldom appears on stage, he emerges as an almost pathetic individual. Ariane's gesture of imperial indifference at the end, when she signals that he should be liberated from the ropes that bind him, emphasizes that in this drama, the noble traits of heroism and honor belong not to Bluebeard but to her.

Maeterlinck's approach to drama varied as the 1890s wore on. The life and destiny of the human soul, always the center of Maeterlinck's philosophy, still retained its deep mystery for the playwright, but after 1895 the tone of his dramas changed from the pessimism of his symbolist plays, where characters are mere marionettes controlled by a destiny they cannot understand, to a more affirmative life view, one in which humans can find happiness in pursuit of their unknown destiny.[27] In an 1894 essay, "The Modern Drama," Maeterlinck explicitly redefines his artistic credo: "To penetrate deeply into human consciousness is the privilege, even the duty, of the thinker, the moralist, the historian, novelist, and to a degree, of the lyrical poet; but not of the dramatist. . . . Do what one will, discover what marvels one may, the sovereign law of the stage, its essential demand, will always be *action*" (Maeterlinck's emphasis).[28]

Maeterlinck's aesthetic redirection stresses the fundamental importance of action in drama. "With the rise of the curtain," he continues, "the high intellectual desire within us undergoes transformation; and in place of the thinker . . . there stands the mere instinctive spectator . . . the man whose one desire it is to see something happen."[29] When the human rabble rushes in to save Ariane, or when Ariane shatters the darkened window of the wives' underground tomb to show them the way to freedom, *Ariane et Barbe-bleue* gives evidence of how far Maeterlinck's conception of drama had evolved away from that of his earlier, more overtly symbolist plays.

Any resemblances that exist between Balázs's version of the Bluebeard tale and Maeterlinck's *Ariane* are superficial in nature. Balázs may have borrowed certain ideas from Maeterlinck's play—for example, the use of seven doors and the symbolic contrast between light and darkness. As in *Ariane*, behind the seventh door the former wives are not dead, but living, a situation that allows each playwright to contrast Bluebeard's newest wife with earlier wives. Judith, like Ariane, brings light to Bluebeard's dark castle, so there may be a parallel between the two female protagonists. Ivan Sanders feels that a similarity also exists between the animism of the two castles.[30] These resemblances can all be viewed as part of a shared symbolist vocabulary, or, alternatively, as the result of something as innocent as both plays being based on the same folk tale. When one reads in Flaubert's novel *Salammbô* of a "long vaulted hall" in which "seven doors" were displaying against the wall "seven squares of different colors," one realizes how much the nineteenth- and early-twentieth-century devotees of mysticism imbibed a common language of symbols and numerology and how difficult it is, therefore, to posit specific precedents for any aspect of a given work.[31] The castle in *Bluebeard* could just as easily have been modeled after Klingsor's magic castle in *Parsifal*.

Yet the differences between *Ariane* and *Bluebeard's Castle* are profound. Balázs changes nearly all aspects of plot and characterization. The opening of the seven doors, to pick only one example, becomes the central focus of *Bluebeard's Castle*, while in *Ariane* this action occupies only the first act and is of secondary importance to the main plot. The quality of the differences between the two plays has caused one writer to question whether Balázs even used *Ariane* as a source: Miklós Szabolcsi feels Balázs wove his version of the Bluebeard story directly from Charles Perrault's original fairy tale.[32] This view is too extreme. It is far more likely that Balázs drew upon his knowledge of both the original Bluebeard story and Maeterlinck's play to fashion the outlines of his own version. Some elements of Balázs's play, too, could not have come from Maeterlinck. The recurrent blood motif, for example, clearly originates with Perrault's fairy tale, where Bluebeard's newest wife cannot remove the blood stains from the magic key she accidentally dropped upon viewing the horrors of the seventh door. Balázs himself held *Ariane* in high regard. He referred to it in his essay as Maeterlinck's "most profound play."[33] Admiration, however, does not necessarily translate into emulation. Aspects of Maeterlinck's drama filter into his conception, but they are radically altered in meaning.

For the true stylistic precedent to the *Bluebeard's Castle* drama, we must instead turn our attention to the example of Maeterlinck's early one-act symbolist plays. In *L'Intruse* (The intruder), one of the better-known of these plays, the invisible figure of Death is introduced early on. Characters gathered around a table in a small, quiet room hear the sound of a scythe sharpening outside in the garden but fail to recognize the source of that noise. For the remainder of the play, the audience is aware of the presence of Death. The family on stage appears oblivious, however; they think the noises they hear are those of a relative coming over to visit. Only at the play's end does Death enter the house, still unseen, to claim its victim, the sick mother in the adjacent room. Death surrounded the family, but they did not perceive it for what it was. The halting, disjunct dialogue in *L'Intruse* is laden with frequent heavy pauses. An anxious atmosphere suffuses the theater. The sharpening scythe heard at Death's first appearance early in the play shapes the expectation that some character will die: the only question is who.

Bluebeard's Castle achieves similar dramatic results through symbols of blood and instruments of torture. The symbols of death in both plays (blood, torture, scythe) are first found toward the beginning, and they resurface from time to time to remind the audience, if not the characters, that death lurks behind all the actions taking place on stage. Balázs's blood symbol is at once more overt and more ambiguous than Maeterlinck's allusive, offstage hints of death, for in its many appearances it also takes on additional overtones of pain and suffering, even of psychological trauma, and thus becomes an image whose meaning for the two participants is not clear. At some level, moreover, the existence of blood, together with its attendant implications, is suggestive of life—specifically, here, the living castle.[34] Thus, an image that Judith may interpret as a symbol of death and suffering may mean something else altogether for Bluebeard: that his castle (read: soul) is coming to life again, bleeding through old wounds and agonizing with each twist of the keys, but nevertheless alive, rather than cold and dead.

Such ambiguities aside, the technique by which tension is introduced and sustained in the drama, the eschewal of secondary plot developments and diversions, and the heavy reliance on silence and gesture as a means of communication are all characteristics of *Bluebeard's Castle* that find their closest analogues in works like *L'Intruse*. Future criticism of Balázs's drama must be deflected away from the supposed model of *Ariane*, which has received the lion's share of attention to date, and onto the more elusive but real connections with these early symbolist plays, which Balázs also admired.

Balázs's Interest in Hebbel and German Romantic Drama

When Judith steps forward to assume her place next to Bluebeard's former wives at the end of *Bluebeard's Castle*, the tragedy of two individuals separated in life, if not in each others' memory, is brought home to the audience with great power. Why must she be entombed? She has done nothing morally wrong in opening the doors. And why does she succumb so willingly, with such resignation? Shouldn't she struggle more against Bluebeard? She has done nothing to merit such punishment other than press Bluebeard into making concessions he did not want to make. Answers to these questions expose the presence of an entirely different sense of tragedy in Balázs's drama. It is in his drama's tragic conclusion that Balázs transcends the symbolist style of Maeterlinck.

Balázs, it has been remarked, was a student of German culture.[35] He had grown up in a German Hungarian household, and throughout his life he moved easily in the world of German arts and letters, albeit from a geographically distant vantage point. His proclivity for things German would manifest itself repeatedly in his literary career. Perhaps the most outward example of this personal inclination may be found in his 1914 *Nyugat* essay, "Paris or Weimar?" where he comes down firmly on the side of German culture, feeling that Hungary could benefit from its influence; he hopes for its eventual victory in the newly begun world war.[36] From 1906 to 1908, his doctoral studies focused on the dramas and dramatic theories of Friedrich Hebbel, the mid-nineteenth-century German dramatist whose ideas were drawing renewed attention across Europe, predominantly in German-speaking lands. The mere fact that Balázs chose to study Hebbel for his doctoral program is indicative of his German-oriented intellectual alignment. At the same time he was writing articles that reveal his fascination with the symbolism of Maeterlinck, Balázs was personally absorbed in a major study of one of Germany's great romantic dramatists. The different quality of his symbolism results from his attempt to impart greater metaphysical depth to the symbolist aesthetic.

Evidence that Balázs viewed German literature and philosophy as more profound and worthy of emulation surfaces repeatedly in his writings from around 1910. This attitude is present even in the otherwise francophile essay on Maeterlinck. There, attempting to put into words the mystic philosophy that emanates from Maeterlinck's plays, Balázs notes that these plays lack the spiritual depth that results from rational thought. Instead, he explains, their depth results from the playwright's ability to suggest or allude to the inexpressible forces of fate that guide humans in their lives. Balázs expresses this qualitative difference as the difference between French and German thinking:

> This German woman [Anselma Heine, author of a Maeterlinck biography] wants at all costs to extract the German from within Maeterlinck. Frightening! . . . What German quality is there in this *thoughtless* depth? Maeterlinck's divingbell is not thought, his depth is not related to the depth of Goethe's, of Hebbel's. He wishes to grasp those thoughts which "we think without thinking"—this is not a German craft.[37] (Emphasis and ellipsis in original)

In finding a lack of Germanness in Maeterlinck's dramas, Balázs wishes to make it clear that merely because Maeterlinck's aesthetic appears to be deep and profound, it is not the result of keen insight into the human condition. Maeterlinck's delicately nuanced style is akin to those of "Verlaine and Debussy, Monet and Carrière," Balázs exclaims, "not the Germans!" (452).

For the same issue of *Nyugat* in which the Maeterlinck essay appeared, Balázs also wrote a short essay assessing Friedrich Hebbel's impact on modern drama.[38] This was in truth his first contribution to the journal, and an offshoot of his dissertation work. In his Hebbel essay, Balázs eloquently stresses that the dramatic theories of Friedrich Hebbel form a worthy point of departure for modern dramatists seeking to impart deeper metaphysical significance to their dramas. He places himself directly in the tradition of dramatists who found inspiration in Hebbel's writings:

> The last great theoretician of drama was Hebbel. That which he dreamt and thought of, the great drama of the future, he himself could not realize. . . . Yet to this day we have not reached the goals that Hebbel the theoretician had set, which live on as unsolved problems disquieting secret thoughts in the souls of those contemplating the fate of drama. . . . He initiated things which have not yet been finished.[39]

Balázs shares the excitement of these unnamed Germans who sensed the considerable potential of applying Hebbel's ideas of tragedy to their own work. His concluding statements reveal that his own dramatic outlook is conditioned by Hebbel and German romanticism: "Our long-starved metaphysical instincts are beginning to torture us and the problem of drama disquiets us, for its pangs of birth and groping for direction have never been so obvious as in our own time. And we return to the [German] romantics, to begin where they left off so as to find a modern form of expression for our modern feeling of transcendence."[40] Such demonstrable enthusiasm for Hebbel confounds our neat picture of Balázs as a symbolist dramatist. His interests were clearly capable of pulling him in several directions at once.

In his attraction to both German romanticism and French symbolism, Balázs was not alone among Hungarian intellectuals and writers working around 1910. His close friend Georg Lukács also felt a spiritual kinship with German romantics like Schlegel, Tieck, and Novalis, a feeling brought about by his realization that symbolism, at its core, remained incapable of communicating the reality underlying human existence. The ultimate failure of the symbolist aesthetic in the eyes of Lukács drove him back to nineteenth-century writers, in whose writing he sought inspiration for a more affirmative cultural and spiritual outlook.[41] According to Mary Gluck, by 1910 Lukács and other young Hungarians of their circle "confessed themselves to be paradoxically related to the romanticists, whose failed task they felt they would finally bring to fruition."[42] Balázs's Hebbel article from 1908 seems to epitomize this relationship with German romanticism. As a dramatist, Balázs's attention naturally came to bear on the great German romantic tragedician who, as he wrote, "initiated things which have not yet been finished." Repeatedly, Balázs emphasizes how Hebbel's ideas looked ahead to the future of drama. The "metaphysical instinct" is being "reborn" among contemporary German writers, he proclaims, and "romanticism is experiencing a renaissance."[43]

Balázs harbored a lingering attraction to the symbolist aesthetic long past the time when Lukács had rejected it on philosophical grounds, probably because he was at heart a creative artist, not a philosopher like Lukács. As his comments in the Maeterlinck essay reveal, however, Balázs—perhaps influenced by Lukács—also felt something was missing, in a spiritual sense, from Maeterlinck's dramas. Because of their intellectual affinities, these two Hungarians approached symbolism not through French poetry and drama but instead through the German literature of Goethe, Novalis, Wagner, and the German romantics.[44] The eventual realization that symbolism, in its Maeterlinckian form, rested on little more than a vague mystical philosophy led both men, in individual ways, to search for firmer metaphysical foundations in the work of German romantic writers.

The perception that his works were shrouded in a fog of German-inspired metaphysics dogged Balázs from the beginning of his career. Mihály Babits, one of Hungary's most prominent men of letters, reviewed *Bluebeard's Castle* and the other *Mystery Plays* in 1913. He admits that the title of the collection worried him; he expected to read "works of a vague, German type . . . like Hofmannsthal's creations."[45] He goes on to express qualified approval for these new dramas due to their Hungarian spirit. "My fears should have been unfounded," he writes. "Balázs . . . took care to seek his homeland tradition and, with truly splendid poetic taste, he sought in his drama not true dramatic form, but as he once expressed to me, 'he tried to enlarge the fluidity of Székely folk ballads for drama.' "[46] Babits is relieved to see this new aesthetic direction in Balázs's writing. He contrasts these "Maeterlinckian symbolical dramas," as he calls the *Mystery Plays*, with some of Balázs's earlier works, "which under a strong German influence wanted to express metaphysical abstractions, the mystical breaths of life."[47]

Baláz's interest in nineteenth-century German drama may be one reason why so many Wagnerian dramatic themes can be seen in *Bluebeard's Castle*. Judith's curiosity about what lies behind the last two doors, and her persistent questioning of Bluebeard, who begs her to stop, recalls Elsa's curiosity about Lohengrin's name in *Lohengrin*. Judith, like Elsa, is motivated to action by love. The strength of her feeling for Bluebeard and the certainty that she must press ahead regardless of the consequences drive the drama forward to its tragic conclusion, as in *Lohengrin*. Bluebeard and Lohengrin are similar, too, in that they both place extreme demands on their new wives: secrets exist, Judith and Elsa are informed, that should not be asked about. Another Wagnerian notion in *Bluebeard's Castle* is that of human redemption, specifically the redemption of a man's love through the agency of a woman. Bluebeard is clearly a stricken soul. Like the Dutchman in *Der fliegende Holländer*, he repeatedly seeks the one woman whose faith and grace will redeem him from his misery. Dark, brooding, mysterious, lonely, and passionate, Bluebeard is in many ways modeled on the Dutchman type. Judith, a modern-day Senta, represents an idealized feminine type: the "Ewig-Weibliche" for which Bluebeard unrealistically yearns. Although Bartók's opera is usually described as anti-Wagnerian in conception, the text itself draws noticeably from the world of German romanticism.

Hebbel's Dramatic Theories and Their Effect on the *Bluebeard* Drama

Balázs's study of the works of Friedrich Hebbel had a perceptible effect on the nature of tragedy in his *Bluebeard* drama. In the German playwright's essays, notably the 1843 "My Word Concerning Drama," he set forth the view, manifested repeatedly in his own dramatic work, that human life was fundamentally tragic. Hebbel expressed the nature of human tragedy as the conflict between individual and universal wills. The opposition of individual and universe invariably seeks an equilibrium within which the individual is subsumed. The tragedy of existence lies in the facts that strong individuals are incompatible with the sense of general world balance and that the more they assert their individuality, the more force the universe applies to restore the balance. From this basic conflict arises Hebbel's concept of "tragic guilt," which occurs when an individual has unknowingly upset the balance and must pay the price for his or her action; the "guilt" stems not from having sinned or from having made a moral transgression, but from having endangered the universal whole. Hebbel expresses this tragic guilt as *Nothwendigkeit*, or necessity.[48]

One of the more puzzling aspects of *Bluebeard's Castle* may be found in the concluding actions of Bluebeard and Judith in the seventh door scene, mentioned above. When Judith sees that her fate, too, is to be entombed within Bluebeard's castle, she does not struggle violently against this unjust sentence, as any normal person might do. Instead, she submits with little struggle as Bluebeard bedecks her with crown, mantle, and jewels. Judith seems to recognize that such an end is inevitable, rendering further contest useless. A Hebbelian interpretation throws some light on her actions. Judith is an individual who asserts herself increasingly throughout the drama. After the crucial fifth door scene, her continued desire to open more doors (to get closer to Bluebeard's soul) passes the point at which knowledge of her beloved's intimate secrets continues to be a positive factor in the deepening of their love. Because she is driven to tragic self-assertion and demands the keys to the last two doors, the universe sets in motion a counterbalancing force that ultimately destroys the individual.

The tragedy of this development is that the agents of both destruction and construction reside in the same person: Judith. The force applied by the "universe" comes from within her; she cannot stop herself, because to live—to express her individuality and find love—requires that she go forward, just as she did initially (we presume) in coming to the castle, a step fraught with danger and, like all her actions in the opera, irrevocable. The poignancy of Judith's decision to continue lies in her simultaneous awareness, and disregard for, the dangers that lurk ahead. "Be it my life or my death, Bluebeard / Open the last two doors," she states before the end of the fifth door scene, her words evoking the familiar hero's words ("Életemet, halálomat . . .") of Hungarian folk tale.[49] What is Hebbelian about the conclusion of *Bluebeard's Castle* is the way in which Judith, after the fifth door scene, drives the drama forward to its tragic conclusion, and ruins herself in the process. She does not struggle at the end because inwardly she had foreseen this eventuality from the minute she entered the castle and because she, too, recognizes that her love for Bluebeard can no longer survive now that his deepest secret has been revealed to her.

Judith embodies the idea, it might be said, of Hebbelian tragic guilt. She has not sinned morally in pressing to open the last two doors, for moral or ethical issues do not come into play in this drama. (Bartók's quotation of the aria "Ach, Golgotha" from Bach's *St. Matthew Passion* at the opening of the seventh door would seem to confirm this view; see chapter 4.) Nor can she be faulted for her desire to open the last two doors, though several critics have demonstrated their readiness to condemn that desire.[50] Judith may be guilty of forcing the drama to its tragic conclusion, but does this mean she is morally guilty, too? No. In attempting to gain greater knowledge of Bluebeard's soul, she has stumbled onto the realization—a universal truth to Balázs, Bartók, and their circle?—that full and total knowledge of man's soul by a woman is possible, but only at the cost of their mutual love (and her life or freedom). The wives before her had also made this discovery, but like her, they made this discovery too late.

As Bluebeard and Judith both recognize, it is a necessity of life that Judith enter into the castle. Life demands that love be sought out. She *must* endanger— to use a Hebbelian formulation—the cold splendor of his isolation, because to not do this would risk spiritual death. Likewise, Bluebeard *must* admit women into his castle, into his soul, for to do otherwise would ensure that it remains lifeless. Her actions conflict, oddly enough, with the normal "curiosity" motive of the Bluebeard story. Only before the last door does Judith seem to show a fearful curiosity; the act of opening the previous six doors is motivated less by curiosity than by her urgent desire to let no impediments stand in the way of their love.

The text to *Bluebeard's Castle* reflects Balázs's multiple interests in the years around 1910. Two of the stronger influences on his operatic text are Maeterlinck and Hebbel. In deriving his dramatic aesthetic from these two sources, Balázs demonstrates strong connections to broader trends in European drama at the turn of the century, one essentially French in origin, the other essentially German. This bivalent influence may explain why we can see in *Bluebeard* connections to both French symbolist drama and German expressionist drama. In one sense, then, *Bluebeard* is international in outlook, part of a general trend toward internalization of the drama in the decades before World War I. *Bluebeard*'s mixture of a modern symbolist style with a nineteenth-century conception of tragedy is not as unusual as it might first appear. Miklós Szabolcsi notes that as the symbolist movement spread outside France, it often coexisted with "certain neo-romantic, even neoclassicist trends."[51] As a dramatist interested in creating a new, identifiably Hungarian dramatic style, Balázs drew on what he found most interesting in western European dramatic trends and synthesized these disparate elements into a modern drama of considerable theatrical power. The fact that Bartók changed so little of Balázs's drama is a testament to the drama's intrinsic merits, and proof that Balázs had created a work that spoke deeply to Bartók's own conscience.

Part II

Music and Drama in
Bluebeard's Castle

3

THE MUSIC OF
BLUEBEARD'S CASTLE

In its most familiar form, as published in Perrault's *Histoires ou Contes du temps passé*, the fairy tale of Bluebeard and his wives tells of a wealthy prince who marries a young woman and gives her the keys to his castle, leaving her free to roam about, with one condition: that she never enter a certain room whose contents he will not reveal. One day soon after the marriage he goes away. His new wife, unable to control her curiosity about the forbidden room, unlocks the door. To her horror she beholds the bloodied corpses of Bluebeard's murdered former wives. Before she can close the door, the key in her hands falls onto the floor, where it becomes bloodstained—a fateful misstep, for the key is magic, and the crimson stains cannot be removed. Her disobedience is thus revealed to her husband upon his return, but she is saved from a similar death by the sudden appearance of her two brothers, who hastily dispatch the cruel husband with their swords. The rescued woman lives out her days among the splendors of Bluebeard's castle, sharing her newfound wealth with her family and eventually marrying a kind man who, in Perrault's words, "made her forget the ill time she had passed with Bluebeard."[1]

Bartók's opera reduces the story to the essential conflict between Bluebeard and his new wife, Judith. All external detail is removed. The story is compressed into an hour-long dramatic scene set within the confines of Bluebeard's cold, dank castle, where seven large, closed doors loom in the darkness. Upon perceiving the doors, barely visible, Judith determines that all of them must open, to let sunshine and breezes penetrate the interior. The drama centers on the contest of wills between her and Bluebeard as she asks for the keys one by one and Bluebeard grudgingly relents. Behind the doors lie his secrets: a torture chamber, a flower garden, a view of his splendid domains. Judith is shocked to find traces of blood revealed behind the first five doors, despite having heard rumors of previous wives' mysterious disappearance. With each successive door the conviction grows in her that within the castle she will find the murdered women. The sixth door, which opens to reveal a lake of tears, confirms her suspicion. The seventh door, much to her astonishment, opens to reveal three former wives who solemnly step forward, alive and resplendently garbed. Judith realizes that she, too, is to be entombed within the dark walls of Bluebeard's castle. She moves to take her place beside the other wives. The door closes behind them, and Bluebeard is left alone on stage. "Now it will be night forever," Bluebeard intones as the light dims to blackness.

There are no scene changes in the opera, and no secondary plot developments. The roster of characters familiar from earlier versions of the Bluebeard tale is empty; no heroic brothers burst in to save Judith at the last moment. An unremittant gloom hangs over the theater. The only action consists of Judith opening the doors and discussing their contents and significance with Bluebeard. Very little actually happens in a physical sense: developments occur within the characters themselves, as they react to the revelations behind the doors. Judith's initial assertiveness yields to a complex emotional ambivalence as she opens further doors. Bluebeard is at turns impassive, assertive, or resigned. The true drama in this play is internal, not external, a point missed by one early writer who summarized the opera as a work where "two people clamor on stage for an hour and nothing happens."[2]

As a major work from Bartók's early career, and as one of the most intriguing operatic creations of the early twentieth century, *Bluebeard's Castle* has attracted the critical attention of many musicians and musicologists in the decades since its composition. It is one of the cornerstones in Ernő Lendvai's harmonic theories about Bartók's music. Mauser, Antokoletz, and Frigyesi, in their specialized studies of the opera, explore issues of form, music-dramatic symbolism, and meaning. Ujfalussy, Tallián, Stevens, and other biographers offer individual insights, generally of a briefer and more philological nature. Providing a foundation for much of the work by these and other writers is a general understanding of the opera's dramatic and musical features first laid out by Sándor Veress (1949) and György Kroó (1961), two Hungarian scholars—the former also a composer of note—whose analyses have framed discourse about the opera for several generations of observers, without precluding the more independently conceived work of scholars like Lendvai and Frigyesi.[3] Yet comprehensive studies have been few. The manifold details of tonal organization, of motivic connections that link dramatic images across the span of the opera, of the music's ability to shape our perception of the two characters and their motivations—all of those features that lend richness and texture to a composition—have not been fully absorbed into the Bartók literature, despite the valuable contributions of individual writers. (Here mention must be made of the recent work of Antokoletz and Frigyesi, which moves discussion of the opera to new levels.) Substantial portions of Kroó's and Lendvai's original research into the opera remain untranslated, so those who do not read Hungarian cannot fully appreciate their work.[4]

The present chapter, therefore, has two purposes. The first is to review the accepted view of the opera's musical design in a way that complements and expands upon the classic studies by Kroó and Veress. Issues of form, musical language, orchestration, and vocal style are taken up in the following pages, together with a summary of Bartók's revisions to Balázs's original *Bluebeard* play, the latter not previously discussed in connection with the opera. The intent is to provide, in one place, an overview of the opera's salient features. The second purpose is to explore in detail the music-dramatic symbolism that unfolds through Bartók's association of flexible musical motifs with events on stage, most prominently the so-called blood motif. *Bluebeard's Castle* rests on a well-defined tonal architecture in which C and F♯ gain symbolic associations with darkness and light during the course of the opera. Exactly how and where Bartók introduces this tonal dichotomy merits extended discussion. Detailed analysis of individual scenes follows in the next chapter.

Musical and Dramatic Organization: The Symbolism of F♯ and C

Bluebeard's Castle is articulated in seven distinct scenes corresponding to the seven doors that Judith opens as she penetrates deeper into Bluebeard's castle, symbolically uncovering the secrets hidden in his mind. These scenes are musically contiguous: the music flows directly from one to the next without any scene changes or interludes, although momentary pauses in the dramatic action sometimes occur between scenes as Judith approaches a new door with her key. A substantial introduction section precedes the actual door-opening scenes. This introduction, sometimes referred to as a "prelude" by Bartók scholars, provides the drama with an exposition that sets forth, in its vague way, the necessary background information about the two characters and their relationship to each other.[5] It comprises Judith and Bluebeard's entry into the castle, her statement of mission, and her sudden observation of the castle's seven doors. Preceding the entire opera is perhaps its most unusual feature, a prologue spoken by the mysterious figure of a bard, or minstrel, who steps forward from behind the curtain to address the audience. He offers a cryptic introduction to the ensuing theatrical event; then he disappears and the opera proper begins. The overall form of *Bluebeard's Castle* is shown in table 3.1.

The opera's conception as a series of relatively brief, individual scenes organized around ever-changing visual images, interestingly, was not without precedent in Bartók's oeuvre. In the years prior to 1911, many of Bartók's instrumental compositions were conceived as collections of shorter pieces gathered together for publication under a descriptive, often visually inspired title. The *Seven Sketches* for piano, op. 9, *Two Portraits* for orchestra, op. 5, and *Two Pictures* for orchestra, op. 10, all written between 1908 and 1910, exemplify the com-

TABLE 3.1 The dramatic organization of *Bluebeard's Castle*

	Tonal center
Prologue of the Bard (spoken)	
Introduction	F♯
Door 1. The torture chamber	C♯–G♯
Door 2. The armory	C♯
Door 3. The treasure chamber	D
Door 4. The garden	E♭
Door 5. Bluebeard's domains	C
Door 6. The lake of tears	A
Door 7. The former wives	C
Epilogue	F♯

poser's predilection for writing music inspired by images or ideas drawn from the world he observed around him. Individual pieces within these collections take the form of portrayals of people (his friends, his wife), actions (folk dances, a bear dance), or outdoor scenes (a field in flower, a village dance). Later in life Bartók reached back to the piano music from the years 1908–11, selected five miscellaneous pieces, orchestrated them, and gave the resulting collection the title "Hungarian Pictures." For Bartók the subjective interpretation of external reality was central to his art. "I strongly believe and profess," he wrote to Márta Ziegler in 1909,

> that every true art is produced through the influence of impressions we gather within ourselves from the outer world, of "experiences." He who paints a landscape only to paint a landscape, or writes a symphony just to write a symphony, is at best nothing but a craftsman. I am unable to imagine products of art otherwise than as manifestations of the creator's boundless enthusiasm, regret, fury, revenge, distorting ridicule, or sarcasm.[6]

At no point in his life was this belief, at its core a romantic approach to composition, more pronounced, or more apparent, than in the music of his early career, with its profusion of character pieces for piano and the deeply personal inspiration for works such as the Violin Concerto and the First Quartet.

The *Bluebeard* play offered Bartók abundant opportunity to exercise his talent for creating musical imagery. The seven door scenes, each centered on a particular visual image and the characters' response to that image, presented him with an overall format not unlike that of the many collections of smaller character pieces he was accustomed to writing. To make the transition to his first continuous, large-scale, dramatic work would not, therefore, involve a radical reorientation in his way of musical thinking. An ever-changing kaleidoscope of musical ideas illuminates and gives life to the activity on stage, yielding a musical form that Veress likens to the movements of a suite, where each movement has its own individual character and form.[7] For Lendvai the result suggests a pictorial metaphor. "Each of the opening doors," he writes, "is a self-contained musical painting."[8]

Bluebeard's Castle represented a new style of opera in Hungary, one that had no precedent and, as it turned out, failed to establish a new path for other composers. Bartók himself, as a young composer, clearly positioned his personal approach to writing opera around the more recent works of Strauss and Debussy, but in an analysis of general trends in contemporary Hungarian opera, he pointed further back, to Wagner, when describing why, in his opinion, Hungarian composers had failed to develop a distinctly national opera tradition. "The Wagnerian spirit," he recounted in his Harvard lectures, "was the absolute antithesis of anything that could be conceived of as Hungarianism in music."[9] Too many Hungarians, he felt, had followed this path, with little success; their music relied on the musical language of German romanticism, overlaid with a veneer of *verbunkos*-inspired Hungarianisms. Some—and here he may have been thinking of men like Ödön Mihalovich, director of the Academy of Music, or Emil Ábrányi Jr., author of the weightily romantic *Monna Vanna* (1906)—developed into "servile imitators of Wagner."[10] "They wrote operas," Bartók averred, "in which the most hackneyed phrases—the offal of the Wagner style—were used throughout. This procedure, in itself, was very bad; indeed, absolutely useless, as it would have been the same in any other country." To his audience at Harvard he further explained that for "a few young Hungarian composers"—a reference to himself and Kodály—"Wagner's music was too heavy in its structure, too German in its spirit."[11] Concentration on authentic folk music qualities would liberate Hungarians from this approach, Bartók concludes. He does not mention *Bluebeard* by name. The thrust of his comments, however, is unmistakable: he had set out along a different operatic path.

In this he was aided by the play he selected. The inherent structural qualities of the *Bluebeard's Castle* play enabled Bartók to organize his music in small scenes or tableaux that did not rely on a dense network of recurrent motives as the principal means of musical elaboration. By organizing the musical material around the seven "pictures" that lay behind Bluebeard's doors, Bartók did not have to sustain a given musical idea over broad spans of time as Strauss had done in *Salome* and *Elektra*, where the entire musical fabric of the opera was spun out from a handful of flexible motives. Instead, every change in dramatic focus would usher in new material. (This does not preclude the presence of deeper-level intervallic and gestural resemblances among the outwardly differentiated musical ideas.) The only nod toward the Wagnerian idiom was found in the recurrent dramatic image of blood, which suggested to Bartók, as it would most composers, a corresponding musical idea that would evolve as the opera progressed. Balázs's play thus enabled Bartók to create an opera comfortably removed from Wagner's influence, although, as Ábrányi demonstrated, and as operas by Debussy and Dukas also affirm, the symbolist dramatic style lent itself readily to an operatic style drawing on Wagnerian techniques.

Bluebeard's Castle opens with a quiet, mysterious theme that rolls slowly through the darkness while the bard, on stage, concludes his spoken introduction. Unfolding in regular four-bar phrases, the unadorned melody is based on the qualities of Hungarian folk song without sounding openly folklike: its pentatonic structure, here a five-pitch collection based on F♯ (F♯–A–B–C♯–E), and parallel phrase construction reflect melodic characteristics Bartók discovered in the oldest authentic Hungarian folk songs.[12] The same orchestral melody, again in F♯, returns at the end of the opera. The idea of bringing the opening music back at the opera's conclusion was Bartók's own, a gesture inspired, perhaps, by the stage direction prescribing "total darkness" for the final moments — a return to the stage lighting of the beginning — and by his firm grasp of the play's inherent symbolic dimension. The rounded form thus inscribed on the drama proves central to Bartók's design. It acts as a musical metaphor for the sense of circularity expressed by Bluebeard and Judith's return at the end to a state of isolation from each other. It also functions as a cornerstone in the opera's musical logic, ensuring the ultimate unity and cohesiveness of a score written in through-composed style. Harmonic closure, in this opera, brings with it a sense of psychological closure. As if molded by some vast dialectic process, however, the melody, when recapitulated at the end, achieves a noticeably different emotional effect. What was merely ominous in the darkened theater at the beginning has now become invested with almost inexpressibly poignant sorrow in response to what has transpired on stage, a transformation made possible by Bartók's harmonization of a melody that initially was heard monophonically. Bartók harmonizes the F♯ melody with slowly shifting successions of chords that sharpen into gentle dissonances, while Bluebeard quietly interweaves among the phrases his pessimistic last line and its echo, "night."

The principal dramatic peak of the opera, at the opening of the fifth door, is set in C. Bartók's use of a tritone F♯–C relationship to define the large-scale harmonic organization of his opera stems from an interest, already evident at this point in his life, in avoiding the language of functional harmony and its ramifications for musical form. By choosing keys that lie the farthest possible distance from each other in traditional harmonic terms, Bartók gives musical expression to the symbolic opposition of darkness and light. Their use mirrors the arc formed by the drama itself, which opens in complete darkness, culminates in a blaze of light at the fifth door, and returns to darkness at the end. Even before C is confirmed as the antipode to F♯ in the fifth door scene, however, Bartók subtly establishes it as a key associated with bringing light to the castle and, therefore, as an opposing force to F♯. While F♯ retains a relatively fixed dramatic association with darkness throughout the opera, the process by which C is introduced musically and gradually accrues meaning is far more subtle, in keeping with the way in which light is slowly revealed as a dramatic force strong enough to vanquish darkness — and all that it stands for — from the castle. The triumphant C major of the fifth door arrives as the logical fruition of a tonal conflict quietly introduced at the very beginning.

When the opening melody descends toward its completion, sixteen measures into the opera, an unsettling woodwind interjection, harmonized in thirds, pierces the atmosphere (see ex. 4.1 in the following chapter). Vaguely ominous in effect, this new, sinuous figure proves to be, in pitch and interval content, a seed from which many of the opera's musical ideas will slowly blossom. Antokoletz has aptly termed it the "menacing motif," in recognition of its eerie sound and forthcoming condensation into a flexible head motif marked by a mordentlike flutter.[13] A C-major triad is projected over its first two beats through the alternation of C–E and E–G thirds with their lower neighbors outlining B major. The tonal context, however, is uncertain. Any sense of C as a focus is further weakened by the phrase's motion to an A–C third at the end, which suggests A minor or a background A–C–E–G seventh chord. Semitones created by the melodic motion between B and C triads introduce into the opera an interval that in its various manifestations will gain increasing significance as a musical symbol associated with the negative effects of Judith's entry into the castle.

When Bartók immediately repeats the motif, the pitch C and its triadic formulation stand out more prominently in the absence of metrically accented references to B major (ex. 4.1, two measures before fig. 1). The lower strings, after a one-beat dip to E, continue to sustain on F♯, momentarily producing a bimodal texture (the pentatonic mode of F♯ is still fresh in the ear) in which the two musical ideas generate opposition through the distinct harmonic realms they occupy and through contrasting orchestration. That Bartók identifies this motif with the pitch C is reinforced by its subsequent treatment. In a rapidly changing chromatic environment, the motif retains its "C"-ness at all appearances from measure 16 of the opera to measure 26 (it is heard six times): its initial gesture invariably incorporates the melodic motion C–B–C, sometimes spelled B♯–B–B♯, in either the upper or lower voice of the third interval. In writing the opening music for his opera Bartók may have taken note of the technique used by Debussy in *Pelléas et Mélisande*, which begins in an analogous manner: A quiet opening theme in the strings representing the dark, mysterious, and oppressive forest is interrupted almost immediately by a second, more active idea in the woodwinds, producing sharp contrast between the initial Dorian mode and the whole-tone harmonies that intrude upon it.[14]

Twenty-five measures into the opera a small iron door suddenly opens on stage to reveal what the stage direction describes as the "black silhouettes" of Bluebeard and Judith, framed by a "blinding white square of light" (fig. 2 in the score). The music abruptly melts back into F♯ for Bluebeard's first words, "We have arrived," sung to a descending F♯ octave leap. The orchestral opening of *Bluebeard's Castle* thus sets in motion the oppositions that will generate the entire music-dramatic design: the static mystery and darkness of Bluebeard's castle (F♯) is disturbed and transformed by the intrusion of light, whose effect on the castle is immediate and palpable but still uncertain, just as Judith has not yet made known her role as the agent through whom light will be brought to the darkened halls. Musically, this symbolic conflict is reflected in the way in which the pentatonic sphere of F♯ is intruded upon by the appearance of a chromatically inflected sphere based around C, a process that begins almost immediately.[15] Like the Chinese yin and yang—a concept Lendvai has invoked in discussing Bartók's music—the two musical ideas associated with these tonalities contrast strongly with each other, yet also form a binding, complementary union, the one theme quiet, passive, and negative (associated with darkness and loneliness), the other assertive, active, and positive (to the extent that it gains an association with the tonality of light). Lendvai, speaking generally about the symbolism in the opera, and without addressing the opening measures, finds that this principle of complementary symbolic and musical ideas lies at the heart of the work: "The world concept of Bartók is dual—it is not light and not dark, but light *and* dark, always together in an inseparable unity —as if polarity were the only framework in which dramatic or spiritual content could manifest itself. . . . Bartók takes up the thought of darkness dialectically into that of light, and vice-versa—the two presuppose and justify each other."[16] It is indicative of the dour philosophy behind this opera that even the more positive side of the duality is undercut, here and elsewhere, by the anxious tension pervading the atmosphere inside the castle. The F♯ theme will return at two points in the opera. Both times, the menacing motif soon responds, as if called forth by its opposite.

In a sense, then, the twenty-nine-bar orchestral opening of *Bluebeard's Castle* functions as a microcosm of the entire opera. It opens and closes in F♯ and encompasses a musical disturbance based around C that becomes associated dramatically with the intrusion of brilliant white light. Dynamic markings further mold the passage in the likeness of its larger context: the music begins at *pp* (and the key of F♯), rises to forte and a sforzando climax at the exact moment the door opens (fig. 2), and then subsides back to *pp* with a return to the realm of F♯ for Bluebeard's entrance.[17] Already, too, Bartók has begun to differentiate musical ideas through orchestration, a procedure that will take on additional, symbolic meaning as the opera proceeds. The remainder of the opera can be interpreted as the dramatization of a purely musical process that passes virtually unnoticed in the darkness at the beginning.

With F♯ and C anchoring the overall form, Bartók arrays individual scenes in tonalities that further demonstrate his reliance on nontraditional methods of harmonic organization. The third door scene opens in D, the fourth in E♭, the sixth in A minor, and the seventh in C minor. (What is meant by tonality in this opera is discussed at length below; here the term is used in the commonly understood sense to describe the music's tendency to emphasize, or center around, a given pitch.) Bartók notates these and other tonalities with accidentals; there are no key signatures in the *Bluebeard* score, in accord with Bartók's general practice throughout his mature composing career. Lendvai has observed that the initial tonalities of the fourth and sixth scenes, E♭ and A, form a tritone relationship around the pitches F♯ and C.[18] Taken collectively, F♯, A, C, and E♭ subdivide the octave into equal intervals of a minor third and thus stand in symmetrical relationship with each other. Bartók cycles through these keys at important structural points from door four to the end of the opera, chiefly in the music that accompanies the opening of each door (see table 3.1). This nexus of harmonic relationships operates at a deep background level to organize the opera's music. A similar plan may be found in the Four Orchestral Pieces of 1912, a work

TABLE 3.2 Parallels between the colors associated with each scene and the colors found in the natural spectrum of light

Door	Colors as listed in the opera's stage directions	Spectrum of light
1	"blood-red"	Red
2	"yellowish red"	Orange
3	"golden"	Yellow
4	"bluish green"	Green
5	"in a gleaming torrent, the light streams in" [white]; "blue mountains"	Blue
6	"darker"	Indigo
7	"much darker" "silver like the moon"	Violet

whose individual movements, set in E major, B♭ major, G minor, and C♯ minor, respectively, circumscribe another symmetrical arrangement of minor thirds.

On a more symbolic level, the opera acquires dramatic thrust and organization through the colored light associated with each door scene. The dark/light duality in the opera has been described by previous writers. Parallels also exist between the sequence of colors revealed by the opening doors and the order of colors in the physical spectrum of light itself. In the natural world, white light comprises seven different spectral components: red, orange, yellow, green, blue, indigo, and violet, where each band of color represents a different wavelength within the overall spectrum. A glass prism or other diffracting medium demonstrates this property clearly. The seven doors in Bluebeard's castle open along this sequence of colors, with minor exceptions (table 3.2). Up to the fifth door, the correspondence is exact. After that point, the general darkening of the stage is not given a precise color gradient in the stage directions. The increasing darkness in the sixth and seventh doors finds a parallel in the increasing darkness of the color progression blue–violet–indigo, a progression that would eventually lead to black, just as the drama ends in total darkness. When all the beams of light fall next to each other on the castle floor, as the stage directions specify, a spectrum could in theory become visible before the audience's eyes, with the exception of the white light of the fifth door. This may have been, for Balázs, an unintentional by-product of the decision to organize the doors according to their effect on the progress of the drama. In an opera where every word and gesture is symbolic, however, the incremental march through the spectrum of light provides one more way—purely visual—of anticipating the eventual return of darkness.

Bartók's Revisions to the *Bluebeard* Play

The text Bartók worked from when composing *Bluebeard's Castle* has not survived. In the Budapest Bartók Archive is preserved the composer's personal copy of the 1912 *Misztériumok* volume in which *Bluebeard* was published. On its pages can be seen deletions and additions made in pencil by an unknown person—not Bartók—that correspond to actual changes made to the play. This source, however, postdates the actual time of composition and appears to represent a later documentation of Bartók's revisions by an outside observer. In all probability Bartók, when composing, worked from the printed play as it appeared in the June 23, 1910, issue of *Színjáték*, his copy of which is now lost. (The only other possibility—that Balázs provided him with a manuscript copy sometime in the second half of 1910 or the first months of 1911—seems unlikely in face of evidence suggesting that as late as June 1911, Balázs was somewhat surprised to learn that Bartók had begun setting his play to music; see chapter 5.) We are left, then, with no text sources that document early stages in the composer's creative work, a situation distinctly different from that pertaining to *The Wooden Prince*, where several manuscript copies of the libretto, wholly or partially in Balázs's hand, offer ample means of evaluating the ballet's genesis.[19] What changes Bartók made, however, can readily be determined through comparison of the opera's first edition with the original, 1910 published version of the play.

The vast majority of the opera's dialogue, as well as the stage directions specifying the characters' movements and reactions as they stand before the doors, were taken over verbatim from the original 1910 play, with appropriate modifications in punctuation necessitated by the transfer from a spoken to a sung medium. No deletion or rearrangement of scenes occurred. Bartók clearly placed great faith in Balázs's writing and trusted his acquaintance's theatrical sense to an unusually high degree, even to the point of composing music that corresponded to suggestions Balázs had incorporated into the play. Revisions were aimed chiefly at minor details of wording in the dialogue and stage directions; they may be characterized, in many cases, as fine tuning. In two locations, seven or more lines were cut to form the largest blocks of removed text.

The most extensive cut took place in the introduction, where Judith, in the original play, offers additional justification for her attraction to Bluebeard and his castle (table 3.3). Bartók deletes seventeen consecutive lines and their accompanying stage indications. Through references to the castle's "dark, wild solitude," clouds rising "bloodily / Above the gloomy tower at night," and "horror-stricken, secret rumors," these lines deepen the ominous undertone already present in the drama, lingering on unpleasant images associated with the castle. They also provide the first textual reference to blood, an event that in Bartók's opera takes place much later, in the first door scene. A smaller cut, more typical with regard to its dimension and relatively minor impact on the drama, is found later in the introduction, following Judith's statement of her mission in coming to the castle (table 3.4). Here Bartók slightly alters a reference to the castle, which now becomes simply "your castle" instead of "your poor castle," and deletes two lines referring to light and windows whose substance is echoed in adjacent references to sunshine and wind. As the example illustrates, at the same time Bartók made small additions in the surrounding text, including, perhaps most important, a tense change to the verb in Bluebeard's terse response "My castle does not gleam," which becomes "My castle shall not gleam." Bluebeard's dispassionate

TABLE 3.3 Excerpt from the introduction, showing the original 1910 text of the *Bluebeard* play and Bartók's subsequent revisions. Bartók's additions are in underlined boldface. Deletions are struck out.

Judith	Elhagytam az apám, anyám	I left my father and mother
	Elhagytam szép testvérbátyám	I left my good brother
	Elhagytam a vőlegényem	I left my intended one
	Hogy váradba eljöhessek.	To come away to your castle.
	(közben lejön egészen)	**(she comes down entirely meanwhile)**
Bluebeard	~~(Hallgat.)~~	~~(Listening.)~~
Judith	~~(Lassan lejebb jön.)~~	~~(Slowly coming down lower.)~~
	~~Megyek, megyek, Kékszakállú~~	~~I'm coming, Bluebeard, I'm coming~~
	~~Csak megálltam, hogy azt~~	~~I stopped only to say that~~
	~~mondjam:~~	
	~~Ez a Kékszakállú vára.~~	~~This is Bluebeard's castle.~~
Bluebeard	~~Ez.~~	~~Yes, it is.~~
Judith	~~Ennek sötét, vad magányát~~	~~People fearfully avoid~~
	~~Félve kerülik a népek.~~	~~Its dark, wild solitude.~~
	~~Borus tornya fölöttéjjel.~~	~~The clouds rise bloodily~~
	~~Véresen dereng a felhő.~~	~~Above the gloomy tower at night.~~
	~~És rettegö titkos hir jár.~~	~~And horror-stricken, secret rumors go forth.~~
	~~(Elhallgat.)~~	~~(She breaks off.)~~
	~~Milyen sötét a te várad!~~	~~How dark your castle is!~~
Bluebeard	~~Nyitva van még fent az ajtó~~	~~The door above is still open~~
Judith	~~Kékszakállú — (Lassan lejön)~~	~~Bluebeard—(slowly coming down)~~
	~~Nappal mindig~~	~~By day I always~~
	~~Rácsos ablakomban álltam~~	~~Stood in my latticed window~~
	~~Mert várad oly fekete volt.~~	~~Because your castle was so black.~~
	~~Éjjel mindig azért sirtam~~	~~By night I always wept~~
	~~Mert várad oly fekete volt~~	~~Because your castle was so black.~~
	(A Kékszakállúhoz simul.)	(She presses close to Bluebeard.)
	Kékszakállú! — Ha kiüznél	Bluebeard—If you would drive me out
	Küszöbödnél megállanék	At your threshold I would stop
	Küszöbödre lefeküdnék.	On your threshold I would lie down.
Bluebeard	(Magához öleli.)	(He embraces her.)
	Most csukódjon be az ajtó.	Now the door above shall close.

observation about the castle now is modified to suggest that he already anticipates that Judith's desire to bring light to his domain ultimately will fail.

A similar instance where Bartók's modifications add portent or ambiguity to the established text occurs at the point when Judith pounds on the closed first door, eliciting an eerie sigh. "Ahh! — What was that?" she asks, "What sighed?" Immediately after these words (the "Ahh!" is repeated in the opera), Bartók inserts an additional query, "Who sighed?" Judith's confusion between "what" and

TABLE 3.4 Excerpt from the introduction of the original *Bluebeard* play. Bartók's additions are in underlined boldface. Deletions are struck out.

Bluebeard	Miért jöttél hozzám, Judith?	Why did you come to me, Judith?
Judith	(Felugorva.)	(Springing up.)
	Nedves falát felszáritom	I'll dry off the castle's dank walls
	Ajakammal száritom fel!	With my lips I'll dry them.
	Hideg kövét melegitem	I'll warm its cold stone
	A testemmel melegitem!	With my body I'll warm it.
	(Ugye szabad, **ugye szabad**, Kékszakállú)	(I am free to do this, **am I not**, Bluebeard)
	Nem lesz sötét ~~szegény~~ [Bartók: **a te**] várad	Your ~~poor~~ castle won't be dark
	~~Majd lesz ablak, majd lesz erkély!~~	~~There will be windows, there will be balconies!~~
	~~Lesz fény szegény Kékszakállú~~	~~There will be light, poor Bluebeard~~
	Megnyitjuk a falat ketten.	We both shall open the walls.
	Szél bejárja, nap besüsse	Wind shall blow in, sun shall shine in,
	Nap besüssön,	**Sun shall shine in,**
	Tündököljön a te várad.	Your castle shall gleam.
Bluebeard	Nem tündököl**jön** az én váram.	My castle **shall** not gleam.

"who" is one of the first indicators of the castle's animism, or the essential symbolic identification of the castle with Bluebeard himself. The "who," of course, may also refer here to the sighs of the former wives as well; the reference is ambiguous.

For the most part, Bartók's revisions to the text involve an occasional addition and deletion of lines, phrases, or single words. The preceding examples represent some of more heavily affected passages and should not be regarded as typical. Certain areas of the text received more attention than others. The sixth door scene, in particular, underwent careful pruning by Bartók to weed out excess repetitions of text lines. The second and third door scenes, in contrast, were set directly, with no modifications to the dialogue apart from an omitted exhalation ("Ah!"—marked "quietly") that Balázs had given to Judith at the very beginning of the armory scene.

One of the more interesting discoveries to emerge from side-by-side comparison of the play and libretto is that Balázs originally included a healthy scattering of musical cues, all of which Bartók observed—though not always to the letter—and subsequently deleted from the stage directions printed in the operatic score. For the opening of the fourth door, for example, Balázs wrote, "The door opens to soft, melodious chords on the harp." The seventh door was to open "with sorrowful, minor-keyed music." During the spoken prologue, as the curtain rises, we are to hear "quiet music," and when Bluebeard first enters, with *Megérkeztünk*, Balázs specifies, "His voice veiled, silent." Such cues or general directives typically were not retained in the score, nor were many of the timing indications woven into the fabric of the dialogues, such as "After a pause," found regularly throughout the scenes; "After a longer pause," from the beginning of the lake of tears; "For several moments it remains dark and silent," from the very beginning of the opera; or "doesn't answer," from the sixth door scene. It is apparent that Bartók took suggestions like these more or less at face value. Almost without fail he composed music to fulfill, or at least approximate, the requested purpose. In this way the text provided more than just a spoken dialogue for Bartók to set; it also made very specific the dramatist's sense of how long certain moments should last on stage, and the subtle inflections in speech or gesture with which the characters should respond to each other.

The Opera's Vocal Style

At the time he wrote *Bluebeard*, Bartók had been engaged in the serious study and collecting of eastern European folk music for over five years. As he became more versed in the instrumental and vocal music indigenous to Hungary, Rumania, and Slovakia, the range of his interests expanded and the diversity of this untapped artistic source was impressed more profoundly on his conscience. Bartók felt that the declamatory style of folk song offered a potential model for an innovative style of vocal art music in which the rhythms of gypsy-inspired Hungarian music would be replaced by a freer style of singing that followed the natural rhythms and inflections of the Hungarian language. *Bluebeard's Castle*, his first vocal work apart from arrangements of folk songs, was the laboratory in which he experimented with this new vocal style. Writing to Delius in March 1911 about his newly begun opera project, Bartók confessed, "I have never written songs before—you can imagine how much and how often—at the beginning—the text bothered me."[20] Conceiving a new means of vocal expression was not an easy task.

The text to *Bluebeard's Castle* observes a consistent, eight-syllable line pattern that derives from properties inherent in old Hungarian folk song. Balázs, when called upon to discuss his *Bluebeard* play around 1915, felt that this magyar folk idiom was one of the text's most characteristic features:

> I created this ballad of mine [the *Bluebeard* play] in the language and rhythms of old Hungarian Székely folk ballads. In character these folk ballads very nearly resemble old Scottish folk ballads, but they are, perhaps, more acerbic, more simple, their melodic quality more mysterious, more naive, and more songlike. Thus there is no "literature" or rhetoric within them; they are constructed from dark, weighty, uncarved blocks of words. In this manner I wrote my Hungarian-language Bluebeard ballad, and Bartók's music also conforms to this.[21]

The Székely region in far eastern Transylvania (present-day Rumania) constituted an area of Hungary that, by the early twentieth century, had come under increasing scrutiny by urban ethnologists who journeyed out from the city to witness, and be inspired by, a centuries-old agrarian mode of life still largely uncorrupted by the influences of urban culture. Hungarians recognized the area as a special place, one whose people, so geographically distant from Budapest, represented a vital source of authentic folk traditions. The young architect Károly Kós, seeking to broaden his knowledge of indigenous Hungarian design features, traveled from village to village studying examples of church and home construction. Bartók and Kodály each made folk-song-collecting trips in the region; on one occasion, in 1906, Bartók was accompanied by Balázs. Though his understanding of Székely instrumental and vocal music would take on added dimension in years ahead, by 1908 Bartók already had begun to recognize the unique qualities it possessed. His first scholarly contribution in the field of ethnomusicology, published that year, was a collection of Székely ballads, a type of narrative folk poetry comprising multiple stanzas sung to a simple melody.[22] The texts to the ballads typically exhibit six-, eight-, or twelve-syllable lines, grouped into isorhythmic quatrains. The music is characterized by its pentatonic modal basis and a rhythmically flexible performance style Bartók later described as "parlando rubato."[23] His *Three Folk Songs from the Csík District* for piano (1907), named after one of the counties in the area, is a setting of melodies he recorded during his field trips.

Judith and Bluebeard's vocal parts are written almost entirely in a recitative-like manner that blends the declamatory features of spoken Hungarian with the melodic features of song. Dialogue unfolds in halting phrases over a continuous background of orchestral music. Individual vocal lines follow a generally descending contour, reflecting the natural tendency of Hungarian prosody. Judith's motto-like repetitions of Bluebeard's name throughout the opera, for instance, respect the stress patterns and intonation of *Kékszakállú* in spoken Hungarian; the first syllable is emphasized through longer rhythmic duration and higher pitch, while the metrically unaccented second syllable commences the melodic descent from the initial pitch, often on a weak beat. The remaining syllables of the name then tumble downward stepwise or by larger intervals.

Claude Debussy's elegant, sensitive setting of the text in *Pelléas et Mélisande* formed a compelling example to Bartók as he searched the Western art music tradition for possible vocal models. The French composer's idea of recapturing the flexible singing style of French Baroque opera in a modern composition appealed strongly to him, for it resonated with his own desire to infuse his vocal music with a native Hungarian spirit. Bartók looked in his own country's past for suitable examples of idiomatic Hungarian declamation, but instead of art music predecessors, he found folk song. "We had no traditions whatever in the Hungarian art music to serve as a basis on which we could have advanced further," he flatly declared in 1920. "The declamatory attempts in vocal works of our predecessors were nothing else but imitations of Western European patterns which were inconsistent with the rhythm of the Hungarian language. . . . We Hungarians have nothing but our *parlando* peasant melodies as the means of enabling us to solve this question."[24] Bartók himself acknowledged the debt his opera owed to *Pelléas*'s vocal style.[25] It showed him the path toward a modern vocal style based on centuries-old native cultural traditions.

In performance, both Judith and Bluebeard exhibit a high degree of rhythmic freedom with regard to the declamation of their lines. In the parlando rubato style of singing Bartók envisioned for his opera, even note values printed on the page are, almost without exception, broken into unequal lengths in accord with natural Hungarian speech rhythms, a technique analogous in some ways to the application of "nobile sprezzatura" in early Italian Baroque monody, although the two approaches have a fundamental difference in expressive aim. The latter uses improvisation to decorate and embellish the printed page in pursuit of a highly artistic result. The former uses improvisation, or the implied departure from the printed page, not so much to gild the music with melodic filigree and rhythmic alterations as to pursue a natural declamatory style responsive to the expressive potential of the language itself. Two eighth notes might therefore be approximated as ♪♪ or ♪♪ or some unnotatable subdivision in between; a series of eighth notes might exhibit a variety of durations. Individual vocal lines move at faster or slower rates than the underlying meter, at times arriving at bar lines slightly before or after the orchestra. This style of performance transcends the limitations of written notation and must be achieved through a sympathetic, informed understanding of Bartók's intentions. The recorded performances of Mihály Székely, who studied the role of Bluebeard under Bartók's tutelage in the 1930s, reveal perhaps most clearly the application of a flexible rubato approach.

The slight temporal dissociation between voices and orchestra achieved through this technique leaves an impression of vocal freedom quite unlike anything else written in the early twentieth century. It is one of the opera's most distinctive musical features. Bartók rarely employs monotone parlando, due to the flexible intonational qualities of the Hungarian language.[26] Recitation on a single note, when encountered, usually has a larger dramatic motivation. For example, at the end of the sixth door scene, from fig. 105 to fig. 117, Judith's determination to open the last door and overcome Bluebeard's resistance is expressed musically by her measured, insistent repetitions on a single tone or tones. Here, too, however, a rubato approach subtly broadens or shortens the rhythmic values.

Bartók's Orchestra: Its Sound and Treatment

The relationship between voice and orchestra in Bartók's opera reveals a close spiritual kinship to the symphonic opera aesthetic that represented the predominant opera paradigm for central European composers after Wagner. Most music of melodic interest is found in the orchestra, which thereby functions as the principal vehicle for music-dramatic narrative. The terse, allusive dialogue between Judith and Bluebeard, with its frequent silences and pauses, offers many opportunities for the orchestra to carry the dramatic action forward or shape the fluctuating emotional dynamic on stage. Here Bartók was guided by the symbolic nature of Balázs's text. What Judith and Bluebeard actually say to each other is not as important as what is left unsaid, and the orchestra is perfectly suited to fleshing out the subtle nuances or unspoken meaning behind the characters' laconic dialogue. A moment emblematic of the orchestra's importance occurs just prior to the opening of the seventh door, when Bluebeard dejectedly hands Judith the final key (fig. 118–121). The anguished weight of this action renders Bluebeard almost speechless; he can only mutter, in a low vocal register, a few lifeless words to prepare Judith for what she will see: "Here, take it. . . . Here is the seventh key." To the orchestra, therefore, falls the task of expressing the pathos of this moment when all hope is extinguished. Over his vocal lines, the orchestra plays a restrained but impassioned melody, enfolding the theater in music of aching beauty, while the two characters on stage, no longer capable of expressing their tangled emotions in words, lapse into a mute or subdued state as the tragedy of their love wells forth around them.

Bluebeard is scored for a massive orchestra replete with organ, celesta, a large battery of percussion, and eight offstage brass instruments. If Bartók was attempting to distance himself, in *Bluebeard*, from German operatic models, he did not choose to make the orchestra part of this stance. In size alone—and perhaps only in this regard—Bartók's orchestra is representative of the grandiose late romantic tradition exemplified in the symphonic works of Strauss and Mahler. The orchestral works from early in Bartók's career typically employ a large and diverse orchestra. With *Bluebeard*, then, he was continuing in the vein already established with *Kossuth*, the first orchestral suite, and *Two Pictures*. The general emphasis in these works, as in *Bluebeard*, is on varied and finely shaded tone colors, frequent solo treatment of the woodwinds, textures thickened occasionally by divisi strings, and flexible use of the overall ensemble, which is reduced at times to an almost chamber music–like transparency.

Pelléas et Mélisande, which gave Bartók inspiration for his treatment of operatic voices, had a noticeably less decisive impact on his conception of the opera orchestra. *Bluebeard* does not sound "French" in the way that, for example, the first of the *Two Pictures* from 1910 does. If anything, it lies closer in spirit to *Salome* and *Elektra* in its use of the orchestra as a powerful dramatic voice. One could perhaps point to a mutual appreciation for the expressive qualities of the lower strings, which both Debussy and Bartók exploit to an unusual degree, and a corresponding tendency to center the orchestral sound in slightly deeper registers. But the *Bluebeard* orchestra possesses a muscular athleticism—a capacity for explosive power and tenacious rhythmic energy—that often thrusts it to the forefront of the drama and illustrates its essential difference from the restrained, opulent, deliberately antidramatic style Debussy cultivated in his opera. Bartók gives the orchestra an impressive, at times exhilarating, presence.

Like Strauss, who in *Salome* had added to an already large orchestra additional parts for instruments not normally found in opera houses, such as the harmonium and what he termed a *Holz-und-Stroh Instrument*, or xylophone, Bartók augmented his opera orchestra with a variety of unusual instruments, some of which were new to him at the time, and all of which would be reserved for special moments in the opera. Parts for organ, celesta, offstage brass group, and keyed xylophone are found in the score. The organ is held back until the opening of the fifth door scene, where its voice lends grandeur to the opera's dramatic climax. It reappears only once, at the very end of the opera, where it supports the final orchestral surge over a B♭ pedal point (fig. 136–38) and subsequently provides a brief but haunting transition back to the opera's opening F♯ melody. To further emphasize the splendor of Bluebeard's domains, Bartók adds a group of four trombones and four trumpets playing on the stage, behind the scenery. In the autograph full score he specifies the exact locations the extra musicians are to occupy.[27] Offstage brass instruments were nothing new to the opera house, having been used for dramatic purposes by Beethoven, Mozart, Verdi, and other composers. What distinguishes Bartók's *banda* is that, like the organ, it represents a purely instrumental effect designed to underscore the dramatic situation without becoming part of it.

Easily the orchestra's most innovative touch is the keyed xylophone, a modified version of the pitched percussion instrument used increasingly for coloristic effect by composers in the early twentieth century. Bartók added what he described as a *billentyűs ksilofón* to the *Bluebeard* score in 1917, after percussion specialists at the Budapest Opera House had designed and built this rare instrument. "Imagine," he wrote to Márta in March 1917, "they are preparing a keyed xylophone so these 'complicated' modern xylophone parts can be played more easily."[28] The new instrument is featured in the torture chamber scene, where its characteristically incisive, brittle sound sharpens the horror of the castle's first revelation. It was also in 1917 that Bartók decided to use a celesta in the third and fourth scenes. The addition of these two instruments to the *Bluebeard* score prior to the first performances—neither had been included in the opera's original 1911 scoring—made Bartók's depiction of the castle's door scenes more colorful.

The Blood Motif and Other Musical Motifs

A tendency for thematic concentration is discernible throughout the music of *Bluebeard's Castle*. Using small rhythmic and melodic ideas, Bartók generates entire passages of music using either a Lisztian thematic transformation process or his own, more personal way of creating harmonic or melodic variants of an original idea. These techniques spring from the same source in Bartók's art: his habitual conciseness of expression. A given musical idea, once introduced, grows and evolves over the span of dramatic action in a scene, or across the opera as a whole. It may be repeated at different pitch levels, reharmonized, augmented or diminished rhythmically, varied in gestural shape, or projected intervallically into the musical texture. The elaboration of musical ideas in this fashion represents probably the single most characteristic feature of the opera's music. The *Bluebeard* score offers a seamless web of outwardly varied orchestral ideas—the strongly characteristic music for each scene—that possess in their harmonic and melodic properties certain indefinable resemblances to each other, as if descended from a common genetic imprint. Innumerable details of gesture and line reveal "new" ideas to be continuations of thematic material that has already been introduced.[29]

One facet of this technique can be seen in Bartók's transformation of the martial principal theme of the second door scene into an expressively lyrical melody (ex. 3.1). The incisive, staccato rhythms of the opening idea, when lengthened to

EXAMPLE 3.1   *Second door scene. Thematic transformation of the principal idea.*

even quarter notes and condensed into overlapping legato phrases for the English horn and other woodwind instruments, take on a new character that imparts glowing warmth to Judith's request for keys to the remaining doors. Still more subtle, and in general characteristic of Bartók's compositional style in this opera, is the way in which the dolce melody gradually metamorphoses back into something resembling the counter-subject that accompanied the theme in its original guise—a process not unlike the thematic transmutation that recent scholarship has identified as a salient feature in the music of Brahms.[30]

Example 3.2 illustrates the process during an otherwise unexceptional moment in the opera, taken, again, from the second door scene. The falling fifth of measure 1 (E–A–A–G) is filled in to become, in measure 3, E–C–A–G, a figure that, thus modified, becomes more animated in following measures, until out of the descending whole step at the end of each measure emerges a triplet figure (mm. 6, 7) that, in this scene, immediately recalls the turnlike figures superimposed above the scene's opening theme. Bartók's effortless merging of these two themes in their rhythmically augmented form is made possible by their mutual incorporation of stepwise melodic motion away from, and back to, a principal tone. Thus, two distinct thematic strands, when woven together, as they are here, reveal themselves to be alternate projections, or variations, of a single idea: the falling fifth so prominently featured in the scene's main theme is also present in the mirror-motion activity of its counter-subject (ex. 3.3). Later in the scene, Bluebeard's arialike passage to the words "I will give you three more keys" opens with another manifestation of the whole-step turning figure (ex. 3.4a). A final allusion to this idea concludes the scene on C♯ (ex. 3.4b). By working with very short, concentrated thematic material, Bartók gains almost limitless power over the shapes it may take. It can move from foreground to background and back and forth between orchestra and voices.

Behind many of the castle's doors Judith finds evidence of blood, whether flowing on the ground of his garden or staining a crown in his treasury. Bartók devises a musical motif that captures the negative emotions associated with this troubling symbol. The opera's blood motif, as it has come to be called, is woven into the texture of the music in ways both subtle and overt. From isolated occurrences early on, eventually it rises to permeate the entire score, a progression that closely links it with the opera's music-dramatic symbolism. The thematic transformation that gives rise to musical events on a local level, therefore, is augmented by the simultaneous application of this technique across the opera as a

EXAMPLE 3.2   *Second door scene, figs. 46/5 – 47/3.*

whole. Developed and varied through successive appearances, the blood motif becomes invested with greater meaning as the opera unfolds.

The first explicit mention of blood in the opera occurs, not surprisingly, in the torture chamber scene. "Your castle walls are bleeding!" Judith observes in horror. Just before her words, the tempo quickens and a new, rhythmically incisive clarinet melody enters. The half-step blood motif appears in the trumpets and oboes as a G#–A dyad that pulses slowly in pairs of half notes (ex. 3.5a). The semitone characterizes much of the music Bartók writes for the opening of this

EXAMPLE 3.3   *Second door scene. Intervallic connections between principal thematic ideas.*

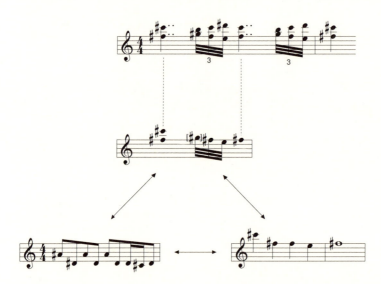

scene, notably the shrill A#/B tremolo sustained almost continuously in the violins and clarinets. What distinguishes the blood motif is its distinct rhythmic and timbral profile. Its chief characteristics are (1) its half-step intervallic content, (2) its repeated longer rhythmic values, and (3) its distinctive tone color within the orchestra. In essence the blood motif comprises two pitches a half step apart; in practice, at least initially, it is defined by a rhythmic aspect as well. Its pitch content, once established, typically remains constant at each occurrence. Until the fifth door, all appearances are scored for pairs of horns or trumpets, sometimes muted, augmented by woodwind complements of varying sizes. The sharper timbral quality of these instruments enables the motif to stand out from the orchestral texture.

The blood motif lies at the heart of the music to *Bluebeard's Castle.* Far more than a Debussyan calling card, it forms an integral part of the opera's overall musical fabric, from which it emerges at periodic intervals to force its way into the audience's consciousness in association with Judith's spoken observations. Possessed of an almost elemental simplicity, it lends itself to unusually far-reaching applications in Bartók's hands. From the fifth door forward, its specific rhythmic profile dissolves, and the motif begins to infect the melodic contours and harmonic content of the music at many levels, leading to increasingly varied and frequent appearances as the drama pushes forward to its conclusion. Elliott Antokoletz has pointed out how the semitone interval itself is woven into the music almost from the very beginning of the opera, after the F# theme has sounded, and thus is introduced without the dramatic connotations it would soon take on.[31] At its one earlier appearance in the opera, the motif's association with the image of blood was not yet known. When Judith touches the damp walls of the castle dur-

a. Fig. 50

b. Fig. 55/6–9

ing the introduction, she starts in surprise. "The wall is wet, Bluebeard!" she exclaims, "What sort of water falls upon my hand?" (ex. 3.5b). At this point a G♯–A half step sounds quietly in the horns, oboes, and flutes, spread across three octaves (Bartók's piano reduction omits the highest octave).

Judith interprets the wetness as tears the castle has shed in sorrow. What will soon become the blood motif, interestingly, is first introduced in the context

EXAMPLE 3.5   *The blood motif.*

a. First door scene, fig. 34

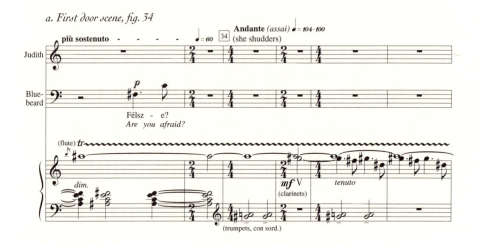

b. Introduction, fig. 11

of tears. Not until several minutes later, in the first door scene, does Bartók's re-assertion of the motif suggest to the audience—in retrospect—that what Judith had felt with her hands on the walls may have been blood, a realization made all the more frightful because it is never confirmed by Judith or Bluebeard's words. Though its identity will become clarified in the first door scene, the half-step motif never loses sight of its original association with tears; in fact, it eventually resurfaces in that context in the sixth door scene. The motif's potential ambiguity is fully realized when Judith, standing before the lake of tears, inquires about the liquid's identity. "What sort of water is this?" she asks, echoing her earlier query from the introduction as half steps thread through the orchestra's melodic lines. Thus Bartók's blood motif shows its Wagnerian heritage. As with many of Wagner's leitmotifs, its meaning is not necessarily clear at its first appearance; meaning accrues only in the context of subsequent appearances. Associations

EXAMPLE 3.5 *(continued)*

c. Second door scene, fig. 45

d. Fifth door scene, fig. 77/11

(continued)

EXAMPLE 3.5   (*continued*)

e. Sixth door scene, fig. 113/4

with more than one image or idea may occur.

In the armory scene, the blood motif intrudes into an extended tertian sonority (B–D–F♯–A–C♯) as a G♯–A dyad corresponding closely, in pitch content and rhythm, to the form it took at earlier appearances (ex. 3.5c). Here, as with most of the motif's appearances prior to the sixth door, Bartók sets the blood motif off temporally as well as timbrally. He inserts it into pauses in the dialogue, allowing it a fleeting moment to be heard, alone, before Judith responds to the vision of blood. (The lone instance where the motif enters simultaneously with one of the character's vocal lines takes place at its initial appearance at fig. 11. There the ambiguity of the wetness Judith observes is reflected, rather ingeniously, by the fact that Bartók does not permit the blood motif to be heard with the same clarity it would manifest in doors one through five, where textual references to blood were explicit. At those appearances the motif is projected at a forte level or higher; here, though, it creeps in pianissimo, its presence obscured, much as the true nature of the wetness is uncertain.)

Bartók's treatment of the blood motif becomes increasingly inventive as the opera proceeds. Although the majority of its appearances in the first half of the opera occur at the same pitch level, G♯–A, the motif is not pitch-specific: in the third door scene it appears at A–B♭; the fifth, at G–G♯. Nonetheless, its initial G♯–A formulation exerts a strong gravitational pull on subsequent appearances, a tendency that, in the context of this opera, is suggestive of Judith's inability to erase the image of blood (and tears?) from her mind, even while presented with an ever-changing array of scenes inside the castle.

After the fifth door scene Judith will uncover no more blood. The motif migrates inward, as it were, losing its specific association with events on stage and the characteristic rhythmic and timbral features that had served to distinguish it from surrounding music. When Judith observes bloody shadows beneath the clouds in Bluebeard's domains, a G♭ tremolo in the upper strings suddenly intrudes into an E-major triad (ex. 3.5d). The clash between major and minor thirds produces the half-step motif. To the strings, not the winds or horns, falls the task of imperfecting her vision of Bluebeard's marvelous realm. In the next scene the motif regains an association with tears, although now in a way that invariably recalls the horrible discoveries of blood. It becomes more malleable in Bartók's hands, and during the final section of the scene it so pervades the music that the very air Judith and Bluebeard breath seems clotted with semitones (ex. 3.5e). This is the type of extremely sophisticated motivic treatment we usually associate with Strauss or Wagner. For Bartók to grasp, in his first attempt at writing an opera, the motif's full potential for enlarging the significance of events on stage was an impressive achievement.

Two other motifs are encountered with some regularity in the opera. The menacing motif has been discussed above. What I term the "sigh motif" is first and foremost a dramatic idea, and only secondarily a musical idea. The castle sighs four times in the opera, always in the context of Judith approaching or opening a new door. Her pounding on the torture chamber door elicits the first exhalation, just prior to fig. 24, an offstage sound described in the stage direction as "deep, heavy sighs . . . like the night wind in long, gloomy corridors." Bartók leaves this sound up to the director's imagination; he merely places a fermata over the bar line to indicate a momentary disruption of the musical flow. Moments later, when Judith turns the key in the lock, the castle sighs again. This time Bartók introduces a musical idea that will reappear several times in the opera, a rapidly oscillating pattern of four thirty-second notes followed by a longer rhythmic value, all in adjacent half steps—music that very realistically reproduces the effect of a sigh (ex. 3.6). The same motif, again moving in predominantly half-step motion, is heard when the lock clicks to open the seventh door.

What seems to define the sigh motif is its particular rhythmic shape (one instance excepted) and its predilection for half-step melodic motion.[32] In this latter aspect we begin to see how Bartók has given the musical motifs in *Bluebeard's Castle* a familial resemblance to each other, as if they were alternate forms of the same musical idea: the menacing motif from the beginning of the opera is based on the half-step interval as well. The motifs in *Bluebeard's Castle* exemplify the thematic

EXAMPLE 3.6   *Introduction. The opera's sigh motif, fig. 29/10.*

concentration that is the hallmark of Bartók's style. Each represents a different projection of the half-step interval, which, in turn, develops a symbolic identity from its aggregate dramatic associations. Sighs, blood, and tears follow from Judith's entry into the castle. Not the legacy of previous wives, as Judith suspects, these dramatic images reveal themselves on consideration to be connected with the castle, and thus with Bluebeard. The context is often rife with ambiguity: If all the previous wives are living, then whose blood is it that flows within the castle? And whose weeping has formed the lake of tears? These questions have no clear answers, though answers are inferred, and acted upon, by Judith.

As the opera proceeds, the negative connotation of such imagery gradually attaches to the half-step interval itself. Thus Bartók can use the motifs interchangeably, as he does during the second door scene when Bluebeard sings to Judith about blood flowing sweetly from open wounds. Here it is the castle—that is, his own soul—that bleeds (ex. 3.7). This is one of the few instances in the opera where the blood motif fails to crop up at the mention of blood. The sigh motif in the orchestra functions as its surrogate, however in the process clouding its own specific identity (there are no sighs here) and revealing its essential connection with the blood motif in Bartók's mind. To further emphasize the connectedness between motifs, Bartók gives them a distinctive tone quality in the orchestra, assigning each to the woodwinds and, in the case of the blood motif, also brass. The full orchestra may pick them up and develop them during some appearances. But in their characteristic and most basic formulation, they inhabit the same chromatically inflected, woodwind-based world that Judith brings into the castle the moment she first sings at fig. 3.

Bartók's Musical Language in *Bluebeard*

In 1924, Bartók urged Weimar music director Ernst Latzko to stress the following features of *Bluebeard's Castle* to his performers. "I would ask you," Bartók wrote,

EXAMPLE 3.7   *Second door scene, fig. 51.*

1) not to overemphasize the folkloristic features of my music;

2) to stress that in these stage works, as in my other original compositions, I never employ folk tunes;

3) that my music is tonal throughout and

4) also has nothing in common with the "objective" and "impersonal" manner (therefore it is not properly "modern" at all!)[33]

Bartók's disavowal of the "objective" label, in this list of desiderata, illustrates his growing distaste for the new directions being taken by Stravinsky and his followers in the 1920s in pursuit of a musical style devoid of human expression.[34] It is apparent from his choice of words, too, that he did not wish *Bluebeard* to earn a reputation as a "folk opera" along the lines of *Jenůfa* or *The Bartered Bride*, with their rustic settings, colorful folk choruses, and incorporation of folklike melodies. He seems eager to avert that potential miscategorization. His distinction between "folkloristic features," which *Bluebeard* possesses, and "folk tunes," which it does not, suggests that the influence of folk music on the opera is deeper and more pervasive than can be apprehended at first glance. In this light, Bartók's claim that the opera is "tonal throughout" warrants further inquiry.

In *Bluebeard's Castle*, purely triadic passages such as that found at the opening of the fifth door coexist with passages of markedly atonal character. Even the jarring, harshly dissonant music that accompanies the opening of the torture chamber door gradually yields to triadic harmonies once the shock of seeing such horrors has eased for Judith. The opera's most shatteringly dissonant passage, the orchestral climax at the very end of the opera directly before the return of the F♯ pentatonic melody, is anchored by a huge B♭ pedal that gives the music an underlying tonal focus. Standing in contrast to passages like these are moments of almost serene triadic repose; the opening of the treasury chamber, for example, is accompanied by a simple D-major triad shining in the brass.

Unusual chord formations, an avoidance of traditional tonal patterns of resolution, and a tendency for bimodal textures and dissonant voice-orchestra relationships give Bartók's "tonality" a broader, less easily defined meaning. In his Harvard lectures, Bartók discusses the use of modes and tonality in his music. The difference between atonality, polytonality, and polymodality, according to Bartók, is that "atonal music offers us no fundamental tone at all, polytonality offers—or is supposed to offer—several of them, and polymodality offers a single one."[35] Bartók concludes that his music is polymodal because it is always based on a single fundamental tone. Applied to his own music, therefore, the term tonality refers to the way in which a given tone acts as a focal point for a constellation of vertical sonorities and pitch relationships based loosely (at this point in his career) on the language of tonality he had inherited as a composer working in the early twentieth century. Bartók's tonality does not necessarily incorporate those harmonic relations (I–IV–V, etc.) that characterize music in the Western art music tradition.

The source for this distinction lies, as always, in folk music. The folk melodies of eastern European cultures feature a variety of styles and modal possibilities within the tonal framework that is one of their most basic properties. In the oldest authentic Hungarian folk tunes, the principal pitches outline a pentatonic collection containing one tone as the final pitch. The absence of minor seconds and leading tones reduces the opportunities for hierarchization of the pitches comprising the tonal system of this music; all pitches are weighted more equally. Bartók was acutely aware of the differences between folklike tonality and tonality as it was understood in Western art music. "Our peasant music," he stressed in a 1928 lecture, "is invariably tonal, if not always in the sense that the inflexible major and minor system is tonal."[36] The absorption of folk music properties into modern music of an increasingly atonal tendency led to works that are not tonal per se but what Bartók described as "quite pronouncedly tonal in type."[37] *Bluebeard's Castle* falls into this latter category. Bartók, we know, felt that his style had moderated somewhat around 1910. In September 1910 he wrote to Frederick Delius in response to the Parisian composer's critique of the arbitrary dissonance in his Second Suite. "Since the piano pieces," he explained, "I have become more 'harmonious' again, so that I now no longer need the contradictory accumulation of dissonances to express the feeling of a mood. This may possibly be a result of my giving way more and more to the influence of folk music.[38]

Bartók broadened his tonal vocabulary through the generous inclusion of seventh chords and extended tertian sonorities. Chords of the major seventh are common in Bartók's music in the years around 1910, and they often carry extra-musical association for the composer. Chords with a flattened seventh degree (e.g., D–F–A–C) also have a special place in Bartók's harmonic vocabulary. Based on his research into old Hungarian folk music, Bartók came to view chords containing any combination of pentatonic pitches as consonances. He felt that one of his musical innovations was the acceptance of the flat seven scale degree as a consonant interval.[39] Seventh chords of both kinds are often extended, in *Bluebeard's Castle*, by the addition of further major and minor thirds to create ninth chords and eleventh chords, and sometimes two seventh chords are linked through a common tone to create an extended structure built of alternating major and minor thirds. After the castle sighs for the first time as Judith pounds on the first closed door, for example, a chain of slowly descending broken thirds in the orchestra leads directly into the return of the F♯ pentatonic melody (fig. 24). Though here they are used melodically, as a transition device, elsewhere in the opera interlocking seventh chords impart structure to entire spans of music, notably in the sixth door scene.

The minor triad with a major seventh above it had special significance for Bartók at this time in his life. The chord of a major seventh, we know from Bartók's other works around 1910, is a musical representation of the idea of love in all its forms, positive and negative. Bartók scholars term this chord the Stefi motif, after the name of the young woman whom Bartók fell in love with in 1907 and to whom he identified the major seventh chord as "your leitmotif" in an often-quoted letter from that year.[40] Bartók employed this chord extensively in earlier compositions from 1907 to 1910, often with a specifically indicated programmatic meaning. Presented as a chord, the seventh has a yearning, unresolved sound that captures the aching, painful side of love as Bartók understood it. The end of his relationship with Geyer in 1908 caused him to pervert the meaning of the motif; the love theme became an expression of emotional pain and even death. A letter from this time explains that "I have started a quartet, its first theme is the theme of the second movement of the Violin Concerto; this is my death song."[41] The motif may be found throughout compositions like the early Violin Concerto, the First Quartet, and the *Two Portraits*. Some indication of its personal meaning for Bartók may be seen in the last two Bagatelles, where it forms the principal thematic material. The first is a funeral march, subtitled "She is dead." The second is a furious, grotesque waltz. Bartók titles it "My dancing sweetheart."

That Bartók should resurrect this motive in an opera dealing with man's thirst for love should not come as a surprise. It forms a basic element in the harmonic language of *Bluebeard's Castle*, and it appears at many moments in the opera. It can be spelled with either a major or minor triad as its foundation. Bartók uses it to underline Judith's words before the first door, "Bluebeard, give

EXAMPLE 3.8   *Introduction, fig. 28/2.*

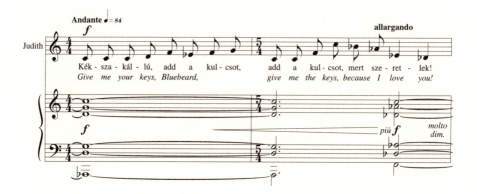

me the key / give me the key because I love you!" where it is placed directly under the words "I love you" (ex. 3.8). It shimmers in the orchestral textures at the beginning of the garden scene and provides a dramatic pause in the seventh door scene before Bluebeard turns to Judith to tell her she will be the fourth of his entombed wives (fig. 130/8). Specifically associated with one woman at first, the Stefi motif gradually developed more generalized associations with femininity and love in Bartók's work. Ujfalussy believes it can also be seen in the characterization of the princess in *The Wooden Prince* and the girl in *The Miraculous Mandarin*.[42]

The permeation of the musical fabric by various, often well-disguised major seventh chords becomes more significant when we realize that its salient interval, the major seventh, has a close relationship to the minor second, which Bartók associates with dramatic images of blood. Harmonically speaking, the major seventh and the half step are two expressions of the same interval. The inversion of one creates the other. (Bartók revisited this relationship many years later in Number 144 of the *Mikrokosmos*, entitled "Minor Seconds, Major Sevenths.") The opera's blood motif thus can be interpreted as a twisted reflection of the theme associated with yearning love. Bartók's interest in exploring the intervallic properties of his thematic material would have led him without much difficulty to the notion of inverting the Stefi motif; all that remained was to give this duality a dramatic form and to realize its expressive potential for the tragedy of Bluebeard and Judith.

The two musical ideas come together openly at the end of the sixth door scene, during the symphonic development of the blood motif. As shown in ex. 3.9, during this passage the moving parts in the strings, bassoons, and horns spell out a steady succession of major seventh chords while, above, dissonant half steps shrilly sustain in overlapping waves of sound. (The first two eighth notes produce vertical sonorities of, respectively, F–A–C–E and G–B–D–F♯, in a pattern that then continues.) Judith has decided she knows what the seventh door conceals: all the former wives, slaughtered in blood. Accusatory words hurl

EXAMPLE 3.9   *Sixth door scene, fig. 115/2.*

forth. The dramatic situation, reflecting the motivic interplay in the orchestra, is laced with seemingly contradictory messages. Judith, acting out of love in asking for the last key, actually fears her own death in pushing forward, and anticipates, nervously, the discovery of others' death. The forceful, vindictive tone of her demand, however, springs from the very real sense of fear she feels—a fear not so much for her own life, for she has already expressed a willingness to die, but more for the irrevocable consequences her action will bring about, the most crucial of which will be a crisis in her love relationship with Bluebeard. Bluebeard's silence is tacit confirmation of his own awareness of how love has pushed Judith to this point; he acts as if he understands, in his sorrow, the costs of such love.

Intimations of death in her dialogue with Bluebeard find aural representation in the continued presence of the blood motif in the orchestra's upper registers. The love that still beats vibrantly, if imperceptibly, beneath the surface of the two characters' actions, meanwhile, is symbolically represented by the flowing major sevenths that rise and fall in lockstep in the orchestra's lower registers. Just as the half step and seventh chord are inextricably intertwined as intervals, their human counterparts, love and death, spring from the same source in Bartók's personal world. The central philosophical message of *Bluebeard's Castle* is reinforced in Bartók's music through the use of these two intervals, whose interconnectedness suggests that human love carries within its very identity the impulses that can cause the death of that love.

ANALYSIS OF INDIVIDUAL SCENES

Bartók's music, with few exceptions, hews closely to the dramatic structure present in the original *Bluebeard* play. While "giving a sharp plasticity to every word and phrase," as Kodály wrote following the opera's premiere, the music also goes one step further in taking its essential form from the dialogue patterns, large-scale dramatic rhythm, and localized stage activity laid forth in Balázs's text.[1] In this chapter, each scene in the opera is analyzed with an eye toward demonstrating how Bartók's music reflects, and breathes life into, the subtle changes in dramatic emphasis that occur within individual scenes. Taken together, the seven door scenes reveal a remarkable variety of musical material keyed to the visions revealed behind the opening doors. Yet beneath the music's variegated surface can be perceived common threads or procedures that help establish links between the scenes and eventually result in a coherent whole. Some of these—namely, the use of certain motifs and the opera's background harmonic organization around a symmetrical cycle of thirds—were discussed in the preceding chapter.

A principal theme in the following pages is Bartók's fidelity to formal patterns discernible in the text for individual scenes. Scenes of outwardly unrelated musical material, such as the first and second scenes, reveal themselves to have almost identical dramatic structure in the way that the characters respond first to the door's contents and, then, to each other. A pattern begins to emerge in which many scenes have three distinct sections: first, a musical depiction of the door, including Judith's response to its contents; second, dialogue in which Judith and Bluebeard work through their emotional responses to the door's revelation; and third, dialogue pertaining to keys and the doors ahead. The dramatic structure of the text thus imposes a certain internal logic and formal rigor upon the opera's music, operating on a local level within a larger dramatic progression also punctuated by a regular series of events: the opening of seven doors. Bartók's music is structured at more levels than appear at first glance; most of that structure, in the tradition of literature operas, was already present in the text.

The chapter begins with a discussion of the spoken prologue, which traditionally has been one of the features most overlooked in analyses of the opera. My investigation of its textual properties and symbolic dimension is intended to restore it to its rightful place as *the* way in which the opera begins. Because the introduction was discussed in chapter 3, here I elect to proceed directly to the first door scene, after which will be found discussions, some more involved than others, of scenes 2 through 7.[2] Issues of larger significance to Bartók's compositional style in the opera are taken up as they arise. The first door scene, for example, reveals in its musical material the manner in which the initial musical ideas are projected into the remainder of a scene using the techniques of variation and transformation. The third door scene, centered throughout on a D-major triad, permits a close analysis of the composer's penchant for bimodal textures.

Prologue of the Bard

The spoken prologue to *Bluebeard's Castle* represents one of the opera's more unusual and, to audiences, challenging features. From behind the curtain, or from the wings of the stage, an actor steps forward to introduce the opera. Speaking in rhymed phrases, the bard, or regős, as this speaker is identified in the score, invites the audience to think about the metaphorical nature of the upcoming drama. "What does it mean?" we are asked. "Where is the stage? Inside or out? / Ladies and gentlemen." Rhetorical questioning like this, put forth by a figure given to such densely ambiguous—and virtually untranslatable—expressions as "The fringed curtain of our eyelids is up," impresses upon the audience an awareness that in this opera, larger implications lie behind the characters' actions and dialogue. We are encouraged to listen closely and marvel at the legendary tale of Bluebeard and his wives. When the orchestra enters with its low, melancholy opening melody, the bard announces that the play has begun and slips silently away, disappearing in the darkness.

Prologues are rarely encountered in the opera house, where the task of preparing the audience for the upcoming drama has traditionally fallen to the overture. In spoken theater, however, the idea of formally introducing a play has flourished ever since the art form originated. Ancient Greek tragedies opened with prologues, usually for a single character, which relate the subject of the drama and the events that have led to the present situation. Shakespeare introduced many of his plays with prologues that have become models of the type. Something of a precursor to the riddling style of Balázs's prologue can be found in the "Induction," as Shakespeare terms it, to *Henry IV, Part Two*, where an enigmatic figure named Rumour relates the history of the conflict between Prince Hal and the usurpers to his father's crown in witty lines so laced with clever allusions as to leave all but the quickest minds breathless in pursuit of his meaning. The dimension and intent of prologues like these can vary, but in all cases they do more than merely narrate information; they also serve to intensify audience interest in the dramatic situation to follow.

The dramatic power of the opening to *Bluebeard's Castle* stems in part from the novelty—to opera audiences—of being addressed directly by a speaker. It is unusual, and a sign of the originality of Bartók and Balázs's conception, that the bard speaks rather than sings. Almost all operatic prologues in the history of the genre have been set to music, dating back to the Baroque era, when sung prologues were frequently incorporated as part of an opera's design. Stravinsky's *Oedipus Rex* (1928) and Busoni's *Arlecchino* (1916) feature spoken introductions, but these were designed by their composers as hybrid operatic works, the one an opera-oratorio, the other what Busoni termed a "theatrical caprice in one act." Their speakers then go on to narrate the entire work, thus serving a fundamentally different function than Bartók's fleeting bard. Bartók's use of a speaker in an otherwise purely operatic context appears to be unprecedented. The closest analogy may be with Berg's *Lulu*, where the Lion Tamer, in a partially spoken prologue, introduces the upcoming characters by symbolic animal names. Speech, *sprechstimme*, and, eventually, full singing voice are heard from this character, who, like the bard, disappears from the stage, never to return.

The fact that the speaker is identified as a bard binds the prologue more profoundly to the subsequent music. The Hungarian word *regős*, which translates equally as "minstrel" or "bard," also connotes a specific type of Hungarian folk music. A "regős song" is a variety of winter-solstice song that Bartók, Kodály, and other early ethnologists were familiar with from their research. In *The Hungarian Folk Song*, Bartók places "regös songs" in his category of old-style Hungarian peasant music (Group A in his classification system). In Bartók's time these were believed to number among the most ancient of Hungarian song types. Citing Julius Sebestyén's *Regösénekek* (Regös songs), published in 1902, Bartók writes that the regös songs and related children's game-songs "greatly differ in character from all other peasant tunes."[3] Kodály explained further that regös songs are ancient New Year greeting songs, or carols, "formerly associated with ancient fertility rites."[4] They feature a wide variety of folk texts and, if the examples cited by Kodály in his *Folk Music of Hungary* are indicative, frequently employ as a refrain or interjection the words "regö, rejtë," "haj, regö, rejtem," or some variant thereof. The latter is, of course, the opening line of the prologue to *Bluebeard's Castle*, which thus can be seen to have drawn—however indirectly—upon this repertoire. Kodály explains, and translators would agree, that these words are "magic formulae" that have no precise meaning. Their chief value is rhythmic.[5]

The image the word *regős* calls forth, of a Hungarian minstrel singing his songs to the people, is reinforced by the bard's first stanza, in which the familiar opening formula of Hungarian fairy tales is invoked. "Hol volt, hol nem: kint-e vagy bent?" speaks the bard in the third line, his words playing upon the Hungarian equivalent of "Once upon a time." Strictly speaking, much of this imagery is inherently contradictory. Neither regös songs nor the repertoire of Hungary's ancient minstrels, it must be pointed out, had a strong connection with fairy tales.[6] Using creative license, Balázs has simply reimagined the regös figure to suit a new context. He invokes, through the name alone, the bard's identity as a professional storyteller, but he begins the prologue with the incantatory formula often found in regös songs, a separate, peasant tradition, after which he introduces words associated with the literary European fairy tale.[7] Given the symbolic nature of the *Bluebeard* drama, where the meaning of phrases and gestures is never clear, one suspects that Balázs savored the polyphony inherent in the regös's name.

The prologue's twenty-eight lines are divided into six stanzas (five of five lines and one of three lines) unified by a regular *aabbc* rhyme scheme and a one-line refrain. Its stanzaic structure was preserved by Bartók for the first edition (ex. 4.1). (Unfortunately, this feature was not retained by Universal Edition in the present-day full score.) References to a stage, the gathered audience, a singer (line 6), and music (line 21) firmly situate the verbal imagery within the world of opera. Each five-line stanza traces a $6-6-8-8-6$ metrical form. The mixture of eight-syllable and six-syllable lines in the prologue, a verse form found nowhere else in *Bluebeard's Castle*, itself represents a departure from the isometric syllable patterns Bartók, Kodály, and other ethnologists ascribed to old-style Hungarian folk melodies. Six-syllable lines are regularly found in the oldest strata of Hungarian folk song, as seen in, for example, the Székely ballads that Bartók published in 1908. There they are typically grouped in four-line stanzas formed solely of six-syllable lines.[8] Balázs's poetry thus employs the external features of what he knew to be authentic folk song style, but in a recognizably nonauthentic and nonspecific manner. The deliberate repetition of certain words and images like *régi* (old, ancient) and *rege* (tale, myth) contributes to the atmospheric evocation of earlier times and places in this text.

The bard's specifically Hungarian identity may offer insight into why Bartók chose to open *Bluebeard's Castle* with an unharmonized melody outlining a pentatonic pitch collection. As the first page of the vocal score illustrates (ex. 4.1), these opening moments are precisely scripted by Bartók. The bard speaks for four stanzas, then the curtain rises; next, four measures of music are heard; at the beginning of the fifth measure, the bard resumes speaking with the words "music sounds, the flame burns / the play shall begin." Why does Bartók take such care in organizing this moment, we might ask? Certainly one reason is to provide conductor and performers with a detailed guide to his intentions, a trait he was to manifest throughout his life. But bearing in mind the deeper significance of all actions in this opera, we also realize that Bartók is using the bard to facilitate the transition from external reality (stage, audience, theater) to internal reality (stage as a representation of Bluebeard's soul). The bard himself and the opening measures of music hold in common an ancestry in the variegated folk and musical

EXAMPLE 4.1   Bluebeard's Castle. *First edition of the vocal score (Universal Edition U.E. 7026).*
Prologue and opening measures of the opera.

HERZOG BLAUBARTS BURG

5

A kékszakállú herceg vára

Béla Bartók, Op. 11.

Prolog

Dies begab sich einst.
Ihr müßt nicht wissen wann, auch nicht den Ort,
da es geschah, Topographie und Jahreszahl.
„Aha", sagt ihr (und es klingt recht fatal) „eine
Legende!"Und fragt–denn es ist nützlich, das vor-
her zu wissen–was in Wahrheit sie bedeute.
Liebe Leute, ich muß euch sagen: die Wahrheit
ist ein Rauch und ist ein Echo nur von eines Seufzers Hauch.

Ihr seht mich an. Ich sehe euch. Ganz offen steht
der Vorhang unserer Augenlider. Ihr sucht die Bühne?
Ja, wo ist die aufgeschlagen? In dir? In mir? Am
rost'gen Pol der Zeit? O liebe Freunde, laßt es dabei
bewenden, beginnt nicht mit Fragen, die nie und
nimmer enden.

Ein Flickwerk ist das Leben. Und was auf Erden
blüht und Frucht wird, ernten Kriege. Aber, liebe
Leute, das ist nicht,woran wir sterben. Woran wir
denn zugrunde gehn? Die Antwort hängt im Strauch,
zerfetzt, befleckt, und ist das Echo nur von eines
Seufzers Hauch.   (Der Vorhang geht auf)

Prológus

Haj regő rejtem
Hová, hová rejtsem
Hol volt, hol nem: kint-e vagy bent?
Régi rege, haj mit jelent,
Urak, asszonyságok?

Im, szólal az ének.
Ti néztek, én nézlek.
Szemünk pillás függönye fent:
Hol a szinpad: kint-e vagy bent,
Urak, asszonyságok?

Keserves és boldog
Nevezetes dolgok,
Az világ kint haddal tele,
De nem abba halunk bele,
Urak, asszonyságok.

Nézzük egymást, nézzük,
Regénket regéljük.
Ki tudhatja honnan hozzuk?
Hallgatjuk és csodálkozzuk,
Urak, asszonyságok.

(A függöny szétválik a háta mögött)

Musik beginnt. Das Spiel hebt an. Hat es euch
Zene szól, a láng ég, Kezdődjön a játék.

gefallen – dann am Ende spart nicht mit Dank und regt die
Hände. Jetzt schließt den Vorhang eurer Augenlider.
*Szemem   pillás   függönye   fent.   Tapsoljatok
majd   ha   lement,   Urak,   asszonyságok.*

Auftaucht das alte Haus. Muß ich es nennen? Ihr werdet's
tief in euch erkennen. Ihr wißt den Ort und wißt den
Namen auch: das Echo nur von eines Seufzers Hauch.
Régi vár, régi már Az mese, ki róla jár, Tik is hallgassátok.

Mächtige, runde, gotische Halle. Links führt eine steile Treppe zu einer kleinen eisernen Türe. Rechts der Stiege befinden sich in der Mauer
sieben große Türen: vier noch gegenüber der Rampe, zwei bereits ganz rechts. Sonst weder Fenster, noch Dekoration. Die Halle gleicht einer finstern, düstern, leeren Felsenhöhle. Beim Heben des Vorhanges ist die Szene finster.
*Hatalmas kerek gotikus csarnok. Balra meredek lépcső vezet fel egy kis vasajtóhoz. A lépcsőtől jobbra hét nagy ajtó van a falban; négy még szemben,
kettő már egész jobboldalt. Különben sem ablak, se disz. A csarnok üres sötét, rideg, sziklabarlanghoz hasonlatos. Mikor a függöny szétválik, teljes
sötétség van a szinpadon.*

Universal Edition Nr. 7026

traditions of Hungary's past. We cannot, and should not, overlook the facts that the bard is still on stage as the music begins and that when it begins, what is heard is a stylized folk melody—the distilled melodic essence of a song a musician like the bard might ostensibly sing. (It cannot be construed as an actual regős song or any other type of folk song.) Hence the absence of supporting harmony, and the baritone range, as if it were an idea crystallizing in the mind of the bard, who decides to sing to the audience (through the orchestra) his song, his memory of this ancient tale. Four measures later, he announces its presence and purpose: "Music sounds . . . the play shall begin." The curtain rises, and we are drawn ineluctably into the bard's "song." When the F♯ melody returns at the end of the opera, it announces the closure of the tale and the transition back to the outer world. This time the bard does not appear.

The First Door Scene: Bluebeard's Torture Chamber

In the first door scene, Judith, having received a single key from Bluebeard, opens the first of the seven doors facing her on the stage. As she turns the key in the door's lock, a deep sigh emanates indistinctly from the castle in ominous warning. She hears this sigh but does not sway in her determination to open the door: "Do you hear that? Do you hear that?" she asks Bluebeard as the door, now unlocked, silently falls open, revealing a blood-red rectangle in the wall. This is Bluebeard's torture chamber. Although the torture chamber's blood-encrusted horrors are enumerated by Judith as she views them, they are not visible to the audience. In a pattern that will become established as further doors in the castle open, the contents of the door are symbolized by the color of the light that emanates from the opening in the wall. Standing in that stream of red light, Judith tries to mask the horror she feels at seeing her new husband's torture chamber revealed. Referring back to her initial desire to let light into the castle, she hopefully suggests, "Look, it lightens already. / Look at this light. / Do you see it? A beautiful stream of light." Her delusions about the light are shattered by Bluebeard's enigmatic response, "Red stream, bloody stream." With this statement, the symbolic red light sheds any remaining possibility of ambiguity, becoming clearly associated with blood and the attendant implications of torture and uxoricide. Judith, however, refuses to believe that the light has no beneficial impact on the castle. Heartened by even this small stream of light, she calls for all the castle's doors to open. "Wind shall blow in, the sun shall shine," she proclaims. Bluebeard warns Judith that she does not know what lies behind the closed doors, but he easily relents to her request for another key. The scene ends on an ambivalent note. "You may open and close every door," Bluebeard says to Judith, but "beware of my castle," he warns ominously. "Beware for us both, Judith."

One of the most striking features about the first door scene, from a dramaturgical viewpoint, is that it occurs where it does. Why does Bluebeard reveal this grisly scene at the very beginning, when Judith, in theory, might be frightened enough to flee the castle? Would it not have been more logical to present

TABLE 4.1   Structure of the first door scene, showing its overall A-B-A' form and the distribution of musical ideas in subsections a, b, and c within this form.

	Location in scene (fig.)	Subsection	Description
A	30	a	Door opens. Sostenuto. Depiction of torture chamber in orchestra.
	33	b	Più mosso. Trill develops melodic characteristics. Judith describes door contents aloud.
	34	c	Andante. Blood motif heard. New clarinet melody. Bluebeard asks if Judith is afraid.
	36	b	Più mosso. Discussion of light's meaning. Music returns to previous material (b).
B	37/4	c	Molto andante. Clarinet melody transformed and developed at quicker tempo. Judith demands that all doors open.
A'	40/5	[c]	Sostenuto. Sudden return to blood motif and clarinet melody at slower tempo.
	41	[a]	Più sostenuto. Dissonant chords from opening brought back. Bluebeard warns Judith about the castle.

the garden or treasury scene first, in order to allay Judith's already growing fears? As we shall see, the placement of the torture chamber behind the first door is of crucial importance to the unfolding of the dramatic action. The disquieting thoughts introduced so early on implant an expectation of certain tragedy in the minds of both Judith and the audience. This expectation dictates how Judith responds to subsequent developments in the opera.

The first door scene has a musical form unlike that of any other scene in *Bluebeard's Castle*. As a rule, the music in *Bluebeard's Castle* is through-composed. Here, though, the musical form is rounded. The opening music depicting the torture chamber is brought back in condensed form to conclude the scene. Years ago, Sándor Veress set forth the idea that the first door scene observes a large-scale structural division into three parts, the last, in his words, a "quasi-free 'reprise' of the first."[9] The first section corresponds to the dramatic action on stage when Judith and Bluebeard describe the torture chamber and the beam of red light emanating from the open door. The second corresponds to Judith's spirited requests for the opening of all other doors in the castle. The third and final section begins at the moment when Bluebeard asks Judith why she wants to open these other doors and she responds, "Because I love you!" Bartók's music traces the changing dramatic focus as attention shifts away from the torture chamber and back onto Bluebeard and Judith themselves. Additional subsections within the scene are suggested by changes in the music's tempo and characterization. The result is a modified ternary form represented schematically as A–B–A' in table 4.1.

The scene opens with a jarring, dissonant orchestral representation the first door's contents. We do not yet know what the door has revealed to Judith, but the excruciating A$\sharp$/B tremolo in the upper strings and clarinet, combined

EXAMPLE 4.2   *First door scene. Opening, fig. 30.*

with irregularly placed, brittle gestures in the xylophone and woodwinds, leaves no doubt that the scene she beholds is a frightful one. Beneath, strings and harp pluck a series of violent, atonal chord clusters whose upper pitches (F#–G#–A#–D#–C#) trace a pentatonic melodic line (ex. 4.2).[10] The tremolo effect is sustained throughout this passage, giving the music a tense, unsettled quality that highlights Judith's anxiety. These and other thematic elements from the opening provide Bartók with the basic compositional material for the remainder of the scene (the various subsections are identified by lowercase letters as "a," "b," and "c" in table 4.1). Through procedures of variation and thematic transformation, he projects the opening music into the scene as a whole.

Shortly after Judith begins to describe aloud the torture chamber at fig. 32, the A#/B tremolo (ex. 4.3a) and the incisive, rapid gestures of the opening music

EXAMPLE 4.3   *First door scene. A♯/B trill (tremolo) figure and its melodic elaborations after fig. 32.*

(ex. 4.3b) combine to form a new horizontal melodic line with a constant rhythmic pattern (ex. 4.3c). This new figure, with its underlying chordal melody, is derived from elements of "a," but it possesses a more lyric character and a regular pulse, as if Judith were beginning to bring her fears under control. The identity of this "b" section is closely associated with its characteristic accompanimental figure (ex. 4.3c), which Bartók presents as an ostinato line that rises and falls repeatedly over the next few minutes of music, breaking momentarily when the blood motif asserts itself at fig. 34. Its rhythm, pitch boundaries (E♯–E), and orientation around a central A♯/B dyad reveal it to be a transformation of an earlier gesture in the winds and xylophone (ex. 4.3d). What was formerly foreground thematic material now moves to the background as an accompanimental figure, created by weaving together the motivic gestures introduced at the very opening of the scene. Whole-tone scale segments (A♯–B♯–Cx–Dx–[ ]) that contributed to the atonal nature of the beginning are carried through as incomplete whole-tone chords (A♯–C♮–[ ]–E–F♯) in the harmony from fig. 33 to fig. 34. Shared musical features between these two sections of the scene stem from their common dramatic purpose. Both provide an orchestral illustration of the torture chamber, first without text and then as an accompaniment to Judith's verbal description.

When Judith observes blood on the castle walls, at fig. 34, the musical flow is suddenly disrupted. A new musical idea is introduced in the quasi-pentatonic clarinet melody at this point, and the half-step blood motif makes an appearance in the horns and oboes. The combination of these two ideas is schematically represented as "c" in table 4.1.

The scherzolike middle of the scene (section B) is characterized by a quicker tempo, a lighter texture, and a fleeting rhythmic figure that diminutes the rhythm of the clarinet melody heard earlier in the scene. The spirited nature of the music derives from Judith's newfound courage. Suddenly agitated, she stands up and, with fierce determination, reiterates her demand to open all the doors. Rather than feeling disheartened by Bluebeard's pessimistic observation about the red and bloody appearance of the light, she appears to take strength; with firm resolve, she looks ahead to the opening of the other doors. The music of section B is found in the score from fig. 37/4 to fig. 40/5.

In composing the music for the middle of the scene, Bartók reworked Balázs's text to bolster the dramatic impact of Judith's demands. What was originally a dialogue between Judith and Bluebeard is turned into a monologue for Judith, interrupted by one terse observation from Bluebeard. Bartók adds four lines to Judith's part, enabling her to reiterate observations or requests, and simultaneously cuts Bluebeard's line "They seldom open—they open poorly." Judith thus is given an almost uninterrupted flow of text, which momentarily alters the balance of power between her and Bluebeard. To underline this transformation, Bartók adds exclamation points to many of the lines she sings. In his hands she is molded into a more forceful, insistent woman than the character found in Balázs's original play. The sight of the torture chamber only steels her resolve to further penetrate the gloom of Bluebeard's castle. Elastic tempi, changes in dynamics, and the rising and falling contour of the musical line all help shape the fluctuating emotional state of the characters on stage. Judith becomes less controlled and more excited as the idea of opening all the doors becomes more certain in her mind. Bluebeard remains impassive.

The third and final section of the scene grows out of the momentum established in section B. This is section A', and it is found in the score from fig. 40/5 to fig. 42/4. The important exchange is heard immediately: Bluebeard asks, "Why do you want it?" and Judith responds, "Because I love you." From this point forward the music slows, the dynamic level eventually tapers to *pp*, and the energy ebbs away. Bluebeard warns Judith about the dangers lying ahead, and the scene ends with a four-measure transition to the second door. The scene comes to a quiet close. Judith's last lines ("Gracefully, gently, I will open it / Gracefully, gently"), in another example of large-scale textual unification, are similar to those she sang at the end of the introduction. Bartók takes advantage of this parallel and, at fig. 42, brings back the pastoral music associated with that text, further rounding out the scene's form.

All of the music Bartók writes for this passage is derived from earlier music, or, in the case of the four-measure bridge passage heard at fig. 42, from the opera's introduction. The recollection of melodic and harmonic ideas occurs in reverse order from their initial appearance, suggesting a possible symmetrical structure for the scene. Bartók does not consistently adhere to this plan, however. At five after fig. 40, the A♯/B tremolo suddenly returns, accompanied this time by two half-note chords that evoke the rhythm, if not the pitch content, of the blood motif first presented in "c." The jaunty clarinet melody of "c" reappears three measures later, now scored for strings and oboes. Originally fourteen measures in duration, it now returns as an incomplete six-measure fragment, set a minor sixth higher and with sharper, double-dotted rhythms. At fig. 41, the dissonant pizzicato chords from the scene's opening are brought back as single, iso-

EXAMPLE 4.4   *First door scene. Tertian harmony sustained in the orchestra at fig. 40/5.*

lated chords whose wide separation from each other and soft dynamic indication fundamentally alters their character. They now act as a gentle, distant allusion to past unpleasantries—a sort of *alter Duft* hearkening back to the violent imagery of the torture chamber. The last sonority in the scene, one measure before fig. 42, a solitary plucked chord (G–A–C♯–D♯–F♯) under the A♯/B trill in the flutes, is the same sonority with which the scene began.

As if to confirm that the harsh world of the torture chamber lies behind Judith and Bluebeard, musical material that originally was presented in a strongly atonal context now develops unmistakable tonal implications. Triadic harmonies underlie the entire last section of the first door scene. The first nine measures of section [A], starting at nine before fig. 41, sustain a single vertical sonority constructed of an extended chain of major and minor thirds (ex. 4.4). Against this purely diatonic sound (the pitches form a gapped C-major scale), a dissonant counterpoint is formed by the A♯/B tremolo and chromatic line of the double-dotted orchestral melody. Bluebeard's final quatrain, after fig. 41, is accompanied by a descending sequence of open fifths on G♯, E, and, finally, C♯. The G♯–E–C♯ root motion evident in the orchestra at this point alludes to C♯ minor, although it does not functionally establish that key. Triadic or pentatonic harmonies outlined in the vocal part reinforce the dominant-tonic relationship between G♯ and C♯.[11] Bluebeard's lines unfold along another extended chain of thirds, this time based on C♯ (ex. 4.5). His last pitch, C♯, coincides with the sustained C♯ in the bass: the end has been reached. The feeble strength of the atonal pizzicato chords itself acts as a musical symbol for the conquering in Judith's heart of the wild horrors inspired by the torture chamber, fearsome music now calmed—overcome—by the emergence of tonality. In this context the atonal chords develop a new role as ornamental flourishes over the stable open fifths projected in the orchestra.

EXAMPLE 4.5   *Chain of thirds present in the harmony at the end of the first door scene, figs. 41–42, reduced to show harmonic organization.*

The Torture Chamber Scene's Placement within the Opera

From a dramatic viewpoint, the entire opera from this point forward could be interpreted as a struggle between Judith and Bluebeard over the eventual expected outcome—the death of one or the other as a result of opening the seven doors. Had the torture chamber scene been placed at another point in the opera, say, behind the fifth or sixth door, the entire thrust and meaning of the dramatic action would have been altered. If we were to rearrange doors one to six so that the more pleasant doors (garden, treasure chamber, domains) were opened first and the unpleasant ones (torture chamber, armory, lake of tears) followed, the resulting dramatic effect would be a crescendo of tension as each scene after the first increases in unpleasantness. Such a dramatic shape is in fact manifest in the corresponding door-opening scene of Maeterlinck's *Ariane et Barbe-bleue*. Although the door openings in Maeterlinck's play are of secondary importance to the overall drama (they take place in rapid succession at the beginning of act 1), a comparison of the two plays demonstrates how Balázs has deliberately ordered his seven door scenes with a view to minimizing this tension-heightening plot device.

The first four doors in *Ariane et Barbe-bleue*, opened by the nurse as Ariane looks on, reveal ever-increasing cascades of amethysts, sapphires, pearls, and emeralds. To these unimaginable riches, Maeterlinck adds a cascade of red rubies behind the fifth door, and a cataract of intolerably radiant diamonds behind the sixth. The order of jewels here is carefully chosen. Starting with the humble amethyst, the gems steadily increase in desirability until the diamond is reached in the sixth door. Surely no jewel could surpass the blinding radiance of these diamonds, Ariane's impassioned words declare. And in fact, none does. The seventh door opens to reveal a dark void leading down into the castle, where this Bluebeard's five former wives can be heard singing a lonely melody. Maeterlinck highlights the seventh door's importance by steadily increasing the radiance of the first six doors' jewels. By the time the sixth door is reached, an atmosphere of tremendous anticipation has been created. All dramatic momentum converges on the moment when the seventh door is opened.

The order of scenes in *Bluebeard's Castle* creates a very different impression. By the time the sixth and seventh doors are opened we have a very good idea of the nature of Judith's fate; the only remaining question is whether the former wives have been murdered or imprisoned. Balázs's dramatic thrust, therefore, is almost the reverse of Maeterlinck's. His seventh door merely confirms what had been suggested back in the first door scene, as if the drama were simply unraveling the various necessary dramatic threads to support a conclusion that was implicit in the beginning. The seventh door fulfills our expectations of Judith's fate. Had the torture chamber been any other than the first scene Judith encounters in the castle, the fatalistic tone that suffuses the rest of the dramatic action in *Bluebeard's Castle* would have been diminished. The moment at which Judith beholds this frightful sight would have been delayed, and she might have responded to it in a different way, perhaps by fleeing. Instead, she meets the torture chamber first, masters her fears, and presses on. Bluebeard no longer offers her the chance to go back. Her fate is sealed.

Ernő Lendvai has assigned positive and negative attributes to each of the seven door scenes in *Bluebeard's Castle*, based on the contents revealed behind each door.[12] In his analysis, the first two scenes are "negative," the middle three are "positive," and the last two are again "negative." Most observers will readily agree that such an analysis is perfectly acceptable: it measures little more than a normative emotional response to things like blood, weapons, gardens, and large piles of gold and jewels. What Lendvai's ascriptions fail to account for, however, at least as he formulates them in writing (a scholar of his intelligence could not have overlooked this point), is the persistent "negative" thread of blood that permeates each scene in the drama up to the fifth. This negativity surfaces even among the "positive" scenes. The riches of the third door's diamonds and gold, to mention one example, are marred by the sight of blood on a crown Judith has picked up.

The continual reappearance of blood in the opera's earlier scenes reminds us (and Judith) that the dark—or negative—undercurrents of the first door never really vanish. The first door scene thus exerts a strong influence on the course of Judith and Bluebeard's actions throughout the opera. It forms a necessary link in the psychological process by which we interpret all later appearances of the blood motif in drama and music. In a way, the unfolding of the drama over the next six doors becomes even more wrenching and tragic because the likely outcome was suggested to us so early on.

The Second Door Scene: Bluebeard's Armory

In the second door scene, Judith again is confronted with a horrible confirmation of her husband's violent past. When the door opens, a yellowish red beam of light falls onto the floor of the castle, cutting into the darkness and revealing to Judith a hall of weapons. To depict the cruel tools of war Bartók writes a nervous, expressionistic march for a small complement of winds and brass, augmented eventually by the strings. Judith responds to the armory as she did to the torture chamber: with an initial fear that transmutes, under the power of her love, into determination to press forward at any cost. She asks for additional keys. Bluebeard, moved by her actions but still guarded in his emotions, offers her three more keys with the admonition, heard here for the first time in the opera, to open what she wishes, "but never question." As if already sensing the eventual outcome of her curiosity, he adds reassuringly, but with ominous ambiguity, "Judith, don't be afraid.—It matters no more."

Three distinct sections can be observed in this scene. The first comprises the music Bartók creates to depict the armory, together with Judith and Bluebeard's accompanying dialogue. The second begins with Judith's demand for additional keys (fig. 45/12). Bluebeard's response, and the dialogue that ensues, injects a momentary note of warmth to the stage. The third section centers around Bluebeard's "aria," a quasi-strophic passage during which he offers Judith the next three keys, warning her to ask no questions when she opens upcoming doors (fig. 48–53). A brief transition section into the next door scene follows (fig. 53–54).

The principal thematic material is epigrammatic and concise, based on two complementary thematic ideas, one a mirror-motion decorative figure in the winds, the other an staccato, martial idea presented first in the trumpets. These two ideas share certain intervallic properties, as discussed in chapter 3. Through varied repetition up and down a chain of thirds (B–D♯–F♯–A♯–C♯) Bartók extends the themes through the first third of the scene, until Judith turns away from the door toward Bluebeard (fig. 45/9), at which point the music's febrile energy subsides and the blood motif appears, initiating a change in dramatic focus.

Judith's psychological response to the castle's newest revelation is complex and unexpected. The appearance of blood ("Blood dries on your weapons / Your many tools of war are bloody!"), oddly enough, only strengthens her resolve. She turns back toward the opened door as if seeing it for the first time. "Beautiful stream of light," she sings, eager to show Bluebeard the transforming power of her love. Even the most fearsome revelations, it is clear, will leave her undeterred. Appropriately, the music Bartók writes to accompany this outwardly rather astonishing reversal is a transformation of the scene's opening thematic material. Slowed down and given lyrical phrasing for solo winds, the incisive trumpet theme gains an expressive beauty, tinged with sadness, that deepens and makes plausible what could easily have been a dramatically unconvincing moment.

Sustained triadic harmonies in the middle and lower strings lend palpable emotion to the orchestral sound, reinforcing the ardor that suddenly suffuses the characters' words. As Judith and Bluebeard stand before the second door, we are again reminded that it is love that guides their actions. "Beware, beware for us both," Bluebeard sings, his words communicating warning but the tone of his voice and the rich sonority in the strings offering encouragement. Additional, veiled associations of hope and desire are suggested by the orchestra after fig. 47, when the seventh chord F–A–C–E♭—one of Bartók's folk-inspired stable harmonies—opens up, through chromatic voice leading, into a major seventh chord, E–G♯–B–D♯. Sustained for five measures, this prominent harmonic placement of the Stefi motif sounds throughout Bluebeard's warning *and* her subsequent request for keys, a glowing musical confirmation of their love for each other.

Bartók deepens the symbolism of Judith's renewed attention to the beam of light by reusing musical ideas already introduced, rather than inventing new ones. Just as visions of Bluebeard's cruel secrets can inspire both fear and love in Judith, so, too, can Bartók take a single idea and shape it into multiple guises, or alternative projections of the same basic vision. The technique of programmatically inspired thematic transformation had been explored previously in Bartók's major compositions from 1907 to 1910, including *Two Portraits* and the last two *Bagatelles*. Here, in the second scene, the "grotesque" and "ideal" visions of the *Two Portraits* find an analogue in Judith's dual perception of the light. Only now it is a woman who, beholding a man's soul, as symbolized by a beam of light, finds what she observes alternately terrifying and appealing.

If like-mindedness and communion of souls had been suggested moments earlier, in the third section of the scene Bartók emphatically underscores the two characters' divergent emotional response to Judith's request. To accompany Judith's words, he launches into a bold, forceful style for full orchestra, punctuated by outbursts of a rhythmic gesture that recall the dotted rhythms of the torture chamber scene (figs. 48–50; 51/7–12). The impetuous quality of her singing (marked "forte appassionato") contrasts markedly with Bluebeard's measured, sober voice in the music that follows, as if to bring out the basic differences in their personalities. Their two styles, and the corresponding orchestral music, shift back and forth, yielding, for Bluebeard, music that resembles the beginnings of a strophic aria. A chamberlike ensemble of low strings, harp, and solo winds accompanies his vocal lines. The controlling power of his presence is reflected in the stable rhythm, consistent mood, and unambiguous tonality of the music he sings.

A nine-measure transition into the next scene unites the second door scene as a coherent entity. A pedal-tone C♯ in the winds helps establish a tonal link with the next scene by acting as a leading tone to D major. Around the C♯, ornamental turns allude to the scene's opening musical idea, now presented without the mirror-motion counter-subject. Bluebeard's last line, "Judith, don't be afraid. —It matters no more," is sung to a descending melody that quotes music he sang at the conclusion of the first door scene—at identical pitch levels, ending on C♯. Although the tonality of the second-door-scene shifts can best be described as "shifting," with a noticeable emphasis on the sharp key areas of D♯, G♯, and C♯, Bartók's return to C♯ at the end in a way that recalls the opening thematic material lends this pitch structural prominence the others do not have. It is both the point of departure and the harmonic goal for the music of this scene.[13]

The Third Door Scene: Bluebeard's Treasury

The first of three scenes revealing the more positive contents of Bluebeard's castle to Judith, the third door scene opens on a fabulous display of Bluebeard's riches. This is Bluebeard's treasury. The audience sees only a golden beam of light emanating from behind the door and, a few moments later, a crown, mantle, and jewels that Judith sets out on the threshold before the audience. The true splendors of Bluebeard's golden chamber are left to our imagination as Judith describes in wonderment the gold coins, diamonds, pearls, and crowns divulged by the opened door. No sooner has Bluebeard told her that all she beholds is hers than Judith perceives blood on one of the crowns. The scene quickly ends. Any discussion of the bloody crown's implications is forestalled when Bluebeard urges Judith to proceed directly to the next door.

The third door scene is the shortest scene in the opera. Several factors contribute to its brevity. At the end of the previous door scene, Bluebeard handed Judith the keys to the next three doors, no doubt confident that their contents would allay her growing fears. When he urges her to open the fourth door, she can do so immediately: the key is already in her hand. Such freedom of action is unusual for Judith in this opera. To open most other doors, Judith must persuade a reluctant Bluebeard to give her a key; achievement of that goal entails a certain amount of additional dialogue and music. Also missing here is the dialogue that would normally ensue from her discovery of blood. The scene moves directly from the revelation of blood to the moment when Bluebeard grants Judith permission to proceed to the next door. Veress acknowledges the third door scene's unusual form when he writes that it has no "reflection music," only "character music" illustrating the door's contents.[14] Bartók makes no changes to Balázs's text for this scene. He adopts it as it stands, omitting only two stage directions that became redundant after he had composed music to represent them.[15]

A sustained, quiet D-major chord greets Judith as she opens the door. The gentle resonance of the brass instruments holding the D-major triad is enhanced by a shimmering orchestral patina of tremolo flutes, harp, celesta, and strings playing open harmonics. Balázs had specified that the third door should open with a "warm, deep metallic sound." Bartók complied, capturing the requested metallic sound in the timbre of the three trumpets.[16] The setting is remarkable for its restraint. Instead of impressing Bluebeard's astonishing wealth upon Judith and the audience with powerful orchestral chords and cascades of wind instruments, as Dukas had done with the jewel-filled doors of *Ariane et Barbe-bleue*, Bartók depicts the glittering surface qualities of the pearls, gold, and diamonds within, choosing to emphasize their visual qualities rather than the emotional impact such riches have on Judith. If Judith is amazed by the sight of all this wealth, it is not apparent from Bartók's orchestral imagery.

By deliberately playing down what easily could have been an exciting moment in the opera — Judith's first glimpse of Bluebeard's wealth — Bartók begins a surge of momentum toward the real dramatic climax of the opera, the opening of the fifth door. The apparent musical slightness of the third door scene, therefore, must be understood as a calculated step in the opera's overall design. In the original play, Judith's initial response to the varied forms of Bluebeard's wealth in doors three through five is roughly equivalent. If anything, the third door seems to elicit a stronger response from her, as she enthusiastically digs among the jewels. A purely theatrical production of *Bluebeard's Castle*, following the cues in Balázs's text, could not re-create the extremes of response present in the operatic setting. Bartók gauges the pace of these middle scenes with a judicious, sure hand. Any differences between their effects on Judith and the audience is due entirely to his creative imagination and to music's capacity to create and guide an audience's emotional response to events on stage.

With the D-major triad providing a firm tonal anchor for the scene's harmony, Judith, Bluebeard, and the two solo violins are free to roam about the tonal spectrum in their individual lines. Both Bluebeard and Judith sing some of their lines in purely pentatonic harmonies (ex. 4.6). Bluebeard sings exclusively in pentatonic modes except at the scene's end, where his two unaccompanied lines pick up the B♭ of the preceding blood motif and widen to a tritone E–B♭ interval. Judith, after an initial line in A pentatonic, tends to express her-

EXAMPLE 4.6   *Third door scene. Characteristic pentatonic pitch formations in Judith and Bluebeard's vocal lines.*

self in chromatic lines that bear little direct relationship to the underlying D tonality. This relationship of voices is in keeping with the general tendency in the opera for Bluebeard to sing in diatonic or pentatonic phrases and Judith to sing contrasting vocal lines of a more pronounced chromatic or whole-tone character.

Individual pitches in Judith's first extended vocal line occasionally cohere into small, local patches of identifiable harmonic formations. The first two measures of ex. 4.7, for example, suggest an oscillation between A major and A minor; the F♯ added in measure 3 extends the A-major triad down a third to form a seventh chord on F♯ (F♯–A–C♯–E). The remainder of ex. 4.7 defies easy tonal analysis, though as a whole, her melodic line could be described as "based on A." Two or more pitches from the A–C/C♯–E pitch aggregate are present in every measure except one. The recurrence of certain pitches gradually asserts the bimodal triad A–C/C♯–E as the predominant tonal focus. Her final cadence, from the word *koronák* onward, outlines a succession of broken triads based on C, B, and A, descending through a minor third and concluding on A. This descending harmonic motion from C to A strongly evokes the "menacing" motif heard earlier in the opera, both of which outline the same harmonic and melodic motion (ex. 4.7). To an analyst they sound related, and presumably Bartók connected them, if only subliminally, though a first-time listener would probably not make the mental connection during a performance. Judith's next line, "How rich you are, Bluebeard!" condenses the cadential passage of ex. 4.7. It omits several pitches but is still recognizably related to what she had just sung. It, too, concludes on A, connecting Judith's vocal line with the D-major triad still sustained in the orchestra.

Two solo violins play a substantial melodic role in this scene, acting as a third

EXAMPLE 4.7   *Third door scene. Judith's first extended vocal line, showing an allusion to the harmonies implied in the opera's menacing motif.*

voice, or refrain, that gently articulates the dialogue between Judith and Blue-beard. Their music appears at regular intervals throughout, either just after a vocal line or partially overlapping it. Essentially a single idea presented four times, this instrumental refrain retains a consistent shape based on repeated downward gestures that swell in range at each iteration, ultimately ending with a cadential formula that mimics the concluding pitches of Judith's first extended vocal line, D♯–B–A–C. At each appearance, the predominance of certain pitches such as G♯, A♯, B, D♯, and F♯ gives the refrain the sound of some nonspecific distant sharp key like G♯ minor or D♯ pentatonic. An essential feature is that no matter what pitches it projects over the first two or three measures, it always dips back to the pitches A–C in its last measure to create a minor seventh chord D–F♯–A–C over the D major held by the rest of the orchestra. Its final appearance is abruptly terminated by the intrusion of the blood motif at fig. 58.

Ernő Lendvai has promulgated an idea concerning the harmonic basis for the third door scene that has become absorbed into the mainstream of literature on the opera. According to Lendvai, the principal pitches in the scene are all derived from a harmonic overtone series based on D.[17] A scale based on the overtone series through the first thirteen partials includes a sharp fourth degree (G♯) and a flat seventh degree (C♮). Lendvai's belief that this altered D major provides the basic harmonic material for the third door scene seems to be substantiated by the orchestral accompaniment. The pitches added to the texture when the horns enter with their syncopated, falling figure at fig. 56 all form part of the D-overtone series, with its characteristic raised or Lydian fourth.

Lendvai's overtone theory offers one way of explaining the unusual modal inflections of the D major in the third door scene. I would like to suggest an alternative. Most of the scene's music centers on two tonal foci, A and D. The fact that both Bluebeard and Judith sing phrases in A-pentatonic mode over a D-

EXAMPLE 4.8   *Third door scene. Twin tonal foci, D and A, with their respective seventh chord and pentatonic formations.*

major triad suggests that harmonies based on D and A can exist simultaneously in Bartók's vocabulary. That is, individual phrases can be related to either A or D, not just D. If we imagine a set of pitches based on the characteristic seventh chord and pentatonic chord for *both* A and D, we arrive at a set of pitch possibilities that accounts for most of the scene's harmonies, vocal and orchestral (ex. 4.8). Analysis of the third door scene using this flexible set of pitches gives a more accurate picture of the music's harmonic identity. Major or minor permutations of the triad and seventh chord are possible, as well as pentatonic modes based on either A or D.

The advantage of viewing the scene's harmonies as a set of possibilities based on either A or D lies in the flexibility of such an approach. In this view, the shifting C/C♯ of Judith's second text line (ex. 4.7) emerges from either the C/C♯ seventh degree of D or the C/C♯ third degree of A—which, is not important. The descending accompanimental figure in the horns is readily explained as the joining of two seventh chords on D and A: **D–F♯–A–C / A–C–E–G♯**. It is not necessary to perceive them as part of an overtone series on D, though here that explanation works as well. But how would Lendvai then explain the G♮ in Bluebeard's part after fig. 56, which sounds at the same time that the "overtone" harmonies sound a G♯ in the horns? He cannot. Viewing the scene's harmonies as a set of possibilities based on the twin foci of D and A, however, readily accounts for this seeming discrepancy. The G♯ stems from a major seventh chord built on A, and the G♮ is part of the D-pentatonic melody Bluebeard is singing at that point. In other words, this music is bimodal. The voice sings in one mode, and the orchestra accompanies it in another. The modes are so closely related that the bimodality is barely perceptible.

From its very beginning, the scene is in D major. This D major is not functionally established through chord progressions that confirm its tonic status. It is simply asserted.[18] The ear gradually accepts it as the principal key of the scene. The continued presence of a sustained D-major sonority throughout the entire scene ensures that all musical events will be heard within the context of that key. What I am suggesting is that the fifth scale degree is treated by Bartók as a separate yet closely related tonal focus with its own seventh chord and pentatonic formations. In the scene as a whole, the two voices tend to outline harmonies built on A, while the orchestra remains firmly rooted on D. We can hear the importance of A as a separate focus in the twenty measures from figs. 56 to 58: Bluebeard sings at times in the D-pentatonic and A-pentatonic modes, Judith sings in a quasi-A-pentatonic mode, and the orchestra accompaniment is based on a pair of interlocking seventh chords based on D and A, all supported by the D-major triad shimmering in the orchestra.[19] As simple as this passage is, to sweep it all under the rug of a D-overtone series misrepresents its bimodal tendencies and completely overlooks the subtle chromatic clashes that vitalize the music.

At the scene's end, blood suddenly intrudes into Judith's vision of the treasury's splendors, shattering once more any delusions she may have entertained about her prospects of future happiness in Bluebeard's castle (fig. 58). The blood motif takes the form of an A/B♭ interval cell that unfolds over the next twenty-two measures in gathering waves of harsh, shrill sound. Boldly reiterated at strong dynamic levels in the upper registers of the orchestra, it emphatically concludes the scene with a period of sustained dissonance that symbolizes the horrors of the bloody crown.

From the moment the blood motif appears at fig. 58, Judith and Bluebeard's vocal lines shift abruptly to a new emphasis on pitches related to B♭. They move away from the A/D orientation of their previous lines, even though the D-major triad is still present in the orchestra. The pitches of Judith's two lines in this part of the scene, "There are bloodstains on the jewels" and "The most beautiful crown is bloody," outline triads on G♭ major and B♭ minor, respectively—triads that, in the context of D major, lie among the most dissonant possible related key areas.[20] Bartók thus maximizes the dissonance between the vocal parts and the orchestra, drawing attention to the emotional shock Judith feels upon seeing blood on the crown.

When Bluebeard takes up B♭ as the central pitch in his unaccompanied invitation to open the fourth door, however, the orchestra has dropped out and the B♭ is no longer heard as a dissonant tone. His final line in the scene enables B♭ to emerge as a new tonal reference, through hints of a new dominant key, F major, present in the pitches A, F, and C sung in the course of his vocal part. In this manner, B♭ major almost seems to be functionally established, a sense only partially diluted by the whole-tone implications (B♭–E) that conclude his vocal line. By placing B♭ as the first and last notes of Bluebeard's four-measure phrase, Bartók underlines that pitch's priority.

The increasing prominence of B♭ at the end of the third door scene facilitates the musical transition to E♭ major, the opening key of the fourth scene, by acting as a dominant to that key. The unambiguous B♭-major scale presented by the gracefully ascending harp glissando that ushers in the fourth door scene is both the logical conclusion of the preceding harmonic motion in the direction of B♭ and the point of departure for the following music in E♭ major. (That this scale begins on its seventh scale degree, A, is a deliberate nod by Bartók to the immediate tonal environment.) Only at this moment is the key of B♭ major truly established. The bridge between the D major of the third door scene and the E♭ of the garden scene is effected by the assertion of their dominant pitches in the form of an A/B♭ interval cell, out of which the B♭ gradually emerges to prepare for the change to E♭: D → A/B♭ → E♭. The half-step blood motif at the end of the third door scene thus serves a specific compositional purpose in addition to its sym-

EXAMPLE 4.9 *Fourth door scene. Opening, fig. 60.*

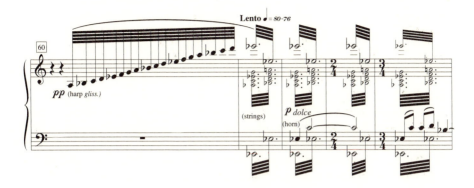

bolic association with the bloodied crown. The music from figs. 58 to 60 is not only an extended appearance of the blood motif but also a carefully designed transition passage leading into the following scene, a transition no less artful for the simplicity of its conception.

The Fourth Door Scene: Bluebeard's Garden

The fourth door opens to reveal a marvelous garden hidden away in the darkened castle. Flowering branches, liberated by Judith's hand, push forward from behind the door frame, bathed in the bluish green light of the open door. "Oh, flowers!" Judith sings in wonder, "Oh, fragrant garden!" To depict the freshness and beauty of this scene Bartók writes some of his finest nature music, of the sort he would use again in *The Wooden Prince* to capture the primal splendor of the uninhabited forest. As in that work, shimmering orchestral textures provide the backdrop for a hushed solo on the French horn, an instrument long associated in nineteenth-century musical thought with images of nature. The horn melody is characterized by an upward leap of a major sixth, from E♭ to C. In the extended lyric line that follows, the instrument touches on this interval repeatedly, each time to initiate phrases that explore—always diatonically—the scene's central tonality of E♭ (ex. 4.9). Against the horn's melody a solo clarinet, followed by other solo wind instruments, gently weaves a contrapuntal line whose pitches result in piquant chromatic clashes. A solo flute adds birdcalls after fig. 64 to complete the image of nature at rest, peaceful and harmonious.

At first the scene unfolds leisurely. The spaciously conceived, thirty-eight-measure orchestral tone picture seems to give Judith pause, and she is long in responding. The ensuing dialogue with Bluebeard is marked by additional, weighty pauses as the orchestra continues to sustain the opening mood. When she suddenly observes blood ("The stems of your white roses are bloody," she exclaims, "The ground under your flowers is bloody"), the dramatic pace accelerates, literally, to permit the orchestra to build the tension that will be released, in a flood of light, when the fifth door is opened. Bartók's tempo markings reflect the change, moving as the scene progresses from "lento" and "andante" to "agitato" and, finally, "vivacissimo" (among other tempo markings). Again, three sections can be observed based on the text's changing dramatic focus. Bartók's depiction of the garden is found in the score from figs. 60 to 65. Dialogue about the garden occupies most of the middle part of the scene, from figs. 65 to 73/3. When Bluebeard urges Judith toward the next door, a brief but powerful transition section follows, from fig. 73/4 to 74/19, when the fifth door opens.

Bluebeard's garden reacts to Judith's presence as if it were human. Like the castle itself, it has animate qualities. The flowers "bow" to Judith and "ring bells for [her] at dawn." The lilies, she quietly observes, are "as large as a man." Through references like these we begin to appreciate the garden's symbolic identity as another facet of Bluebeard's soul. Bluebeard tacitly acknowledges its larger meaning when he projects his own emotions onto its contents. If not tended correctly, he warns, the flowers can just as readily wither in her presence. "You make them grow," he assures her, "you make them wilt / You make them sprout anew, and beautifully."

Out of the opening picture emerges, inconspicuously at first, a rhythmic motif that will grow increasingly prominent in the scene's music, eventually taking shape as a bold gestural idea sounded repeatedly in the orchestra after fig. 69. Possessing a rhythmic shape that reflects the prosodic patterns of spoken Hungarian, the motif issues from the opening horn solo after fig. 62 (ex. 4.10a). Oboe and English horn appear to echo the horn melody's contours with their rising sixth, but they immediately transform the melody into a sharp, accented figure that encompasses, in its most characteristic form, a descending tritone or other chromatic interval. Judith's mental absorption in the vision before her is reflected by the contours of her opening vocal line, which mimics the rhythms heard in the orchestra: she sings two statements of the motif, slightly varied, to the words *Oh! virágok* and *Oh! Illatos kert!*, phrases whose natural speech rhythms lend themselves readily to this declamation (ex. 4.10b). The orchestra, as she sings, echoes the motif, a sign of its growing thematic weight. As the scene moves toward its conclusion, the orchestra seizes upon the motif, leaving aside other musical ideas introduced in the opening picture, and, through varied repetition, uses it to punctuate the dialogue with forceful, dissonant outbursts (ex. 4.10c) that underscore the rising tension on stage. Bartók sustains and intensifies this mood in the transition passage that follows, thus preparing the audience—and Judith—for the brilliance and overwhelming emotional effect of the fifth door. In the final moments before the music converges onto a pounding, syncopated rhythm that will lead into the moment when Judith throws open the next door, what sounds like an allusion to the clarinet melody of the first door scene fleetingly sounds forth at fig. 74—a symbol, perhaps, that for Judith each forward step in the opera is also a step backward toward a fate suggested by the first door.

EXAMPLE 4.10 *Fourth door scene. Emergence of the rhythmic motif associated with this scene.*

The Fifth Door Scene: Bluebeard's Domains

After the extreme dissonance and febrile, nervous energy of the music that brings the fourth door scene to a close, the fifth door opens to powerful chords bursting forth in C major from the full orchestra, augmented by instruments Bartók held in reserve until this point: the organ and a small group of offstage brass instruments (ex. 4.11). Brilliant light pours in from the opened door as Judith beholds the breathtaking grandeur of Bluebeard's domains, visible from a balcony revealed behind the fifth door. Emotionally, this represents the climax

EXAMPLE 4.11   *Fifth door scene. Opening, fig. 74/19.*

toward which the preceding doors have been driving; the tension on stage between Judith and Bluebeard, the anxiety that has built up as a result of the blood
that keeps surfacing behind the doors, and the uncertainty about what Judith
will still encounter—all this is momentarily washed away by a flood of bright,
unambiguous, affirmative C major. Bluebeard, as if drawing strength from the
orchestra's brilliance and power, makes every effort to impress upon Judith the
splendors of his lands, singing in a stentorian voice of the "silken meadows, vel-
vet forests / and blue mountains far in the distance" that can be hers—are hers—
if she ceases her demands to open all the doors. If moved by the sight of this
wealth, however, Judith gives little outward indication of it. With a hollow, ex-
pressionless voice, she quietly affirms that, yes, "your land is beautiful and
grand," in a tone which indicates that she remains deeply troubled by the presence of blood in his castle.

Veress and Antokoletz have described how the personalities of Judith and
Bluebeard undergo a gradual transformation during the course of the opera, as
expressed in their dialogue and accompanying orchestral music.[21] Initially it is
Bluebeard who is quiet and reserved, but as Judith moves farther into the castle,
the way in which he warms to her presence is reflected in the more active role he
plays in their dialogue, while she, in turn, becomes increasingly preoccupied by
the meaning of her discoveries, and correspondingly quieter. This pattern is by
no means rigorously enforced; it represents a general tendency. Judith, for example, in her requests for additional keys or in her reactions to seeing blood behind the doors, shows a consistent capacity for forcefulness that, if provoked, results in agitated vocal lines throughout scenes one to six. Viewed in context of the
entire opera, however, the pattern is undeniably present, though complicated by

the continuing emotional flux of the two characters. Here, in the fifth door, the reversal is complete. Bluebeard is now the voluble, emotive character, while Judith turns inward, becoming withdrawn and taciturn.

Balázs explains the transformation that takes place: "And when, through the fifth door, a flood of light and warmth engulfs the castle, and Bluebeard — liberated, redeemed, luminous, grateful in his happiness — wants to embrace the woman in his arms, already the daylight is no longer visible to the woman who brought it to him. She sees only the bloody shadows."[22] By the end of the opera, Bluebeard will return to a state of quiet resignation and pessimism, to what might be described as his basic personality. Judith, too, will leave quietly, as she entered, but not before having hurled forth, in a sustained monologue, the most bitter accusations of murder, in a situation parallel in tone and dramatic effect to her mission statement heard earlier in the introduction. A large-scale symmetry thus becomes evident in the emotional states of the two characters, deepening the dramatic symmetry (stage lighting, progression of hope) inherent in the opera as a whole. The fifth door scene is, in many ways, the turning point of this form.

Bluebeard, as the scene progresses, sings Judith's praises for making his castle gleam with light. He makes one last, desperate attempt to turn her attention away from the remaining two doors, the sad delusion of a man who cannot see — or does not want to see — that for her no other option remains. Judith, shocked yet again by the discovery of blood, this time in the shadows beneath the clouds, slowly regains her sense of purpose and becomes increasingly assertive, at the end demanding in her most strident voice, "Be it my life or my death, Bluebeard / open the last two doors."

Bartók's music for the fifth door scene falls into three distinct sections whose succession mirrors the changing dramatic situation on stage. The first comprises the music Bartók writes to depict the beautiful expanse of Bluebeard's lands (fig. 74/19–79). Opening in C major, the parallel chords that characterize this section pause at regular intervals to enable Bluebeard's voice to be heard over the full orchestra. The section ends with Judith's observation of blood. The middle part of the scene launches into a scherzolike sound to accompany Bluebeard's vainly optimistic words about the presence of light in the castle (figs. 79–85). Fleet, dancing rhythms animate his voice. When Judith fails to acknowledge his open arms, the energy dissipates, providing a momentary lull in the scene that prepares the way for the third dramatic section, in which Judith reiterates the request to let her proceed (figs. 85–91). Bluebeard hands her the key to the sixth door with the futile plea, "Judith, Judith, don't open it!"

As Bluebeard's confidence and optimism slowly crumble under the weight of Judith's disinterest and, then, her continued demands, Bartók's musical language changes to reflect the dissipation of hope in an atmosphere of increasing tension. After the diatonic purity of the opening picture, the music steadily increases in chromatic content until, by the end, the triadic harmonies Bartók uses to characterize the domains have been supplanted by music of strongly atonal tendencies. A similar progression was already heard in the fourth door scene and will be en-

EXAMPLE 4.12   *Fifth door scene, fig. 79.*

countered again in the sixth, reflecting the ebb and flow of the two characters' emotions.

The second section opens with music (ex. 4.12) that alternates C-major and E♭-major harmonies beneath a surging melodic line in the orchestra, a line whose pitches project incomplete whole-tone scale segments in each measure (i.e., C–[D]–E–F♯ in measure 1, E♭–[F]–G–A in measure 2, etc.).[23] Triads based on these same pitches form the basis for Bartók's music at the beginning of section 3 (ex. 4.13), but now beneath an intensely chromatic melodic line that undermines the music's tonal sense, a feeling reinforced by Bartók's increasingly frequent use of chords based on a wide range of intervallic contents as the scene moves to its conclusion. As he had done previously, in the fourth door scene, Bartók steadily increases the music's tempo, moving from the stately pace of the opening music ("larghissimo") to the "vivace" middle section and, finally, to the "agitato" and "presto" markings of the conclusion.

The opening of the scene provides an exemplary demonstration of a compositional technique Bartók uses throughout *Bluebeard's Castle*, in which a musical

EXAMPLE 4.13   *Fifth door scene, fig. 85.*

idea is extended, or varied, by rotating triadic harmonies around a given pitch or pitches. Following their initial statement in C major, the parallel orchestral chords are heard three times, the last time in a more muted statement by the lower brass. The four statements are set in, respectively, C major (opening), F major (fig. 76), Ab major (six after fig. 76), and F minor (fig. 77). In its initial appearance the orchestral melody outlines a pentatonic pitch collection based on A (A–C–D–E–G), pitches that Bluebeard will pick up in his opening parlando vocal line. The key of C major, Antokoletz has noted, is established by the prominent metric placement of the major triad and by the shape of the melody itself, which, among other features, begins and ends on C.[24] Using these pitches as a cantus firmus, Bartók creates variants by reinterpreting the melodic line as the tonic, mediant, or dominant pitch in a series of parallel triads (ex. 4.14). The melody may be abbreviated, as in statements 3 and 4, or extended by the addition of a new finalis at its end. In each instance, though, it remains in fixed position for the instruments to whom it is assigned; the first violins, for example, playing in their uppermost range, never depart from the initial "C major" melodic line as Bartók cycles through the keys. The progression of tonalities so strongly heard—and felt—as Bartók cycles through his four statements of the opening parallel chords has a dramatic motivation that helps articulate the opera's overall form: the lifting of such a powerful, grandiose, musical idea, through successive tonal regions, each audibly higher than the last (for the first three statements), has the effect of magnifying the grandeur of Bluebeard's domains while simultaneously accentuating the emptiness of her response. The more he speaks of his lands, the more passionately he sings their glories to Judith, as if to overcome with his words the lack of interest revealed in her lifeless responses. In the context of the opera as a whole, by sustaining and magnifying this moment bathed in brilliant white light, Bartók reinforces its position as the music-dramatic climax toward which the first scenes have been aiming. Ahead lie only the darkness and sadness of the last two doors.

The Sixth Door Scene: The Lake of Tears

In the sixth door scene, Judith opens the door and perceives a still, silent lake. Bluebeard tells her that the water is formed by tears. The horrid implications

EXAMPLE 4.14   *Fifth door scene. Separate appearances of the parallel orchestra chords at the scene's beginning, arranged to show their shared cantus firmus.*

confirm Judith's growing suspicion that Bluebeard has had previous wives who have met a tragic end. Momentarily faltering in her resolve to open the last door, she steps toward Bluebeard and they embrace. Although the meaning of this gesture is not without its ambiguous points, it suggests that love can still blossom as long as the last door remains closed. Judith's curiosity now develops a new personal tone, however. Knowing that Bluebeard possessed other wives before her, she now wants to know what they were like and how much Bluebeard loved them. His evasive replies ("Judith, love me, ask me nothing") frustrate her, and she separates from the embrace, demanding that the last door be opened. In an uninterrupted flow of words whose length and intensity recall her earlier statement of mission in coming to the castle, Judith hurls forth accusations that Bluebeard has murdered the wives whose blood she has seen behind each door. "Ah, the rumors are true," she exclaims. Seeing that Judith must know all his secrets, Bluebeard defeatedly hands her the last key.

The sixth door scene merits extended discussion not only for its clearly delineated musical structure but also as the scene featuring the consummate manifestation of the blood motif. Bartók articulates the music in three distinct sections that, as in previous scenes, correspond to the changing focus of Bluebeard and Judith's actions. The first depicts the lake of tears in the orchestra, continuing as Judith makes observations about the sight before her and Bluebeard responds (figs. 91–100). The second comprises the two characters' dialogue about Bluebeard's former wives (figs. 100–112). The third section begins when Judith separates from the embrace and demands that Bluebeard open the last door (fig. 112–end of scene). For the purpose of analysis I label these sections A, B, and C.

More than any other scene in the opera, the sixth door scene relies heavily on the technique of verbal repetition. This may have been meant to symbolize Bluebeard and Judith's increasing inability to communicate with each other at this critical last moment before their love collapses under its own weight. Instead of responding to each other directly, both characters frequently fall back on repetitions of portentous sentences or phrases. Bluebeard can describe the lake of tears using only one word, "tears," sung a total of nine times at the scene's beginning. His unwillingness to tell Judith about earlier wives finds expression in the pleas "Judith, love me, ask me nothing," or "Kiss me, kiss me, ask me nothing," which together are uttered five times (six in Balázs's original). Judith is equally repetitive. She begins four sentences with the phrase "Tell me, Bluebeard . . ." Bartók retained most of the repetitive lines in the sixth door scene. He even added one of his own creation, Bluebeard's reiteration of "You are my castle's radiant splendor / Kiss me, kiss me, ask me nothing," which replaced some lines of similar meaning.

When comparing the operatic text with the original play, one senses that Bartók found Balázs's dialogue a little cumbersome in this scene, or at least unnecessary at times. Of the alterations he did make, many involve a reduction of repeated lines. This is particularly evident in the final section of the scene, where he cuts nine of the twenty-eight lines spoken by Bluebeard and Judith, an amount equal to approximately one-third of section C. Judith's two interjections "All your former wives are there!" are reduced to one, while her five commands "Open the seventh door!" are reduced to two. Bartók also cuts a repetition of Judith's two-sentence declaration of trust and fidelity, "I came here, because I love you. / I have one life, one death, to give." This important statement is found elsewhere in the drama and acts as a large-scale textual unifying device.[25]

By making these revisions Bartók alters the dynamics of the relationship between Judith and Bluebeard, in what must be seen as the composer's personal interpretation of the two characters' roles in the drama taking place. Judith now has a succession of uninterrupted lines whose accusations swell in power as they go unanswered by Bluebeard. In the original play, Bluebeard protests when Judith demands the seventh key. He asserts one more time that he won't open the last door: "Judith! / I won't open it." Bartók cuts these words. In his hands, the figure of Bluebeard becomes more passive, more victimlike, at this final moment of confrontation. In contrast, Judith is stronger, more assertive. This increased polarization of character has the effect of portraying Bluebeard in a more sympathetic light. What few traces of obstinate defiance Bluebeard had retained at this point are excised by Bartók.

Bartók streamlines the conclusion to the sixth door scene and shapes it into a unified dramatic moment for Judith: her first blunt demand to open the seventh door is followed by a sharpening litany of (now-uninterrupted) accusations terminating in a final, climactic imperative to open the last door. Even those stage directions for Bluebeard that would have interrupted Judith's monologue are removed. Bartók's reasons for making these minor textual revisions become clearer on examination of the musical score. The rapid alternation of musical ideas that characterizes earlier parts of the scene (sections A and B) yields in section C to an intensive symphonic development of the chromatic half-step motive (figs. 112–18). The gradual orchestral accelerando and crescendo sweeps along with the rising tide of Judith's own emotions, reaching a climax immediately after Judith's shrill final command (fig. 118). The unity and cohesion of Judith's dramatic moment are paralleled in the musical material itself. The omnipresent half-step motif permeating the harmonic and melodic motion of this passage dramatically underlines the danger of Judith's decision to open the final door. This is the opera's climactic development of the interval symbolizing blood and death. Recognizing this, an early conductor of Bartók's opera scrawled the words *Vér, vér, vér!* (Blood, blood, blood!) in his copy of the score at the moment when this final rise by half steps begins to surge forth at fig. 112.[26]

In the sixth door scene, as in the rest of the opera, Bartók shows himself to have been sensitive to the fundamental importance of stage gestures in Balázs's dramatic conception. Balázs placed an unusually high value on the use of silence, as measured by the frequency of stage directions such as "long pause" and "[he/she] does not respond." The sixth door scene included many such stage directions. They function in much the same way as the textual repetitions: as symbols of Bluebeard and Judith's difficulty in communicating with each other. Bartók treats these directions literally. If Balázs writes "long pause" or "long kiss," Bartók composes music to allow the gesture its full dramatic weight. A "does not respond" indication, likewise, is accorded an appropriate musical representation in which the character refrains from singing while the orchestra plays.

Bartók's fidelity to dramatic gestures in Balázs's text can be appreciated only through comparison with the original play. He sometimes removed stage directions from the musical score after composing music to take their place. The orchestral opening of the scene (mm. 1–11), for example, is not only a brilliant musical representation of a lake of tears but also a musical substitute for Balázs's original specification, "a longer pause." Once the music was composed, Bartók deleted the stage direction, no doubt finding it redundant. Examination of the original play also shows that the ominous B♭-based melodic intrusion one measure after fig. 93 has a specific purpose not marked in the score: it represents Bluebeard's unspoken response to Judith. Bartók omits the direction "he doesn't respond" that appears in the drama, replacing it with a musical phrase that becomes closely associated with Bluebeard's responses in the next few lines.

Throughout the scene, distinct musical ideas are identified with Judith, Bluebeard, and the lake of tears, a procedure not yet encountered in the opera in such scrupulous detail. (Bartók makes frequent use of this technique, however, as can be seen in the music at the end of the second door scene or at the beginning of the fifth). The music associated with Bluebeard in section A differs markedly from the music representing him in section B. Similarly, Judith's music in section A is superseded by new musical material for her in section B. Section A's music is, for the most part, quiet and emotionally restrained, reflecting the mute horror of the lake of tears and Judith's reaction to this sight. The music in

TABLE 4.2   Distribution of musical ideas from example 4.15 across the sixth door scene

	Section A	Section B	Section C
Lake of tears	a		
Judith	b	d	(development of d)
Bluebeard	c	e	
Sorrow music			f

section B alternates between impassioned emotional outbursts and sinuous, menacing half-step passages. It covers a much wider dynamic range. The careful apportioning of musical ideas from section to section and, within these sections, between the two characters suggests that Bartók was conscious of the text's inherent structure and chose to reflect that structural framework in his music. The scene's principal musical ideas are set forth in ex. 4.15, where they are identified by letter name as "a" through "f." Their distribution is illustrated in table 4.2. Throughout the scene, Bartók is very direct in his presentation of ideas, almost never employing the orchestra's vast potential for hints or references to offstage events or hidden emotions. When Judith sings, we hear her music alone; when Bluebeard sings, we hear his. An example illustrates how this is done.

At the scene's beginning, three distinct musical ideas—one associated with the lake of tears, and one each for Bluebeard and Judith—alternate in a seamless flow of music. The order of their appearance reflects the actions and dialogue pattern of the characters on stage. Judith sings each of her lines accompanied by simple sustained pentatonic chords in the lower strings and horns (ex. 4.15b). Bluebeard sings his repeated words "tears" to a slightly quicker, B♭-based melody in the orchestra (c). The orchestral tone picture of a motionless, silent lake is captured by pulseless orchestral sighs capped with a haunting G♮/G♯ flutter (a_1) and a one-measure falling melodic figure (a_2), both identifiable subelements within the lake of tears music (a). Together, these three musical ideas (a, b, and c) constitute the entire musical substance of section A. They are sometimes joined by small connecting passages; at other times they abut each other directly.

The lake of tears music, once introduced in the opening picture, is reinserted at regular intervals to separate Judith and Bluebeard's observation-response couplets. It therefore assumes a structural function in addition to its pictorial quality. As table 4.3 demonstrates, the lake of tears music (a) resurfaces between all but the first two couplets. Bartók organizes his music with great care around the dramatic structure of the text: every appearance of (a), for example, is associated with a stage direction, sometimes later deleted by the composer. The harmonically static arpeggiated sighs (a_1) lend themselves readily to the sort of flexible treatment Bartók displays in this scene; they can be repeated to fill any required amount of stage time.

The recurrent patterns of musical ideas heard in the opening of the sixth door thus derive in part from the text itself, where lines by Judith and Bluebeard are clearly paired. Structural implications inherent in the original text are further

EXAMPLE 4.15 *The principal musical ideas of the sixth door scene.*

Section A

a. Lake of tears

Csen - des   fe - hér   ta - vat   lát - ok.
I   see   a   silent,   white   lake.

b. Judith

c. Bluebeard

Kön - nyek, Ju - dit   kön - nyek.
Tears,   Judith   tears.

Section B

d. Judith

three distinct elements

and

e. Bluebeard

EXAMPLE 4.15   *(continued)*

Section C

f. Sorrow music

delineated by Bartók's creation of unique musical ideas for each character and for the lake of tears. Variety is achieved by the inclusion of flexible elements within each idea, which enables him to generate new expressive possibilities, here and in the remainder of the scene. Dynamics, tempi, and harmonization are frequently altered, as is the relationship of the voice part to the orchestral music associated with it. Bluebeard's melodic line (c), for example, features a melodic tail that concludes differently each time, with new harmonic consequences for the following music (ex. 4.16). Variants may be extremely subtle, as in the rhythmic placement of Judith's eight-syllable lines in her opening music (b); alternatively, they may completely alter the harmony and overall shape of a musical idea, as in the orchestral music framing Bluebeard's repeated lines "You are my castle's radiant splendor / Kiss me, kiss me, ask me nothing." The first appearance of this text at fig. 104 is initially harmonized in D♭ major; this tonal sense is

TABLE 4.3   Sixth door scene, section A. The association of specific musical ideas with Judith, Bluebeard, and the lake of tears. Bartók deleted from his score selected stage directions given in the play (shown here as overstruck text).

	Text	Music	Location in score
	(After a long pause)	a	91
J.	I see a silent white lake	b	92/4
	A motionless, white lake.		
B.	(Doesn't respond)	c	93
J.	What sort of water is this, Bluebeard?	b	94
B.	Tears, Judith, tears, tears.	c	94/3
	(Judith shudders)	a	95
J.	How deathly silent, motionless.	b	96
B.	Tears, Judith, tears, tears.	c	96/3
	(She bends down and scrutinizes the water)	a/[c]	97
J.	Calm white — pure white.	b	98
B.	Tears, Judith, tears, tears.	[c]	98/4
J.	(She slowly turns and silently faces Bluebeard.)	a	99
	Long pause.		

EXAMPLE 4.16   *Sixth door scene. The conclusion of the melody associated with Bluebeard in the orchestra (c) at its first three appearances.*

quickly transformed into a bimodal harmony that combines E♭ pentatonic with a tertian sonority (F–A–[C]–E–G), crescendoing to a fortissimo climax before fig. 105. Repeated a few bars later, the text is reharmonized in a tonality resembling B major, and the entire dramatic gesture is changed. The music now tapers gracefully into Judith's entry at fig. 108 after settling on D♭ major at its *conclusion*. The melodic identity of the two textual statements remains essentially the same, however, despite the striking harmonic and gestural differences.

Bartók applies the technique of variation unevenly: Judith's music in the sixth door scene (b and d) is treated with far less harmonic and melodic flexibility than Bluebeard's (c and e), which tends to vary on each repetition. Bartók's differentiated treatment of the characters' musical ideas has the effect of underscoring Judith's single-minded obsession with opening the last door. Just as she does not sway from her goal, so, too, her music pursues a single path, reluctant to change character.

The scene concludes with one of the opera's most moving passages, the mournful orchestral lament expressing sorrow as Bluebeard yields to Judith's demand for the final key. In the tradition of musical laments from Beethoven onward, Bartók sets the music in a distant flat key, in what appears to be A♭ minor. Root-position triads on strong beats firmly anchor the music in that key. To say that this music is "in" A♭ minor, though, would misrepresent its bimodal tendencies, for it achieves its considerable expressive power from the juxtaposition of A- and A♭-based harmonies. Coming directly after the extended symphonic development of the blood motif, it presents another, more lyrical manifestation of the semitone relationship, now transferred to a background harmonic level, where entire chord formations lie a half step apart from each other.

In Bartók's vocabulary, A♭ (and its various pentatonic, modal, or tonal formations) is related to the scene's opening tonality as the major seventh of the chord A–C/C♯–E–G♯. Much of the scene's music is organized, either directly or indirectly, around these two pitches, A and A♭. From the unequivocal A minor/ pentatonic of the beginning, through a long middle area of uncertain harmonic identity suffused with the semitone blood motif, we are finally led to the bimodal A/A♭ of the music representing Bluebeard's sorrow at the end. In retrospect, A♭ can be seen emerging from the very opening A-minor lake of tears motif, where it is present as the G♯ seventh atop the arpeggiated chord (a_1). With the addition of a dropping melodic semitone figure E–D♯ in the fourth measure of the scene (a_2), the lake of tears music outlines the principal tonic-dominant pitches of both A and A♭: A–E and A♭–E♭. The scene's first bars are thus a harbinger of things to come, though A♭ is still far from prominent.

Bartók leaves no doubt that this "sorrow music," as I have come to label it, is based on the pitch A♭ (ex. 4.17). From fig. 118/5 to the end of the scene, only two pitches are found in the bass, E♭ and A♭. The ear hears this alternating root motion as a V–I motion in A♭ minor, and in most measures, inner voices in the orchestra complete the implied triads. Signs of the music's bimodality, however, can be seen in Bluebeard's vocal part. His few lines here ("Take it, take it, here is the seventh key" and "Open it, Judith, and see them. / There are all my former wives") are sung to pitches based on A, either A major or minor. The orchestral melody moves easily between the realms of A♭ and A, its bimodal nature, too, concealed through enharmonic spellings (e.g., B♭♭–D♭–F♭).[27]

Here, at the end of the scene, Bartók reveals the logic behind his choice of A♭ minor as a complementary key to A. One of two chords supports the melody in each measure, either an A♭-minor triad or a tertian sonority based on E♭ (E♭–G♭–B♭♭–D♭–F♭), the latter a sort of dominant ninth chord. A collection of pitches drawn from these chords can be arranged to form an extended chain of thirds, as Bartók partially demonstrates, producing a two-octave network of tertian relationships that ultimately cycles back on itself to come full circle, with A as its foundation. Interestingly, it is not until the scene has almost run its course that this method of organization becomes manifest. A-major segments of the orchestral melody are always presented over a tertian harmony that extends the A–C♯–E (or B♭♭–D♭–F♭) triad down to include two lower minor thirds, that is, D♯–F♯–A–C♯–E. At four measures after fig. 120, Bartók links this segment of thirds with another descending figure outlining a separate group of third-related pitches heard over the A♭-minor chord in the middle of the bar. This new melodic segment (F♭–A♭–C♭–E♭–G♭) gains prominence a few measures later when it is presented alone, without any harmonic support. With F♭ acting as a common tone, the two tertian segments combine to create an interlocking chain of thirds spanning two octaves (ex. 4.18). A-major and A♭-minor triads form the backbone of this chain, as the first two consecutive triads that can be extracted from the sequence of thirds A–C♯–E–G♯/A♭–B/C♭–D♯/E♭–F♯–[A].

Extended chains of thirds form the harmonic foundation for other areas of *Bluebeard's Castle*, notably in the armory scene, with its loosely defined B–D♯–F♯–A♯–C♯ harmony, but rarely are the harmonic potentials as fully developed as in the sixth door scene. Early in the scene, Bartók hints at A♭ as a tonal goal, but he postpones the full arrival of this key until the scene's end, where the great

EXAMPLE 4.17   *Sixth door scene. Bluebeard's "sorrow music," fig. 118.*

EXAMPLE 4.17 *(continued)*

lament of lost love sounds in the orchestra as Bluebeard hands Judith the last key.

The Seventh Door Scene: The Former Wives

In the Bluebeard fairy tale, the newest wife opens the forbidden chamber and discovers to her horror the bloody corpses of Bluebeard's previous wives. All along in Bartók's opera, the signs of blood have led Judith to believe that behind the seventh door she would find a similar sight. Bluebeard's reluctance to open the last two doors convinces her, and through her, the audience, that he is hiding a terrible dark secret. "All your former wives are there!" she exclaims at the end of the sixth door scene, "slaughtered, frozen in blood!" Bluebeard does not contradict her; he merely hands her the key, with the ambiguous words, "You shall

EXAMPLE 4.18   *Chains of thirds in the melody and harmony at the end of the sixth door scene, fig. 120/7–8.*

see them. There are all my former wives." The entire drama has been converging on this point, which forms the opera's second dramatic climax.[28]

How surprising, then, to see three resplendently dressed women step forward from the seventh door once it is opened. Judith, astonished, backs away slightly. "They live, they live!—They are alive in here!" Balázs's description of this moment in his comments about the *Bluebeard* play leaves no doubt that he felt it to be *the* point of arrival in the drama, a moment of great symbolic significance.[29]

> And when the woman looks inside, she staggers back in alarm: not as if she had seen the dead women, no! The women are *alive*! From behind the seventh door the wives—who had been loved at one time by the man—rise to their feet, dreamlike, from the deep recesses of slumbering memory. And wreathed with diadems and halos they are more beautiful than all women presently living. Oh, how plain, how miserable Judith feels when Bluebeard sings in dreaming ecstasy of his past loves.

Having discovered Bluebeard's deepest secret, Judith now moves to take her place next to the other wives, alive, entombed within the castle. The symbolism of her action, and of the entire seventh door scene, becomes dense with ambiguity. What can it mean that the wives are still alive? Why does Bluebeard cherish them and sing of their beauty yet keep them locked up? Balázs partially explains, continuing:

> But she doesn't shudder in horror until he begins to beautify her, to adorn her with jewels. "Ah, Bluebeard, you are not dreaming, I am your poor, living wife." But the man covers her with glittering ornaments, and Judith gradually grows numb with death. The man's dream kills her, the very dream she herself has conjured up in him. And the dreaming man remains alone once more, his castle again locked and dark.

Judith and Bluebeard's actions in the seventh door scene unfold slowly, enfolded in gravity and portent, and with this feeling comes a related sense of how events on stage now depart even further from any semblance of reality, proceeding in a noticeably disjointed, dreamlike manner. Unexplained gestures and unexplained statements multiply in a bewildering sequence of events not easy to comprehend. In general theatrical effect, this is the most expressionistic scene in the *Bluebeard* play.

Bartók sets the music of the opening in C minor: the "sorrowful, minor-keyed music" Balázs had envisioned and specified in his play. The music will eventually lead back into the recapitulation of the F♯-pentatonic melody that opened the opera. By returning to C at this point in the opera, Bartók takes the tonality of light and twists it into the minor mode, revealing here, perhaps more openly than in the rest of the opera, the hidden tragedy inherent in bringing light to the castle. Both of the opera's climactic moments, it might be noted, are set in the tonality of C. Altering the mode does not completely erase the sense of light's presence, only its quality. Light now reveals a sight both disturbing and, in a way, relieving: the women are still alive.

When the door opens, somber chords pulse slowly in the orchestra's middle register while an English horn weaves contrapuntal arabesques around the soulful clarinet melody. Benjamin Suchoff has remarked on the resemblance between the English horn motif, a four-note figure curling around the pitch E♭ with upward motion of a minor third, to G♭, and a similar melodic figure in the alto arioso "Ach, Golgotha" from Bach's *St. Matthew Passion*.[30] By no means obvious at first hearing, this apparent quotation proves remarkably prescient and subtle on Bartók's part, for Bach's text reads, in part, "The guiltless must die here guilty. That strikes deep into my soul; Ah, Golgotha, hapless Golgotha." Bartók in 1911 was certainly not in the habit of making quiet reference to Christian theology in his music, but this oblique commentary may be his way of underlining, for those few likely to grasp the connection, the larger meaning of Judith and Bluebeard's final actions on stage. Into the orchestra's soul, or into Bluebeard's, comes this unspoken thought absolving Judith of any guilt for having opened the final door. Like Christ, its presence suggests, she is blameless (and the rest of the scene bears this out, for Bluebeard accuses her of nothing but, rather, praises her), but she must nevertheless die, as Christ did on Calvary. Symbolically "killed" by entombment in the castle, Judith does not actually die in the opera, but, like Christ, lives on forever in the soul of him whom she has saved. This helps explain what Balázs was writing about when he describes Judith growing numb with death, even though she remains very much alive on stage. She is killed in an emotional or psychological sense, as Bluebeard, in the dream that is this opera, locks her up in the castle of his soul, forcing the actual object of his love away in order to idealize her memory. (Further discussion of the opera's meaning may be found in chapter 5, where it is shown that themes like those discussed here also surface in other retellings of the Bluebeard story dating from the turn of the century.)

Through orchestration Bartók guides the audience's emotional response to the events on stage. The orchestral timbre at the beginning is wind-dominated, supported by a sustained, pianissimo C-minor chord in the low strings. Abruptly, when Bluebeard holds out his arms to address the wives at fig. 123/4, the upper strings enter for the first time and begin to lead the melodic lines, yielding a more string-dominated sound that, in the opera, is often heard in the context of his vocal lines. For the duration of his address to the former wives, a warm string sound, supported by plucked chords in the harp, predominates. When the three wives step back behind the seventh door and he turns to Judith (fig. 131), the timbre reverts to the woodwind-dominated sound heard at the scene's opening. Coincident with these changes is a shift back and forth between the chromatically inflected realm associated with Judith throughout the opera and the diatonic/pentatonic music to which Bluebeard sings the majority of his lines. He addresses the first wife in B♭ major (fig. 127), the second in C major (fig. 128), and the third in D minor (fig. 129/12). The dialogue eventually returns to focus on Judith, whom he addresses in an intensely chromatic harmonic environment suffused with the half-step interval and, therefore, with reminiscences of the blood motif.

The welter of confusion and powerful emotions building up on stage is given magnificent musical expression when the orchestral begins to surge upward around Bluebeard's lines "You are beautiful, beautiful, a hundred times beautiful," leading inexorably to a shatteringly dissonant orchestral climax over a B♭ pedal tone (figs. 135–38). Beginning diatonically, in a Lydian-inflected B♭ major, the short, six-note figures rise higher in ever-increasing waves of sound to incorporate chromatic neighbor tones that resolve and move in half-step motion. The orchestra turns increasingly strident and dissonant as Bluebeard sings his last line to Judith, "You were my most beautiful wife," and finally reaches the point for which this scene has been heading: a tremendous crash of dissonant sound (fig. 137) at the moment the seventh door closes in upon Judith. All the horror and tension, all the uncertainty and anxiety of the entire opera is released in a wrenching dissonance reminiscent of the famous moment at the end of *Salome*: ten of twelve possible tones are heard simultaneously, triple forte, on the downbeat at fig. 137. Unlike in *Salome*, however, where dramatic tension is maintained until a frighteningly abrupt end, in Bartók's *Bluebeard* the sound quickly melts away to prepare for the return of darkness and of the F♯ theme from beginning of the opera, now harmonized with F♯-minor triads and other tonal harmonies. Tonality, in this context, gains a dramatic association with darkness and, therefore, with stability. The catharsis it represents comes as something of a paradox. That which Bluebeard sought to escape, through Judith, in the end he welcomes with weary, sad resignation.

ᢗᡂ 5

BARTÓK'S REVISIONS TO
THE OPERA, 1911–1917

Almost a decade lapsed from the time *Bluebeard* was composed until it appeared in print from the Viennese firm Universal Edition in 1921. For Bartók, having a major composition lie unperformed and unpublished over an extended period of time was not an altogether unfamiliar situation during the years around World War I, when the disruption of commerce and cultural life, together with the composer's avowed lack of interest in maintaining a public profile as a musician in Budapest, combined to delay the appearance of works that, in some instances, were composed many years earlier. The *Ady Songs*, composed in 1916, waited three years for their first public performance, in 1919; they were published only in 1923. The *Wooden Prince* ballet, begun in 1914, was not finished until 1916–17, victim in part of the composer's war-induced depression; it was premiered in 1917 and published in 1921. More protracted still, and unusual for Bartók in the length of their gestation, were the Four Orchestral Pieces, written in two-piano score format in 1912 but not orchestrated or performed until 1921–22. The circumstances that led to the deferred premiere or publication of works like these varied considerably in origin. Completion of the *Wooden Prince*, for instance, was slowed by worries about its orchestration, while suitable German translations for the *Ady Songs* proved difficult to obtain. Perhaps more than anything else, however, the absence of a committed publisher for his music, either in Budapest or abroad, contributed to the sharply reduced rate at which new works by Bartók flowed into the public sphere.

In Budapest, both Rozsnyai and Rózsavölgyi had lost interest in publishing

125

Bartók's original compositions after 1912, though they continued to work with him on new editions of the classic piano literature. Their reduced association with the composer meant that when Bartók sat down to write, it was without any hope of seeing his music in print in the immediate future, a hardship—at times self-imposed—whose psychological and financial implications weighed heavily upon him at a time when he was already beset with frustrations over the development of his career in Hungary. It was only after he secured a new contract with Universal Edition in mid-1918 that most of the compositions written in the 1911–18 period began to appear in print. "This year's great success for me," he confided in a 1918 letter to Romanian ethnomusicologist János Buşiţia, "was not [the positive reception of *Bluebeard* after its premiere] but rather my success in entering into a long-term agreement with a first-rate publisher. . . . This is of great significance because for approx. 6 years nothing of mine has appeared— thanks to our home publishers."[1] In July 1918, a month after this letter was written, *Bluebeard's Castle* was sent to Universal to begin the process of engraving. Three years later, the score was printed.

The long period in which *Bluebeard's Castle* existed only in manuscript state afforded Bartók several opportunities to critically reevaluate his opera. That he took advantage of this situation, and in many instances revised his original thoughts, is confirmed by the state of the opera's surviving sources. Extensive changes are entered into the autograph scores and their contemporary copies. Music for several scenes was revised, the vocal parts rewritten in places, and the general appearance of the score significantly modified in terms of orchestration, dynamics, and tempi. Orchestral instruments that were not available to Bartók in 1911 (or had not occurred to him), the celesta and xylophone, were added to the instrumental textures by 1917. Overall, an estimated five minutes of music had been deleted by the time Bartók delivered the score to the Budapest Opera House for its premiere. Further alterations, mostly minor in scope, were made in the publishing stage. The result is an opera different in many respects from the work Bartók composed in 1911. After being filtered through the refractive lens of ten years' time, *Bluebeard* emerged in a slightly more compact form, its orchestration vividly enhanced and the dramatic force of its ending shaded with deeper poignance and pessimism. The story of this evolution is recorded in the unpublished manuscripts, which read like palimpsests: beneath the scratched-out notes, rewritten bar lines, pasteovers, and deleted measures, an earlier version of the work can be detected.

In 1981 György Kroó, who has devoted much of his scholarly research to Bartók's stage works, attempted to unravel the tangled web of relationships linking the extant manuscript sources for *Bluebeard's Castle*.[2] His insights into the opera's long history brought to light, for the first time, the existence of unpublished versions of the ending, a finding of great significance for our understanding of Bartók's compositional development in the 1910s. Kroó traces the progress of Bartók's revisions from 1911 to 1921 and even later, when the composer condoned minor changes in the vocal parts for stage and radio performances in the 1920s and 1930s. Bartók's urge to revise, he points out, did not cease with the appearance of a definitive published version of the opera in 1921; he was open to the possibility of further changes or improvements, some of which were entered into the personal scores of the singers involved. Kroó concedes that Bartók's reworking of the *Bluebeard's Castle* scores creates a "complicated trail" for the researcher to follow.[3]

This chapter represents a response to, and enlargement of, Kroó's work on the opera's genesis, with emphasis on the musical and dramatic changes Bartók made to the opera's concluding moments. Three versions of the ending were created from 1911 to 1917, all focusing on Bluebeard and Judith's last words to each other and the return of the opening F♯-pentatonic theme to conclude the work. They differ significantly from one another in their harmonic language and overall music-dramatic aim, their pages a silent testimony to Bartók's difficulty in dramatizing the profound sense of finality and despair that emerges from the characters' last actions on stage. Viewed collectively, they also attest to the certainty of his original vision, for Bartók never lost sight of a design element he had conceived in the opera's earliest completed form: the orchestral recapitulation of the F♯ theme from the opera's opening moments. In all versions this feature is retained, though its orchestration, length, and inner voicing were modified each time the composer returned to the score.

By tracing the sometimes halting process by which Bartók shaped *Bluebeard's Castle* into a form he considered suitable for performance and publication, we can gain further insight into the creation of what György Kroó has called, not inaccurately, "the greatest and most perfect of his compositions from 1900 to 1915"[4] —a subject intrinsically interesting to scholars, for the history of this work has always admitted some degree of uncertainty, particularly with respect to the two competitions in which Bartók entered the opera in 1911 and 1912. More exact dates for the principal sources—and the revisions they contain—are suggested below. Perhaps even more important, however, the opera's three endings provide a rare opportunity to gauge the progression of Bartók's style over a period of time that led, ultimately, to works such as the Second String Quartet and the *Miraculous Mandarin*. Once we recognize that parts of the published *Bluebeard* score were written not in 1911 but in 1917, and that the entire opera benefited from comprehensive revision six years after it was first composed, it becomes easier to understand why *Bluebeard's Castle*, stylistically speaking, at times sounds like a work of the later war years.

Manuscript Sources for *Bluebeard's Castle*

Six complete manuscript scores of *Bluebeard's Castle* and one six-page fragment survive. Five of these scores originated during the years 1911–12. The other two date from 1917–18 and ca. 1922, respectively. Table 5.1 lists the opera's principal sources in chronological order, beginning with Bartók's autograph draft. Also relevant to the study of Bartók's revisions are (1) the performing materials prepared by the Royal Opera House in Budapest for the first production: a pair of manuscript vocal parts for Judith and Bluebeard, and a conductor's score, all

TABLE 5.1 The manuscript sources of *Bluebeard's Castle*, 1911–22. Sources originating in the 1911–12 period are given expanded listings showing the manuscript's physical characteristics, date of origin, and current location.

VS1	**Bartók's autograph draft**
Hand	Entirely in Bartók's own hand.
Length	50 pp. plus 2 additional pages, 48 and 49, which are attached to the end of the manuscript.[a]
Paper size	16-line staff paper throughout.
Date	February to July 1911; "missing ending" (part of seventh door scene?) added in August or September 1911. Largely finished by July 8, 1911, when Bartók left Hungary to summer in France and Switzerland.
Current location	Budapest, Hungary. Bartók Archívum (Manuscript number A-76/62; new number BBA 492).
Translation	German translation by Emma Kodály entered directly into score in violet ink in the hand of Zoltán Kodály.[b] Corrections to translation made in pencil by Emma Kodály.
VS2	**Márta Bartók's copy of *Bluebeard's Castle* in piano-vocal format, used as an engraver's copy for the 1921 Universal Edition**
Hand	Márta Bartók, with numerous corrections and revisions in Bartók's own hand. A possible copyist's hand on pp. 21, 61, 64, 65, 67, 68 is probably a later form of Márta's own writing, ca. 1917. Also present are occasional performance markings in an unidentified hand (pp. 20, 68), and many engraver's markings in the form of numbers.
Length	68 pp. plus a dedication page ("Mártának / Rákoskeresztur, 1911. szeptember havában"), a title page in Hungarian and German, and an unruled outer wrapper on which the German title *Herzog Blaubarts Burg* is written in an unknown hand.
Paper size	16-line staff paper throughout.[c]
Date	Begun in July 1911, possibly earlier. Revised in 1917. Finished by Márta in fall of 1911 in original form with first ending of the opera.[d] Score heavily revised by Bartók prior to 1918 performance (i.e., mid-1917), with some sections recopied by Márta at that time, including a third version of the opera's conclusion. Further corrections were made in conjunction with first performances and possibly afterward (vocal part, fig. 17–18), before being sent to Universal Edition on July 16, 1918.[e]
Current location	Bartók Records, Homosassa, Florida, in the collection of Peter Bartók (manuscript number 28VOSFC1).
Translation	German translation by Vilmos Ziegler entered directly into score in unknown hand (Márta?) after 1919 and before 1921. The score would have been in Hungarian only until that time.
FS1	**Bartók's autograph full score**
Hand	Entirely in Bartók's own hand. German translation added in unknown hand.
Length	119 pp. plus 1 blank cover page with title in German in Bartók's hand ("Burg des Herzog Blaubart's" [*sic*]).
Paper size	Both 20- and 24-line staff paper, with approximately three-quarters of the score written on 24-line paper.

TABLE 5.1 *(continued)*

	20-line pages: 1–4, 37–60, 113–17 24-line pages: 5–36, 61–112, 118–19
Date	Late July 1911 to Sept. 20, 1911. A new ending was added in late 1911 or early 1912.
Current location	Bartók Records, Homosassa, Florida, in the collection of Peter Bartók (manuscript number 28FSS1).
Translation	German translation by Emma Kodály entered directly into score.

FS2   **Márta Bartók's copy of the full score**

Hand	Márta Bartók, pp. 1–99, 101–4, 129–30; unknown professional copyist, pp. 105–28, 132–42; Béla Bartók, pp. 100, 131, 143–49 (end). Numerous corrections and revisions in Bartók's hand throughout.
Length	149 pp. plus 4 introductory pages: (1) Title page in Hungarian with later changes; (2) dramatis personae in Hungarian; (3) instrumentation list and a small attached notecard of later origin with corrections for engraver; (4) Prologue of the Bard, in Hungarian only.
Paper size	Heterogeneous mixture of 20-, 24-, and 28-line staff paper. Bartók's later pasteovers, small and large, made in a variety of paper sizes.

20-line pages:	1–16	37–44	49–72	
24-line pages:		17–36	45–48	73–99
28-line pages:				100
20-line:		129–30		
24-line:	101–28		132–42	
28-line:		131	143–49 (end)	

The pages entirely in Bartók's hand, it will be noticed, are also the only ones on 28-line paper.

Date	Ca. August 1, 1911, to October? 1911. Revised in summer of 1917. In 1917, portions of the original ending were detached from the score and a new ending was substituted.
Current location	Bartók Records, Homosassa, Florida, in the collection of Peter Bartók (manuscript number 28FSFC2).
Translation	None. Text in Hungarian.

Márta Fragment   **Márta Bartók's copy of the second version of the ending**

Hand	Márta Bartók's hand throughout. No corrections or revisions by Bartók.
Length	6 pp. Numbered 195–200 in upper corners.
Paper size	24-line staff paper throughout.
Date	February 1912? At the very earliest, late 1911 (November or December). Contemporaneous with Bartók's revised ending of the opera.
Current location	Bartók Records, Homosassa, Florida, in the collection of Peter Bartók (manuscript number 28FSID1).
Translation	None. Text in Hungarian only.

[FS3?]	[now-lost remainder of a full score in which the Márta Fragment was once inserted; late 1911 to early 1912; presumed to be the work of a professional copyist due to high page numbers found on Márta's insert]

(continued)

TABLE 5.1 (*continued*)

Opera House Score	Score in an unidentified copyist's hand used at performances of *Bluebeard* at the Royal Opera House in Budapest during 1918 and 1919. Date of origin: sometime during the second half of 1917 to very early 1918. Collection of Peter Bartók, manuscript number A-651/65.
Opera House Parts	Pair of vocal parts in a professional copyist's hand; used to prepare for the first performances in 1918. Collection of Peter Bartók.
FS4	Copy of the full score used by Universal Edition as a rental score, ca. 1922. Collection of Peter Bartók.

Notes

    a. In the VS1 manuscript, Bartók numbers the two added pages as simply "48" and "49," intending thereby to replace the existing pages 48 and 49.

    b. More on the physical appearance of the German translation in this score may be found in Kroó, "Data on the Genesis," 116. I have been unable to examine the manuscript in person.

    c. The dedication page, on 20-line staff paper, may have been a later addition. The original title page is on 16-line paper.

    d. A facsimile of the original last page of this manuscript showing the 1911 ending of the opera is reproduced as facsimile 20 in Kroó, "Data on the Genesis," 100.

    e. Kroó recounts the history of the manuscript from 1918 to 1921 as it was sent back and forth between Budapest and Vienna ("Data on the Genesis," 117–19).

written in an unknown copyist's hand; (2) Bartók's marked proofs of the Universal piano-vocal score, dating from late 1921, and his personal copy of the opera's first edition, in which a handful of minor corrections are entered directly into the score; and (3) a copy of the full orchestral score prepared by Universal Edition around 1922 for use as a rental score. All of the known *Bluebeard* source material is preserved in one of two locations, the Bartók Archívum in Budapest or the collection of Peter Bartók in Homosassa, Florida.[5]

    In the accompanying table, abbreviations are assigned to each manuscript in order to facilitate reference. These sigla are of my own device and are intended to replace the cumbersome array of archive accession numbers by which these scores are usually identified. Ease of remembrance prompted the naming system. Thus "VS1" means "Vocal Score Number 1," while "FS1" refers to "Full Score Number 1." A concordance of these symbols with the manuscripts' existing accession numbers (e.g., A-76/67, 28FSFC1) may be found under each entry. Also found in the table are detailed descriptions of the four principal manuscripts for the opera and of the fragment in Márta Bartók's hand, showing their physical appearance (page length, paper size), date of origin, subsequent history, and current location. It is from these five manuscripts —VS1, VS2, FS1, FS2, and the Márta Fragment, a six-page excerpt from the opera's conclusion—that earlier versions of the opera's ending can be reconstructed. The Márta Fragment excepted, they are also the principal participants in the creation process that yielded *Bluebeard's Castle*; almost all revisions Bartók made to the opera were entered into their pages. Later sources such as the Opera House Score, FS4, and Bartók's marked copies of the Universal

Edition proofs transmit a version of the opera that postdates the major layers of revision.

Only a single, one-line sketch survives for the opera. In his early years Bartók did not make a habit of keeping sketches once a work was completed. Kodály recollected that in the late 1910s Bartók burned some of his manuscripts; if Kodály's memory is true, this act may be responsible for the almost complete absence of any preliminary sketchwork for *Bluebeard's Castle*.[6] In a notebook used sporadically over a fifteen-year period from 1907 to the early 1920s, however, Bartók notated a melodic line that would become the English horn theme from the opera's ostinato passage (seven measures before fig. 20).[7] It is found in close proximity to sketches for the *Two Pictures*, op. 10. Given the magnitude of an opera project, it seems reasonable to assume that additional sketch material existed at one time. A list of missing manuscripts Bartók drew up in 1938 prior to his departure from Hungary includes one item described as a "Bluebeard two-staff sketch," but this is probably a reference to the complete autograph draft of *Bluebeard* (VS1) that Bartók had given as a gift to Zoltán and Emma Kodály in 1921.[8] If any compositional sketchwork for *Bluebeard* once existed, Bartók seems not to have counted it among his missing manuscripts in 1938. Nothing further has surfaced since then.

The "Missing Ending," Summer and Fall 1911

The earliest surviving manuscript of *Bluebeard's Castle* is the autograph draft (VS1), which Bartók began in February 1911 and had largely finished by early July 1911, when he left Budapest for a summer in France and Switzerland. It would be completed by September of that year. Written in piano-vocal format, this score appears to represent Bartók's first attempt to establish the opera's final form. The music is copied straight through, in a manner that suggests confidence in the opera's overall plan: new scenes start in the middle of pages, or at other irregular points, as if their music had previously been worked out and needed only to be fixed in place (hence the suspicion that earlier sketches may once have existed). Sprinkled throughout are instrumental cues and other notations Bartók wrote to himself, as well as corrections and other signs of spontaneous creative activity which indicate that this was a working score as well.

When Bartók departed for Paris on July 8, his first destination after leaving Hungary, he left the *Bluebeard* draft with Márta in Rákoskeresztúr so she could begin the process of making a clean copy. For the next nine months, until March 1912, the two Bartóks, husband and wife, would be deeply involved in the task of completing the opera and preparing clean copies in time to enter the work in two separate opera competitions in Budapest. After their marriage in 1909 Márta soon assumed the role of principal copyist for her husband; she would remain so until they divorced in 1923.[9] Possessing a careful, elegant script, and familiar with her husband's sometimes difficult handwriting, she was a logical choice for the preparation of attractively written scores or parts suitable for performance. In the summer of 1911, for unknown reasons (possibly relating to the care and nurture of Béla Bartók Jr., born a year previously), she remained home in Hungary while Bartók traveled abroad, a separation that engendered a steady stream of correspondence between her and her husband. In keeping each other up to date on household matters and, for Bartók, his movements across France and Switzerland, the pressing matter of *Bluebeard's Castle* and its progress toward completion came up with regularity. From these letters, and taking into account evidence drawn from other quarters, we can partially reconstruct the chronology of the opera's creation during a period when Bartók left it incomplete, lacking the ending he would put in place by September 1911.

When Bartók left Hungary for the summer, he did not take the *Bluebeard* draft with him, despite the urgency of committing an ending to paper and beginning the orchestration process. To Frederick Delius, whom he was planning to visit once he reached France, he explained, "I was too busy to get away before the middle of July, in spite of all I did not manage to finish the compositions I wrote to you about recently, so I came to Paris empty-handed."[10] (In a letter to the reclusive English expatriate in March, he had made mention of his new opera and the *Two Pictures*.) It was not his intention, however, to take a sustained break from writing the opera, for within two weeks of his arrival in Paris the *Bluebeard* draft was back in his hands, together with a new copy prepared by Márta: Bartók had placed her under considerable pressure to forward the autograph draft to him as soon as possible. On July 15 Márta protested, "It's impossible to send *Bluebeard* off so soon."[11] Three days later, however, on July 18, she had finished her assignment: "I'm sending *Bluebeard* by today's post."[12] Bartók received the score of *Bluebeard's Castle* in Paris several days later. To his surprise, he found that Márta had sent both his draft and her newly prepared copy. His response was swift and sharp. Because of its relevance to the history of the *Bluebeard* scores, his letter of July 22, 1911, is quoted at length here:

> [Paris] Saturday, July 22, 1911
>
> The package luckily arrived. It is very nicely written—but how should I have thought it would be ready by Tuesday, when I had asked for it by Wednesday and you wrote that such a task was impossible. Now I will soon send *back* 8 pages (2 folios) of the score as well as the copy of the piano reduction. Silly girl!! Why would I have needed both? It's enough that the original is here. It's *dangerous* to send the original and the copy at the same time, keeping them in the same place. Among other things, if the original gets lost, at least the copy still remains. And for just this reason—("how he scolds again")—I hasten to send it back. Now then, the entire piano reduction copy has to be bound at the bookbinders, together with many empty pages on which you will then write the missing ending. It will be good to have this done as soon as possible. (Not having the book cut and trimmed binds our souls ten times, too!!)
>
> Detailed instructions on the copying of the new full score then follow.
>
> The writing of the score will be hard work. Because I'm afraid that with your round script it's not possible to write the text as small as I do. Yet

if you adopt a bigger style of writing now, the thickness of the lines will change; perhaps then the text will fit more or less within the system according to whether more instruments are found in your system arrangement, or whether instruments will be omitted.

Before you begin to write a page it has to be measured out. It will be better to write with more room, and only on *twenty-line* paper; it doesn't matter if a page has on it, for example, only a 10- or 11- or even only an 8-line system.

Like this. [Bartók draws a little diagram showing five staff lines bound by a system brace at the left-hand edge.]

For example, the first page can remain as I have done: this is rather roomy.

The second page already has space for only one system on the page; thus the second six-line system really should go on the next page, together with the twelve-system line already there (this, too, is pretty roomy). In this last case, it's a bad spot for the gran cassa to go. Its true location is marked.[13]

This letter provides an extraordinary amount of information related to the writing of the *Bluebeard* scores. (Its alternately scolding and instructive tone also offers a glimpse into the relationship between Bartók and his wife.) Apparently Bartók had not asked for Márta to send him the copy she was making; he wanted only his autograph draft, which he would need in order to begin the process of orchestration. After only a few days in France, then, the copy was sent back to Márta with instructions to have it bound. From the preciseness of his instructions for copying "8 pages of the score" it is possible to identify these as the first pages of what would become the autograph full score (FS1) over the next two months.[14] Bartók's letter to Márta makes plain that the orchestration of *Bluebeard's Castle* was begun in Paris. Evidently the first few pages of the opera had already been orchestrated by July 22, for he describes the eight resulting pages of full score as if they were lying in front of him.

The composer's passing reference to a "missing ending" (*hiányzó befejezés*) indicates that, for whatever reason, he apparently had not succeeded in finishing the opera before he left for Paris on July 8, a fact corroborated by his communication to Delius. We have no way of knowing the dimensions of this missing ending. It could have comprised only a few pages from the very end of the opera, or it could have been the entire seventh door scene, perhaps even more. It is possible, too, that Bartók had already composed the entire opera but grew dissatisfied with its conclusion and left for Paris with plans to rewrite the affected parts. Little evidence can be gathered in support of this latter scenario, however. On the "many blank pages" Bartók instructed Márta to include at the back of the bound copy, Márta did eventually copy down an ending, of which a single page (p. 66) still survives among the extensive alterations Bartók later made to the manuscript—the sole remnant of what must have once been a complete ending in her hand. Enough music is included on this page, however, to conclusively identify it as part of the opera's original ending, thereby making almost certain the opera's unfinished status prior to July 1911.

On July 23, 1911, Bartók departed Paris for Switzerland. For the next six weeks he vacationed in that country, making Zermatt his base for the first month.[15] Though ostensibly on vacation, he worked diligently on *Bluebeard* the entire month of August. Balázs, who joined Bartók and the Kodálys for a week at a "nature resort" in the mountains outside Zurich from August 20 to 28, recalled that Bartók worked six to eight hours a day on the orchestration of *Bluebeard* during the week they spent together.[16] The constraint of finishing the score prevented Bartók from fully enjoying his summer. "I am very weary of my hotel's monotony," he wrote to Márta from Zermatt on August 14, "and if the score weren't hanging around my neck I would long ago have been somewhere else."[17] A few days later he wrote to a friend saying that he had been unable to get away for hiking because of the "needed score-writing."[18] The orchestral score grew rapidly in August. It would be finished only after he returned to Budapest at the beginning of September to resume another year of teaching at the music academy. It was then that he inscribed the date, September 20, on the score's last page.

The composition of *Bluebeard's Castle*, these letters reveal, took place in two distinct phases. The sketchwork (if any) and draft occupied Bartók from February to early July 1911. Following a short break, he commenced the orchestration in later July, while abroad. When writing orchestral works Bartók normally worked from draft to full score; the procedure he followed for *Bluebeard* was not unusual. What stands out in the otherwise orderly creation of a major musical work, however, is the absence of an ending at the time Bartók began orchestration. This, perhaps, was the first sign of Bartók's anxiety over a passage that would continue to leave him dissatisfied in the months and years ahead. As of early August 1911, four manuscript scores of *Bluebeard's Castle* were in existence, each in a different state of completion, and each—significantly—still lacking an ending. Márta's copy of the full score (FS2) can be assigned a tentative date of origin around August 1, 1911, or when she received the first shipment of eight pages in the mail from her traveling husband. The first 104 pages of this manuscript are copied in an exceptionally neat, attractive hand that László Somfai has identified in other manuscripts as Márta's "calligraphic" hand, which suggests that FS2 was designed from the start as one of the scores to be entered for competition, where neatness and legibility were paramount concerns.[19] Individual notes are carefully and precisely placed within their measures, and the Hungarian text and stage directions are entered into the score in a handsome, stylized script that recalls the Gothic typeface of old German print.

The orchestral score (FS1) was completed in only two months' time, from ca. July 22 to September 20, an impressive achievement by any standard. Bartók was in the habit of dating his manuscripts throughout his life, and on the autograph full score of *Bluebeard's Castle* he inscribed the dates "(1911 febr.)" and "1911. szept. 20" on the first and last pages. These dates, quite logically, have been taken as the times when Bartók began and finished the opera. The first date is less precise than the final date because Bartók had actually only begun the preparation of the full score in July 1911; after he finished the scoring on September 20, he went back to the head of the score and wrote down a rough approximation of when he began to compose the opera (notice the parentheses surrounding the February 1911 date, as if it were remembered imprecisely). At what point the missing ending was added to complete the opera is a matter of conjecture, but it must have taken place sometime during the two months from late July to September 20. Our knowledge of Bartók's working habits enables us to assume that the draft was completed prior to the orchestral score. VS1 can therefore be assigned a date of completion no later than September 20, 1911.

The original ending of *Bluebeard's Castle* is transcribed in example 5.1.[20] The exact dimensions of what Bartók identified as the opera's "missing ending" cannot be reconstructed with any degree of certainty, but in all likelihood it was this passage, if not more, that had yet to be written when he left for Paris. Other parts of the seventh door scene also would be revised, notably the music heard when the three former wives step forth from behind the seventh door (figs. 123–25 in the published score). This deeply symbolic section at the very end, however, never performed or published, underwent the most significant transformations. The excerpt begins at the point in the opera where Bluebeard places the crown, jewels, and mantle on Judith as she moves to take her place with the other wives as the stage light fades to darkness, leaving Bluebeard alone on stage at the very end. It comprises the last two to three minutes of the opera and corresponds roughly to the music found starting at fig. 133 in the published score. How Bartók eventually scored the music can be seen in example 5.2, a facsimile from page 111 of the autograph full score that illustrates the corresponding passage (beginning only) in its orchestral form.

One of the most immediately striking features of the original ending is the almost purely triadic nature of its harmonic language. The music Bartók wrote in late summer 1911 consists largely of major and minor triads moving in gentle parallel motion to support Judith and Bluebeard's vocal lines. At points of repose, the harmony tends to sustain on quiet chords of a major or minor seventh —relatively uncomplicated sonorities that bear only a faint resemblance to the more dissonant chords of the final version. The compositional technique evident here of slipping rapidly from one key area to the next via nonfunctional triadic motion shows the influence of the contemporary French music Bartók admired so much at this time in his life. Through the waves of Debussyan parallel triads, particularly on the first two pages of example 5.1, Bartók's personal voice shines only weakly. It emerges in the occasional chromatic clash or bimodal sonority (D major/minor in the last system of page 3 in example 5.1) or in the pentatonic outlines of Bluebeard's vocal part. Were it not for the Hungarian language and the occasional Hungarian rhythmic inflection in the vocal lines, large parts of the original ending to *Bluebeard's Castle* might easily be mistaken for the work of Debussy.

Another noteworthy feature is that after the dialogue between Bluebeard and Judith concludes, the orchestra ends the opera with not one, but two statements of the F♯-pentatonic melody, first in the winds, then in the strings an octave lower. Bartók would later remove the first of these statements. The music from that point forward, however, remained largely unchanged from 1911 to

EXAMPLE 5.1 *The original ending of* Bluebeard's Castle, *September 1911. Transcribed from Bartók's autograph draft (VS1), pages 48–50. An English translation has been added to facilitate reference. Bartók's orchestral cues, also found in the draft, are rendered into English here.*

EXAMPLE 5.1 *(continued)*

(continued)

EXAMPLE 5.1 *(continued)*

Te vol - tál a leg - szebb asz - szony.
Your were my most beautiful wife.

(They look each other in the eye for a long time.)

138

EXAMPLE 5.1   (*continued*)

(The seventh door closes.)

(strings)

(oboes)

(flutes)

(Total darkness,

in which Bluebeard disappears.)

(clarinets)

(violoncellos
+
contrabasses)

(*continued*)

EXAMPLE 5.1   *(continued)*

1921. When the closing melody first appears, its four-note phrases are each harmonized identically over a F♯-minor triad that resolves by chromatic voice leading to a D-minor seventh chord at the phrase's end. The melody's second statement varies points of resolution at phrase endings and adds a counter-idea taken from earlier in the opera, the menacing motif fluttering in the woodwinds. A further addition in the shape of a four-note motif rising stepwise from C♯ to F♯ in the middle voices helps establish continuity between each phrase.

It is in the cumulative dramatic effect of these musical differences that we see how profoundly Bartók's conception of the opera's final moments changed with time. As originally written, the opera draws to a close in a passive, restrained manner, as if the experience of love Bluebeard had just relived in his mind were but a distant memory. The entire conclusion is written at a dynamic level that exceeds piano only for a few brief surges to mezzoforte and one rise to forte. The huge orchestral climax over a B♭ pedal that we know from the final version is nowhere to be found, reducing the immediate psychological weight of Bluebeard's last gestures. By not lingering at the words "You were my most beautiful wife" (ex. 5.1, m. as on preceding page), Bartók further downplays the dramatic potential of Bluebeard's last declaration. The accompanying orchestral music commences at mezzoforte, crescendos to a four-measure forte, and then quickly melts back into the pianissimo return of the F♯ pentatonic melody. Compared to the final version, this is understatement indeed. Bartók's first attempt at an ending thus seems consciously antidramatic in a way familiar from Debussy's *Pelléas et Mélisande*. Lacking a culminating orchestral statement to summarize and interpret the drama, the music wanders weakly in search of a dramatic moment that

EXAMPLE 5.2   Duke Bluebeard's Castle. *Bartók's autograph full score (FS1), page 111, showing the beginning measures of the ending transcribed in example 5.1. Deleted measures visible on the right-hand side of the page are later revisions made in late 1911 or early 1912. Reproduced with the permission of Peter Bartók.*

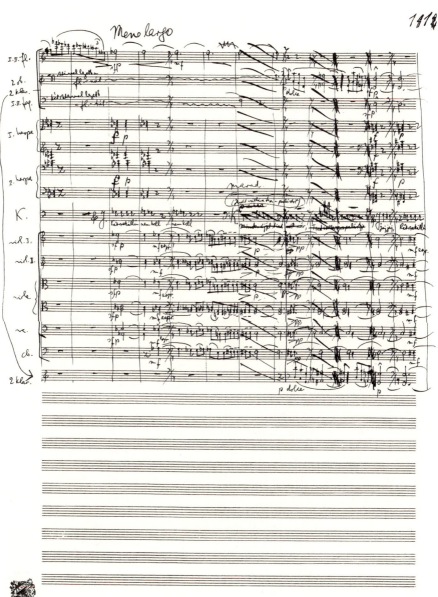

never arrives. This conception nicely suits the static theater aesthetic espoused by the libretto's author but lacks the sure operatic sense—and larger-than-life emotional impact—of Bartók's later version.

An Intermediate Stage: The Second Version of the Ending, Late 1911–Early 1912

We have to use our imagination to reconstruct what the opera's manuscripts looked like in the fall of 1911, for it would not be long before Bartók began to revise the opera's conclusion, making the first of what would become many changes to the scores. As they are preserved today, the four manuscripts all contain revisions made after the time of their initial completion. Two were revised extensively; two were not. Those that Márta copied, VS2 and FS2, became Bartók's working scores when he returned to the opera in 1917 to prepare for the premiere. He used her clean copies to make the revisions, thereby relegating his own, somewhat messier scores, VS1 and FS1, to the status of artifacts preserving an earlier, soon-to-be-outdated version of the opera. In September to October 1911, these four scores all transmitted a single version of the opera. From that point on, however, their subsequent paths diverged, and they now record different stages along the long trail leading to the first published edition.

Within months of finishing the opera Bartók had already revised its ending. At some point in late 1911 or early 1912, he returned to the score and recast the existing music in slightly different form, adding a newly composed section of music that profoundly altered the effect of the opera's final minutes.[21] Bartók's revisions at this time were directed only at the seventh door scene, and, within that scene, primarily at the music illustrated in example 5.1. No other areas of the opera were affected.[22] The changes were significant: (1) At the moment when Bluebeard bestows upon Judith the crown, mantle, and jewels (beginning of ex. 5.1), Bartók removed all of Bluebeard's words, starting with "Now all nights are yours / Yours the starry mantle." To compensate for the loss of text, he shortened the duration of the sustained chords in the orchestral accompaniment. (2) Bartók then replaced a twenty-measure section of music from the original ending with an early version of the powerful orchestral climax over a B♭ pedal point that we know from the opera's final form (see ex. 5.1, where the deleted measures are marked). Bluebeard's text at this point, "You were my most beautiful wife," was simply removed. (It would be restored by 1917.) Toward the end of the newly composed orchestral insertion, Bartók wrote in a part for the organ, whose melancholy, haunting sound would lead the music back into the return of the F♯-pentatonic theme. This memorable feature of the opera was not present in Bartók's original conception. (3) In the first statement of the F♯ theme (which would be removed in 1917), Bartók added to the texture a small ornamental figure whose half-step contours and fleeting thirty-second-note rhythms recall the castle's sigh motifs heard earlier in the opera. Bluebeard was given a final line of text to sing: the pessimistic "And now it will be night forever," intoned in a hushed voice over the unfolding F♯ melody in the orchestra.

TABLE 5.2 Changes made to the conclusion of *Bluebeard's Castle* to produce the second, revised version of the ending, ca. February 1912. Bartók's additions are in underlined boldface. His deletions are struck out.

J.	Kékszakállú nem kell, nem kell.	Bluebeard, I don't need them, I don't need them!
B.	(Judit vállára teszi a palástot.)	(He places the mantle on Judith's shoulders.)
	~~Minden éjjel tied most már.~~	~~Every night is yours now.~~
	~~Tied csillagos palástja.~~	~~Yours the starry crown.~~
J.	Jaj, jaj Kékszakállú vedd le.	Oh, oh, Bluebeard, take it away.
	[The second door closes.]	
B.	(Judit fejére teszi a koronát.)	(He places the crown on Judith's head.)
	~~Tied gyémánt koronája~~	~~Yours is the diamond crown.~~
	~~Büvös gyémánt koronája.~~	~~The splendid diamond crown.~~
J.	Jaj, jaj, Kékszakállú vedd le.	Oh, oh, Bluebeard, take it away.
	[The first door closes.]	
B.	(Judit nyakába akasztja az ékszert.)	(He places the jewels on her neck.)
	~~Tied a legdrágább kincsem.~~	~~You are my most precious treasure.~~
	~~Szép vagy, szép vagy,~~	~~You are beautiful, beautiful~~
	~~százszor szép vagy~~	~~A thousand times beautiful.~~
	~~Te voltál a legszebb asszony.~~	~~You were my most beautiful wife.~~
	[They look at each other for a long time.]	
	<u>És mindig is éjjel lesz már.</u>	**<u>And now it will be night forever.</u>**

By deleting Bluebeard's vocal lines and their orchestral accompaniment in the manner illustrated in example 5.2, Bartók transformed Bluebeard into an almost mute character. His textual revisions are illustrated in table 5.2. With these changes in place, Bluebeard now sang only one line in the entire closing section of the opera. Instead, he pantomimes, silently placing the mantle, jewels, and crown on Judith's body. In light of Bartók's future development as a composer, this retreat from the world of language to the world of gestures at the end of *Bluebeard's Castle* takes on a larger significance. In *The Wooden Prince* and *The Miraculous Mandarin*, dialogue was left behind altogether as he moved in the direction of ballet. Bluebeard's inability to speak when he bids farewell to Judith may be a reflection of Bartók's own inability to articulate the anguish of his spiritual loneliness: music alone, without words, could speak more profoundly than the human voice. And when Bluebeard, alone on the darkened stage at the end, does open his mouth to sing, it is with words that are addressed not to Judith but to himself—addressed, as it were, to his inner conscience, which we in the audience are privileged to hear.

Kroó, who has examined this second version of the ending, rightly notes that the added orchestral music had great importance for the opera. With the new music in place, he writes, "Bartók had essentially found what he was seeking: the great transition and culmination, the final musical and dramatic climax of the opera before the epilogue."[23] The revised ending projects the tragedy of Judith and Bluebeard's lost love with far greater immediacy. Wordless gestures, an extended *fff* outburst in the orchestra, and a final line of text that encapsulates the depth of Bluebeard's sorrow all combine to transform the dramatic effect. Bluebeard's emotional response to the loss of Judith is amplified in the revised ending. He is no longer the purely passive sufferer portrayed in the opera's first ending. His suffering is greater, and somehow more believable.

The Two Opera Competitions

Apart from their names, very little seems to be known about the two opera competitions *Bluebeard* was entered in following its completion in September 1911. Their rules for entry, their closing dates, their eventual winners—none of this has been brought to light. The rejection of *Bluebeard* at these opera competitions has become part of the lore surrounding the opera. One finds it mentioned in most Bartók biographies, the wording slightly changed to suit each author's taste. The very word "rejection" conveys the degree to which later observers have fashioned a suitable mythology for this episode in Bartók's life, a mythology that perpetuates the image, popular in Western music history since Beethoven, of the composer as beleaguered artist, misunderstood by lesser minds and in constant battle with the forces of musical conservatism. Are works "rejected" from competitions, or do they simply fail to win? And if *Bluebeard* was actually rejected, when did that event—or events—occur? István Kerner has traditionally been identified as the demagogue who, in Kroó's words, "pronounced the opera impossible to perform and rejected it" from the first competition.[24] New evidence indicates that Kerner, the music director of the Royal Opera House, was not the only distinguished musical or theatrical judge who passed negative judgment on the opera. Far more damaging to the fate of *Bluebeard's Castle* in Hungary was its failure to win the second and more prestigious of these competitions, the Rózsavölgyi, and there it was opposition to Balázs's play, not Bartók's music, that proved to be the opera's undoing.

The impetus to complete *Bluebeard* in the fall of 1911 was provided by the Lipótvárosi Kaszinó, one of Budapest's well-known coffeehouses—a club, really, whose membership was composed largely, though not exclusively, of the upper strata of the Jewish bourgeoisie in Budapest.[25] In honor of the hundredth anniversary of Ferenc Erkel's birth, members of the casino sponsored an opera competition with the presumed intent of promoting the further development of the national Hungarian operatic tradition. *Bluebeard's Castle*, one of two entries for what was known in musical circles as the "Ferenc Erkel prize," was submitted for consideration in October 1911 (see below). The prize amount was 3,000 crowns.

The second, and more lucrative, of the two competitions was sponsored by a leading Hungarian music publisher, Rózsavölgyi, with whom Bartók had enjoyed a productive business relationship since June 1908. In addition to publishing many of his early piano pieces, in its capacity as concert bureau the Rózsavölgyi firm had sponsored the Waldbauer-Kerpely Quartet concerts of March 1910

at which Bartók's first quartet—a work they also published—received its premiere.[26] In June 1910 a competition was announced for a Hungarian one-act
opera in honor of the firm's sixtieth anniversary. For a "work of absolute value
and stageworthiness" (*absolut becsű és színielőadásra mű*), submitted on or before
March 31, 1912, an award of 5,000 crowns would be given, to be shared by composer and librettist. Notice of the competition was reported in Hungary's leading
music journals. *A Zene* printed a brief summary of the conditions for entry in its
June issue. A more detailed announcement appeared in the June 1, 1910, issue
of *Zeneközlöny*, where the specific rules for entry were enumerated:[27] The length
and legal detail of this announcement, reproduced in full in Table 5.3, was necessitated by the dual role its sponsors wished to take. Winning works would not
only be given a prize but would also be added to the roster of Rózsavölgyi
properties, to be promoted by the firm within and outside Hungary. The contest's prestige is amply demonstrated by the roster of judges, drawn from Budapest's leading musical and theatrical institutions. It offered a substantially
higher sum of money to the winning authors and, with performance at the Royal
Opera House a strong likelihood, if not absolutely guaranteed (point 6), held out
the prospect of instant recognition within Hungary's leading musical circles.
Bartók was personally familiar with many of the firm's officers, including Dezső
Demény, editor of its house-sponsored journal *Zeneközlöny*, who had accompanied him to Rome early in 1910 for a music conference. His piano works were
beginning to appear under the Rózsavölgyi imprint with some regularity. At the
very least, based on his prior relationship with the firm, *Bluebeard* ought to have
had a fair chance at winning.

A comparable announcement for the Lipótvárosi Kaszinó competition never
appeared in these journals. Its terms and conditions appear not to have been
widely publicized, or, if they were, channels other than Hungary's musical press
were used to draw attention to the contest.[28]

The two competitions' successive closing dates, separated by six months,
appear to have been the chief reason Bartók returned to the *Bluebeard* score and
revised it following its initial completion. That the second ending postdates October 1911—and therefore was not ready in time for the opera's entry in the Lipótvárosi competition—is supported by evidence drawn from letters and the
scores themselves. Perhaps the most important clue to dating this first layer of revisions lies in the sudden appearance, in the second version, of a line present in
neither the original play nor the original ending: Bluebeard's words "And now it
will be night forever." This was a creation of Balázs, who forwarded it—as part of
a reworked conclusion—to the composer in October 1911. Balázs, in Paris, had
been editing and revising the text to the *Bluebeard* play in preparation for its publication in the *Mysteries* volume. (This is why the 1912 edition of the play dis-
agrees in certain details of wording with the operatic text.) Writing in mid- to
late October, he explains why he thought his new ending represented an im-
provement over the old one, and he queries the composer for news of the two
competitions.

TABLE 5.3 The announcement of the Rózsavölgyi opera competition in *Zeneközlöny*, June 1, 1910.

Rózsavölgyi & Co., Budapest's Imperial and Royal Court music publishing firm, announces a competition for a one-act opera on the occasion of its sixtieth anniversary, with a prize of 5,000 crowns offered.

Competition rules are as follows:

1. All composers who are Hungarian natives and Hungarian citizens may take part in the competition.
2. The prize is 5,000 crowns, which will be given only for works of absolute value and stageworthiness.
3. Entrants may choose freely the librettos for their entries.
4. The prize belongs to the author of the libretto and the composer together, who between themselves shall come to an agreement regarding the division of the winning amount before the delivery of the prize. The prize will be paid to the composer, and the above-named firm hereby fulfills their obligation to the text author, too.
5. Rights to the prizewinning works of all composers, with the exception of performing rights, belong to the firm of Rózsavölgyi & Co. All proceeds arising from performances belong to the authors after deducting commission in the customarily administered way.
6. Rózsavölgyi & Co. reserves the right to offer the Hungarian Royal Opera House first rights to the prizewinning work. In the event the Hungarian Royal Opera House does not accept the work, or would be unable to produce the submitted work in the course of two seasons, performance rights can be offered to other houses or foreign theaters. If Rózsavölgyi & Co. does not succeed in obtaining a production of the prizewinning work within three years, at that time the work's performance will be at the discretion of its authors.
7. With respect to foreign performances, Rózsavölgyi & Co. will represent the authors in negotiations. All translation expenses will be paid in advance by the firm; after the performances these expenses will be deducted from the proceeds.
8. The competition closes March 31, 1912, at 12 noon, when the following shall be sent to Rózsavölgyi & Co.'s address: libretto, orchestral conductor's score, and piano reduction, all neatly copied (the committee has the right to disqualify unreadable works from the competition), and with a sealed envelope bearing a code name and containing the real name of the competitor. Works received after this time will not be considered.
9. At the competition's close, judgement on the entries' stageworthiness will be requested of a jury comprising dramaturgs from the Hungarian Royal Opera House and the National Theater, together with distinguished representatives of our own firm.
10. Only works deemed excellent in terms of stageworthiness will be admitted for musical judgement.
11. For its musical judges the firm shall obtain outstanding members of each of the following institutions, the Hungarian Royal Music Academy, the National Conservatory and the Hungarian Royal Opera. The committee will be completed by the addition of one or two judges appointed by the firm.

Dear Béla

Herewith I'm sending you the new form of Bluebeard's ending. I hope I'm not late with it, so that you can still set it to music for the "serious" competition. At one time you used to complain: saying that Bluebeard is short, too, and that couldn't I make it longer. Here is a little extension. It's not much but it's something. But in terms of its sense, even its theatricalness, it may be a lot, and important. It is important that at the point where the drama is settled, or where in effect it happens, the words should be brighter (with the skeleton standing out a little), and before our eyes the stream pauses for a minute; in a word, so it should last longer and get warm on the stage. This is all a matter of an additional line or two here and there.

I hope I'm not late with it, the more so since it would be a big blow to my conscience, considering I had it a month ago and haven't mailed it. The reason is that I'm writing a new drama, I'm short of time, and I'm a little absent-minded. . . . When will the big money be awarded for Bluebeard? It would help much trouble and worry if it would be soon.[29]

On an accompanying two-page attachment Balázs sent his expanded version of the drama's ending, beginning at the point when Bluebeard turns to Judith after addressing the three former wives.[30] He adds lines to the existing dialogue in an effort to change the effect of the closing moments, or, as he says, "so it should last longer and get warm on the stage." Here, in this enclosure, Balázs contributed the final line that Bartók needed.[31] Though composer and librettist would go about revising in their respective ways, both seemed to recognize how the crucial final moments might have greater theatrical impact if they were granted more time to sink in. Instead of accepting the dramatist's additional lines, Bartók highlighted Judith and Bluebeard's separation through the addition of an orchestral interlude — lengthening the moment, but also transforming it into something of greater emotional power. Balázs worked the new dialogue into the play's 1912 edition.

The Budapest Bartók Archive contains a presentation copy of the libretto in Márta's hand. Its text transmits a variant of the opera's ending that corresponds exactly to the text illustrated in table 5.2 and, therefore, to the revised ending of late 1911 or early 1912.[32] Balázs's new last line is included. On the title page is written "A Kékszakállú herceg vára / irta / Balázs Béla," followed by a list of characters. Bartók's name is omitted. At the very top can be found, in Márta's writing, the words *Jelige: Omega,* or "Code name: Omega." This, we can safely assume, was the libretto submitted to the Rózsavölgyi jury in March 1912 as part of the required entry materials, all of which were to be identified by code name only. By inference (assuming score and libretto agreed in all details), the revised ending must have been completed by Bartók prior to the March 31 deadline.

Márta's copies can be extremely useful in establishing the chronology of *Bluebeard's Castle.* A separate source in her hand, the Márta Fragment, provides unexpected confirmation of the revised ending's dating. On February 15, 1912, Márta wrote to her mother-in-law with recent news from the Bartók household.

She mentions that Rozsnyai had just brought out Bartók's *Sketches*, op. 9b, an event that gave her great pleasure because two of its seven pieces were written for her. She then turns briefly to the subject of *Bluebeard's Castle*: "I have copied down the ending to the Bluebeard score, too (the part that the copyist wrote), and at the end of February Béla is entering it in the Rózsavölgyi competition (which may draw to a close sooner than the Erkel competition, in which he entered Bluebeard last October.)"[33] Several questions immediately present themselves. Which "ending to the Bluebeard score" had Márta just copied in February 1912? And what can be made of her reference to "the part that the copyist wrote," when no copyist scores exist from this time other than her own? Barring the possibility that Márta is speaking of a score that has not survived, her words can only be a reference to the Márta Fragment, a six-page copy of the opera's revised passages, as represented on pages 111–17 of Bartók's autograph full score. (The term she uses here, *partitúra*, indicates that she was speaking of a full score; in letters from this time she and Bartók generally referred to vocal scores as *zongorakivonatok* [piano scores], *másolatok* [copies], or *kották* [scores, in a general sense]). Like the pages of FS1 from which it was copied, the Márta Fragment shows no evidence of ever having been used in performance. There are no rehearsal numbers or other performance markings in the score. What prompted Márta to copy only these pages from the end of *Bluebeard's Castle*? We can reconstruct the events as follows.

The physical state of Márta's copy of the orchestral score (FS2) is strongly suggestive of a project finished under increasingly urgent time pressure, such as that provided by an imminent competition deadline. In the surviving manuscript, the hand of a professional copyist begins in the middle of the sixth door scene, starting on page 105.[34] (A third hand, Bartók's own, was added in 1917.) Márta, who from the start had been entrusted with the copying of this score, for some reason was unable to finish what she had begun. Because Bartók completed the opera in late September and the copied score was due the following month, it is easy to envision a situation in which Bartók enlisted the aid of an outside copyist, recognizing that Márta would need some help in the weeks before the competition. The copyist was given the music that Bartók had most recently scored, starting in the middle of the sixth door scene and continuing to the seventh door scene and the conclusion of the opera. The *original* ending was copied into FS2. Had the revised ending been done at that time, Bartók naturally would have had it copied instead. As the now-crossed-out page 142 clearly shows, the copyist prepared a score that corresponded to the earliest version of the opera's conclusion.[35] Within months, Bartók had revised the ending, rendering the music on page 142—and the remaining pages of the manuscript at that time—obsolete. This newer ending needed to be recopied.

The attractive physical appearance of the FS2 manuscript strongly suggests that this score had been intended from the beginning as a score that would be submitted to the jurors of the competition, upon whom its legibility and carefully prepared look would not be lost. This hypothesis is corroborated by the absence of Bartók's name on the original title page. A common prerequisite of music competitions is that scores be submitted anonymously, as can be seen by the wording of the Rózsavölgyi firm's 1910 announcement. Márta wrote only the title *A Kékszakállú Herceg Vára* and the words *szövegét írta Balázs Béla* (text by Béla Balázs) on FS2's title page.[36] In all likelihood, it was this score that was submitted to the Lipótvárosi competition in October 1911. The fact that Márta wasn't able to finish the score herself argues in favor of the earlier competition; by February 1912, ample time would have passed to complete a score she had begun six months earlier.

When Bartók decided to revise the opera's ending, either VS2 or FS2, or both, were already in the hands of the competition judges, so revisions could not be entered into those scores, even allowing for the remote possibility that Bartók had revised the opera so soon after it was completed. Therefore he made the revisions in his two autograph scores, starting first with VS1 and then orchestrating the newly composed passages and inserting the additional pages into FS1. Existing pages were simply reworked (see ex. 5.2). For the Rózsavölgyi competition, another copy of the full score needed to be made. Though this manuscript (FS3) has not survived, the mere fact that Márta was asked to copy down the revised pages of the ending in full score tells us that at one point it transmitted the original ending, or what she later remembered as "the part the copyist wrote." Once written out, the Márta Fragment was probably then inserted in the appropriate place in FS3 and given the page numbers 195–200. In its combined state (FS3 plus the Márta Fragment), this score would then have been sent to the March 1912 competition.[37]

The first two versions of the ending to *Bluebeard's Castle* thus can be correlated to the two competitions held in late 1911 and early 1912. The opera was submitted to the Lipótvárosi Kaszinó competition in original form in October 1911. Revised slightly, it was submitted to the Rózsavölgyi competition six months later.

Results of the competitions were not announced in Budapest until the second half of 1912. A tersely worded notice in the July 1912 issue of *A Zene* indicated that two operas had been submitted for the Lipótvárosi Kaszinó competition and that neither was awarded a prize.

> The Lipótvárosi Kaszinó's 3,000 crown "Ferenc Erkel prize," for which this month two operas competed—to no avail—will reopen with a new closing date of October 1, 1913, for three prizes.
> 1. Four-movement symphony, 1,500 crowns.
> 2. Orchestra overture, 750 crowns.
> 3. Cycle of six songs, 750 crowns.
> Dr. Géza Molnár, university professor at the National Music Academy, can provide full information.

Five months later, in November 1912, the fate of Bartók's opera in the Rózsavölgyi competition was announced in *Zeneközlöny*, the firm's own house organ.[38] Presumably, then, the following announcement represented the "official" opinion concerning the opera competition. Again, only two operas had been entered. The identity of the other opera has not been discovered.

> The firm Rózsavölgyi & Co. announced, on the occasion of their sixtieth anniversary, a competition for a one-act opera and a Hungarian-style orchestral work. Two entries were received for the first competition which, in the judgment of Sándor Hevesi, stage manager at the opera house, were completely unsuitable for staged performance [*teljesen alkalmatlanok voltak színi előadásra*], and therefore were unable to come up for musical judgment [*zenei bírálatra még csak nem is kerülhettek*]. Six works were received for the second competition.[39] The judging committee—whose members were István Kerner, Jenő Hubay, Alajos Gobbi, and Dezső Demény—stated unanimously that, among them, not a single work of absolute value turned up, and that therefore it would not be possible to give out the prize.

The competition's rules had stated clearly that determination of the winning works would be based first on their theatrical quality. Works that failed to meet standards of excellence in terms of stageworthiness, as adjudicated by a committee of leading Hungarian dramaturgs, would not be admitted for musical judgment. *Bluebeard's Castle*, in other words, never made it to the music committee of the Rózsavölgyi competition. It was found lacking from a theatrical standpoint.

That it was deemed "unsuitable for staged performance" by Sándor Hevesi, a long acquaintance of Balázs's from Budapest's professional theater circles, came as a sad irony. In 1912 Hevesi was appointed stage manager of the Opera House, a position he held until 1916. From 1922 to 1932 he would go on to assume the directorship of the National Theater, an institution he had started with as stage manager in 1901. In his early days at the National Theater he had lent his support and expertise to the small theater group called Thália that Balázs, Lukács, and Kodály helped cofound in 1904, and it was his work with Thália that exposed him to modern trends in European theater.[40] He had known Balázs for at least eight years by the time he was asked for his assessment of the *Bluebeard's Castle* libretto. From his perch as a rising talent in Hungarian theater, it is likely that he was familiar with at least some of Balázs's previous literary efforts. His low opinion of the opera's theatrical merit, from one who earlier had willingly thrown his weight into the battle to raise Hungarian theatrical standards, appears, on the surface, to be at odds with his record. His ruling, in any event, meant that the music committee, whose members may have included some of the same men who adjudicated the orchestral competition, would not have the opportunity to weigh the opera's musical merits.

When Hevesi took up duties at the Opera House in the fall of 1912, his presence sharply diminished any hope that *Bluebeard* would soon be heard on its stage. It wasn't that he was hostile to new musical or theatrical ideas; his legacy indicates quite the opposite. During his tenure the Opera House continued its longstanding tradition of advocacy for new Hungarian stage works, scheduling several premieres each season in rotation with periodic performances of contem-

porary operas and ballets that had earned some degree of popularity, such as
Hubay's *A cremonai hegedűs*, Dohnányi's *Pierette fátyola*, and Ede Poldini's *A
csavargó és a királylány*. Of the eleven new productions Hevesi mounted during
the 1912–13 season, two were new operas by Hungarians: Ákos Buttykay's
Hamupipőke and Sándor Szeghő's one-act *Báthory Erzsébet*. New works from
abroad, including Debussy's *L'enfant prodigue*, heard May 3, 1913, and Mus-
sorgsky's *Boris Godunov*, receiving its first Hungarian performances in December
of 1913, were introduced to Hungarian audiences through Hevesi's staging.[41]
Both Bartók and Balázs met with Hevesi and other decision makers at the Opera
House around this time, including Miklós Bánffy, the general director. Balázs relates in his diary a story that illustrates how deep a gulf existed in matters of
artistic taste between Bartók and the men whose support he needed to produce
his opera. "I met with Béla Bartók and Zoltán in Pest," he wrote in the summer of
1912.

> From Béla I heard the following incident. They had come to him to ask him
> to write music for a ballet which Margit Vészi and Jenő Mohácsi had writ-
> ten. They said that Bánffy had already seen it, and liked it, Hevesi, too—it
> was everyone's wish that he should do the music; they rushed off to Zoltán
> to try to persuade him, too, they even spoke about it to the Academy's jani-
> tors, perhaps. They needed to "arrange" it like this. "Heart," however (the
> ballet) was bad, and Béla didn't take a liking to it. If you want opera music:
> here is *Bluebeard* (Upon hearing that, they wanted to get around Béla, so
> they said: be sensible. don't put off the opportunity to be on good terms with
> the Opera.) They admitted he nearly succeeded. Business is business—
> that's what is written above the gates of Parnassus.[42]

The Opera House wanted to work with Bartók, this story shows, but only on
projects deemed more palatable to the general public. That its directors could simultaneously court Bartók for a separate project while ignoring *Bluebeard* may be
indicative of how little enthusiasm they could muster for the opera. For the right
project—one that was less gloomy, perhaps—they would be willing to work with
him. (This is, of course, what eventually happened with *The Wooden Prince*.) On
another occasion Balázs himself tried to persuade Hevesi and Bánffy to stage the
opera, possibly in the period after the competitions closed. So memorable were
Hevesi's words of rebuff that Balázs could still remember them thirty years later:
"Too dark."[43]

In 1922 Balázs recalled the struggle to get *Bluebeard* performed at the Opera
House as another example of his unceasing support for Bartók, something he
felt the composer had failed to appreciate. The bitter tone of Balázs's story, directed not just at Hevesi but also, unmistakably, at Bartók, stems from the circumstances surrounding its publication, for in 1922 he had publicly broken his
friendship with Bartók (see chapter 1). Nonetheless, his reminiscence sheds light
on the fate of their first collaboration, and here, too, Hevesi's dismissive words
ring forth.

Bartók didn't want to submit *Bluebeard* to the Opera. He was arrogant and detested useless experimenting. I encouraged Sándor Hevesi, to no avail; Hevesi at that time had been taken on as director by Miklós Bánffy. Never was there such hopeless hopelessness. I got a piano score stolen and smuggled out to Bánffy. And Bartók was right. He didn't like *Bluebeard's Castle*. "Far too dark [*túlságosan sötét*]," said Doktor Hevesi, who was then working in rococo. Well, Bartók wasn't exactly a cheerful man. But at that time he had become entirely black.[44]

After crossing swords with Hevesi over *Bluebeard* for several years, Balázs appears to have been only too eager to cast his former ally as chief scapegoat for the opera's delayed premiere. In actuality it is unlikely that the blame rested solely with Hevesi, for others at the Opera House, chiefly Bánffy, had the power to place the work in production, and could have overcome his objections had they themselves believed deeply in the work, which they apparently did not. In light of this information, it seems clear that we must alter our understanding of why *Bluebeard* met the fate it did. To view István Kerner as the opera's principle nemesis misrepresents the actual situation. His legendary denunciation of *Bluebeard* as "unplayable" may have had some basis in fact, but he played no apparent role in determining the results of the Rózsavölgyi competition. Whether or not he served on the Lipótvárosi Kaszinó competition's jury (whose makeup has not been ascertained) and made his statement there, or perhaps privately to Bartók, remains unclear. At the very least, future biographers will have to acknowledge that the "rejection" of *Bluebeard's Castle* was not the isolated act of one man. Nor was it, in this case, a decision based solely on the music. Hevesi's low opinion of *Bluebeard's Castle*, formed when he first reviewed the materials entered in the Rózsavölgyi competition, hindered or prevented acceptance of the work among those who might otherwise have given it fuller consideration—including the members of the music jury Rózsavölgyi had assembled.

Bluebeard's failure to win either of the two opera competitions in which it had been entered, when combined with the folding in 1912 of the short-lived *New Hungarian Music Society*, an enterprise Bartók and Kodály had helped found only two years earlier, precipitated a period of crisis in Bartók's life that took many years to overcome. He withdrew from musical life in Hungary, bitter over the apathetic and even hostile reactions his music had met. For several years after 1912 he made no public appearances as a pianist, composed little, and merely fulfilled his duties at the Academy of Music. "I have resigned myself to writing for my writing-desk only," he wrote to Géza Zágon in August 1913.[45] He traveled extensively in pursuit of folk song material, visiting locales in eastern Europe as well as more exotic destinations; the summer of 1913 found him in Biskra, Algeria, collecting the music of North African peoples. The onset of World War I forced the curtailment of even this activity, however. In 1915 he wrote in frustration to his wife Márta, "Actually what do I desire? Purely impossible things! I would go to my dear Wallachians to collect; I would go off, far, to travel; I would go to hear wonderful music, but not in Budapest; I would go to rehearsals of *Bluebeard*; I would go to a performance of *Bluebeard*! Now I know that never in my life shall I hear it.—You asked me to play it for you—I feel I would not be able to play it through. Yet I shall try it some time, at least we can weep over it together."[46] Two years later the success of *The Wooden Prince* signaled a change in public opinion about Bartók's music. Performance of *Bluebeard* were scheduled for the spring of 1918 at the Opera House. Preparing for the premiere inspired Bartók to cast a critical eye over the music once again. On June 17, 1917, he informed Bánffy, "I will be looking over the *Bluebeard* score until July 15, and then I can submit it to you."[47] It was at this point that the third and most substantial layer of revisions began.

The Third Version of the Ending, 1917

A description of the myriad changes Bartók made to the opera in the months leading up to the May 1918 premiere rapidly develops into an endless catalogue of minutiae. In a complete review of the score, from beginning to end, Bartók reevaluated the music on all levels, revising dynamics, tempi, agogic markings, and, in places, the harmonic and structural content. Every page of VS2 and FS2, the scores he worked with, shows evidence of this comprehensive revision process. The bulk of this work had already been completed by mid-July 1917, in order to accommodate Bánffy's wish that he deliver a conductor's score, piano-vocal score, and libretto to the Opera House library so copying could commence.[48] Example 5.3, a facsimile of page 61 from Márta's piano-vocal copy, illustrates how extensively Bartók reworked certain passages.

This example comes from the beginning of the seventh door scene, where the three former wives step forth, accompanied by a plaintive melody in C minor. The middle two systems on this page represent a pasteover, difficult to see in black and white, on which Bartók wrote a reharmonized version of the music that appears in the published score from figs. 122 to 123/5. Keeping the melodic line at its original pitch, he shifted the underlying C-minor chords up a half step, to D♭ minor. Measures at the top and bottom of the page had to be deleted to make the pasteover fit. (The first measure of what was once the melody's original C-minor harmonization can be seen beneath the hatch marks at the end of the first system.) Bartók had Márta recopy the affected passage—on the illustrated page, we see a 1917 version of her writing in the middle two systems, set against the calligraphic neatness of the first and fourth systems, which date from 1911, all overlaid with a thin layer of Bartók's own modifications. It is not unusual to see revisions of this magnitude in the surviving scores, though the first and seventh door scenes were by far the most heavily affected.[49] The smudging barely visible in the vocal part of the first measure arose when Bartók displaced Judith's exclamations *Élnek, élnek* by one beat: he scratched out the eighth notes originally placed on beats one and three, replacing them with a rest, and moved

EXAMPLE 5.3   Duke Bluebeard's Castle. *Márta Bartók's copy of the vocal score (VS2), page 61, showing Bartók's revisions from 1917 and later. Illustrated is the music from the seventh door scene, beginning at fig. 122/4 in the published score. Reproduced with the permission of Peter Bartók.*

the words to beats two and four, in the position where they are now known. At some point before he sent this score to Universal Edition to be engraved in June 1918, Bartók revised the tempo markings and added metronome indications.

Beyond changes of this nature, the ending also underwent significant structural and harmonic change. Bartók removed the first of the two F♯-pentatonic melody statements and condensed Bluebeard and Judith's last lines so that their vocal parts were superimposed rather than separate, as they had been before. The sounds of the solo organ now led directly into what was formerly the second statement of the F♯ melody. Bartók then trimmed seventy-two measures from elsewhere in the score to further shorten the opera's overall duration.[50]

His primary motivation in going back to the ending was, no doubt, to find a more satisfactory way to bring the work to a close, musically and dramatically. Inevitably, though, his musical style was colored by the compositional advances in the intervening years. If his earlier music seemed at times an eclectic mixture of elements drawn from folk song and the Western art music tradition, through the years of World War I these disparate strands of influence began to coalesce into a personal style of great power and originality. In harmonic terms, this was expressed by a gradual distancing from the language of tonality. Symmetrical and other nontraditional modes of pitch organization became more pronounced. Dissonance was more pervasive. As a result, the harmonic language of *Bluebeard*'s 1917 ending at times more closely resembles the music of works like the Second String Quartet, the *Ady Songs*, and *The Miraculous Mandarin* than it does the original *Bluebeard*. This aspect of the opera's development has received little attention from Bartók scholars. Kroó, in examining the stages that led to the opera's final form, asserts that "no stylistic changes" were made to the score over the ten years from 1911 to 1921.[51] As the manuscripts clearly show, this is not the case.

In 1911 Bartók's music, *Bluebeard* included, was still redolent of the contemporary French music he admired so much. While much of this influence can still be seen in the score Bartók eventually published, the imprint of Debussy was even more pronounced in the opera's original, unrevised state. The coloristic, nonfunctional parallel chord motion found in the first version of the ending (ex. 5.1) strongly evokes the Debussy of "La cathédrale engloutie" and other pieces for piano. Such a style, which sounded fresh and innovative in 1911, especially when couched in the sharp rhythmic patterns of the Hungarian language, by 1917 may have appeared to Bartók as a weakness needing correction. Many of the triadic harmonies found in the 1911–12 ending were simply removed or altered. The extent of Bartók's harmonic revisions can be seen by comparing the published version of *Bluebeard's Castle* with the manuscripts showing what corresponding passages looked like in 1911. One measure before fig. 132, for example, Bartók changes a V⁷–I cadence in C major to a succession of unrelated chords with no clear tonal focus (ex. 5.4). In another passage, after fig. 124, parallel triads on G♯, F♯, and G were given a new form that changed their rhythmic duration and obfuscated the parallel relationship (ex. 5.5; see also the facsimile in ex. 5.3).

A dramatic illustration of how Bartók's harmonic language evolved from 1911 to 1917 can be found in the music starting at fig. 133 in the published score,

EXAMPLE 5.4   *Seventh door scene, fig. 132. Original and revised form.*

most of whose basic elements were already present in the original ending of 1911. Four measures after fig. 133, Bluebeard and Judith begin to sing words that closely resemble the 1911 text. Bluebeard places the crown and jewels on her, and she responds with pleas to remove them. Bluebeard, however, now sings and makes symbolic gestures simultaneously, and Judith responds immediately; text and actions that formerly occupied eight or nine measures now occupy four. In rewriting and superimposing the two voice parts, Bartók expresses the resulting music in a more advanced harmonic idiom. What were originally, for the most part, simple triads and seventh chords are now rendered as complex dissonant chords whose bottom two pitches maintain a constant fixed interval of a tritone. Echos of the original ending can also be seen in Judith's half-step intervallic content and in the way the entire passage descends in sequential fashion through three successive pitch levels. Bluebeard's vocal line outlines an A♭ triad at *Tied csillagos palástja*; an F♯-minor triad at his next line, *Tied gyémánt koronája*; and an E-minor triad at the last line in the example, *Tied a legdrágább kincsem*. The descending stepwise motion A♭–F♯–E is taken directly from the original ending, where, however, it is arrayed over a broader span of music.

1911/12 Version, FS1, pp. 103–4. Reduction by the author.

1917 Version

The first three bars at fig. 133 were added to the opera in 1917. Present in none of the early manuscript sources, they serve as a brief orchestral interjection that prepares Bluebeard and Judith's final dialogue together. This is exactly the type of writing that would not have been encountered in *Bluebeard* in 1911. Abrasively dissonant chords oscillate under a melodic line that shares no pitches with the harmonies, thereby adding to the dissonance. It could be argued that the increased levels of dissonance found in the 1917 form of the ending were not entirely alien to the conception of *Bluebeard's Castle*, but merely intensifications of a harmonic element already present in the original score. The tritone interval was very much a part of Bartók's harmonic and melodic language in 1911; it is present in the F♯–C overall tonal plan of the opera, as well as in many vertical sonorities. Nonetheless, Bartók appears to have consciously revised individual chords throughout the opera with an eye toward making them less triadic. This seems to have occurred mainly in those parts of the opera where he was making revisions for other reasons related to structure or orchestration. This is why the seventh door scene, particularly its ending, was so heavily affected.

We tend to think of *Bluebeard* as a work of 1911, as a culmination of his early period. It is not just a work of 1911, though, but a work of 1911 *and* 1917—or, more precisely, 1911–early 1912 and 1917–18. This is reflected at least in part by stylistic differences observable within certain passages. To a body of music composed in 1911 and early 1912, Bartók added a conclusion written in the more harmonically advanced, confident style of 1917. The revised ending would sit uncomfortably with the rest of the opera, stylistically speaking, had Bartók not gone back through the entire score at the same time and made a thin layer of changes, effectively updating the opera from beginning to end. The original ending, despite its appearance as an exercise *à la manière de* Debussy, was therefore stylistically consistent with the rest of the opera as it existed in 1911. Another part of the opera composed in essentially the same style, the opening of the fifth door scene, Bartók revised only minimally following its original composition. He left that music intact from 1911 to 1921, no doubt because of its dramatic effectiveness.

Part III

Contextual Studies

6

THE BLUEBEARD STORY AT
THE TURN OF THE CENTURY

> Look how he suffers. . . . He is no longer so monstrous.
> —Paul Dukas, *Ariane et Barbe-bleue* (1907), act 3

> It is precisely this tragic obscurity, this suffering withdrawal into
> seclusion, that attracted the woman with strange power.
> —Béla Balázs, notes for the *Bluebeard* play (ca. 1915)

For the subject of his first and only opera, Bartók turned to a modern retelling of the age-old Bluebeard fairy tale, for centuries a familiar children's story in France, Germany, and England and elsewhere in Europe. Originally one of the Mother Goose tales written by Charles Perrault, where it kept company with such beloved classics as Cinderella, Puss in Boots, Sleeping Beauty, and Little Red Riding Hood, "Bluebeard" was first published in story form in 1697, and it quickly became a fixture in the pantheon of world children's literature. Adults from the eighteenth century onward encountered it in dozens of literary recastings, in operas, and in the theater, where the story of the cruel prince who murders his wives for disobeying him was brought to life with a rich variety of plots, settings, and characters.

The first literary adaptations of the Bluebeard story began to appear in the late eighteenth century, with Ludwig Tieck's five-act dramatization, *Ritter Blaubart* (1797), and a series of libretti for European opera houses by Michel-Jean Sedaine (*Raoul Barbe-bleue*, 1789, set to music by Grétry) and Monvel (*Raoul, sire de Créqui*, 1789, music by Dalayrac). Since then, hundreds of short stories, plays, and theatrical entertainments have been created using the tale's traditional outline as a point of departure. Among the more prominent retellings are Jacques Offenbach's operetta *Barbe-bleue* (1866); Maurice Maeterlinck's play *Ariane et Barbe-bleue* (1899), later the basis for an opera of the same name by Paul Dukas; Anatole France's facetious short story "Les sept femmes de la Barbe-bleue" (1908); and, of course, Bartók's one-act opera. It continues to inspire writers up to the present day. Angela Carter's feminist-inspired revision in *The Bloody Chamber* (1979), Max Frisch's *Bluebeard: A Tale* (1982), and Kurt Vonnegut's novel *Bluebeard* (1987) offer new interpretations of a subject that appears to become no less relevant, or intriguing, with the passing of time.

Musicologists and others who have written about Bartók's opera over the years have pieced together a general history of the Bluebeard tale in European literature, so important precursors to Bartók's version have been identified and examined for their possible impact on the story presented in the opera. György Kroó's work in this area has been of central importance.[1] His comprehensive study of the opera's cultural context established for Bartók scholars an essential body of information to which subsequent research remains deeply indebted. In the decades since his study, however, scholars from outside disciplines have brought to light numerous additional Bluebeard retellings from the years around Bartók and Balázs's opera, in studies that provide, in some cases, significant insights into the tale's reception in the nineteenth century.[2] Until now their findings have not been absorbed into the literature on *Bluebeard's Castle*. In addition, close examination of the many interpretations of the tale contemporary with Bartók's opera helps restore a sense of the deeper cultural and historical context in which *Bluebeard* is situated. Springing primarily from the literary, rather than the musical, world, and not from Hungary but from France, Germany, England, and North America, these long-forgotten Bluebeard interpretations demonstrate that other authors, like Balázs, were exploring the tale's psychological dimensions—fleshing out motives or delving into the characters' mental states— and thereby inventing a Bluebeard story at some remove from the traditional, fairy-tale outline.

Toward the end of the nineteenth century, and into the twentieth, a notable softening of Bluebeard's ruthless outlines took place in European literature. The fairy-tale Bluebeard is a rapacious man who shows no mercy toward the women he has married—"our childhood's monster," in the words of one later observer.[3] His heart is "harder than any rock," Perrault had assured us in the original tale, and he shouts so fiercely at his doomed wife that his cries "make the whole house tremble." In the nineteenth century the horrors of his crimes, if anything, were accentuated, but, ironically, the man perpetrating the violent deeds—Bluebeard himself—in some portrayals emerged as a tortured soul wracked by loneliness and guilt. This trend accelerated in the work of later writers such as Anatole France, Maurice Maeterlinck, Alfred Döblin, and Herbert Eulenberg, who pried loose hidden meanings and motives from the story's familiar outlines, seeking greater insight into the psychological motivation for Bluebeard's deadly behavior. The relentless wife-murdering was, in their view, less the capricious habit of a cruel man than the unfortunate consequence of repeated disappointments encountered in a fruitless quest for love. Bluebeard, in short, became a man to be pitied as much as feared. His wives shared his discontent and, in some versions, survived their visits to his forbidding castle. Bartók and Balázs clearly were not alone in finding the story to be a meaningful metaphor for the difficulties men perceived in their relationships with women. The underlying spiritual and philosophical beliefs that make the opera such a powerful statement about the inevitability of loneliness were prefigured, if not with the same voice or temperament, in the work of other authors. By the time Balázs wrote his *Bluebeard* play, the following pages will demonstrate, the trend toward sympathetic examination of the love relationship between Bluebeard and his newest wife was already well established among writers of serious literary pretension.

Most people experience Bartók's opera with memories, often childhood memories, of the Bluebeard fairy tale stirring about in the back of their mind, conditioning their response to the dramatic situation. This is nothing other than the human mind's natural response to a new experience: to consciously or subconsciously measure unfamiliar sights, sounds, or emotions against a lifetime of accumulated experience. The classic Bluebeard tale, unfortunately, carries heavy baggage into the modern world. Its overt misogyny cannot be shrugged off, as may have happened in earlier eras, nor can its patronizing attitude toward women and their supposed foibles prove endearing to observers sensitive to changing perceptions of women in Western culture. Everything in the story, from the woman's tearful pleas for mercy to her agreement to marry such a monster in the first place, and from Bluebeard's controlling presence to his willing use of violence, bespeaks a dependence on cultural stereotypes of male/female behavior that late-twentieth-century people find increasingly difficult, and uncomfortable, to accept without qualification. Constructing a mental landscape for Bartók's opera based on landmarks familiar from the fairy tale therefore runs the risk of overlooking the vast gulf that separates Bartók's two characters from their colorful but tradition-bound antecedents.

To put it another way, failing to distinguish between the fairy-tale villain and his Bartókian counterpart can prevent observers from appreciating what is really new and noteworthy about the opera's treatment of the Bluebeard story. Bartók's opera transcends the traditional story lines to achieve a less judgment-laden — and therefore more profound — view of Bluebeard and Judith's attempts to find spiritual union in love. The metamorphosis of Bluebeard from villain to improbable object of compassion took place relatively quickly, beginning in the 1880s, under the impress of a surge of interest in the man often credited as the historical inspiration for Perrault's fairy tale, the fifteenth-century French nobleman Gilles de Rais. What resulted was a peculiar, turn-of-the-century image of the character in European literature. This melancholy, lonely individual, rather than the fairy-tale murderer, is the Bluebeard that steps onto the stage in Bartók's opera.

The Theme of Female Curiosity

"Bluebeard," "Cinderella," "Puss in Boots," and other classic fairy tales come down to us invested with what one folklorist calls "the moral dimension of fairy-tale life."[4] These stories of cruel ogres, talking animals, beautiful princesses, and clever children are not merely idle tales. Like biblical parables, they resonate with a didactic quality that enables readers to draw lessons from them, lessons that reinforce the value of commonsense wisdom and craftiness applied to good ends, or, equally, lessons that impress upon young children an awareness of the dangers that follow bad behavior. Cinderella, humble and virtuous, becomes a princess, to the dismay of her ill-behaved sisters. A gullible Little Red Riding Hood, too credulous for her own good, is gobbled up by a wolf posing as her grandmother. "Bluebeard," too, has a message that many later writers would pick up and expand upon. The title of one nineteenth-century English stage production sums up the basic point rather neatly: *Blue Beard, or Female Curiosity!! and Male Atrocity!!!*[5] The perils of excess curiosity, specifically feminine curiosity, emerge as a common theme throughout the tale's lengthy history, no doubt inspired by the moral that Perrault appended to the story:

> O curiosity, thou mortal bane!
> Spite of thy charms, thou causeth often pain,
> And sore regrets, of which we daily find
> A thousand instances attend mankind.
> For thou, O may it not displease the fair,
> A flitting pleasure art, but lasting care;
> And always costs, alas! too dear the prize,
> Which, in the moment of possession, dies.[6]

The fairy-tale Bluebeard is a man of few redeeming qualities, yet Perrault tells the story in such a way that the woman's relatively minor transgression receives a disproportionately high share of blame for her close scrape with death. The moral, cited here, ironically makes no mention of Bluebeard's cruel behavior. Succumbing to temptation, the Bluebeard story teaches, is a greater crime than murder. The paradoxical tendency to fault the women in this story, rather than their husband, would form a persistent theme in Bluebeard retellings from Perrault's time forward. It finds its source in the original fairy tale, though precedents can also be found in the stories of the biblical Eve, the Greek Pandora, and other curious women of ancient lore.[7]

The Brothers Grimm included a German translation of the Bluebeard story in the first edition of their *Nursery and Household Tales* (1812; 1815). Their "Blaubart" tells of a wealthy nobleman who marries young women from his region and murders them, one after the other, for betraying his trust and entering the one room in his castle that he expressly forbids them to visit. It follows the narrative established by Perrault in that, at the last minute, the new wife is saved by the sudden appearance of her brothers, who promptly dispatch the cruel prince. A slight modification was introduced through the Grimms' emphasis on the close family bond between the newest wife and her three brothers. Convinced, however, that the story's French origin stood out too sharply in a volume devoted to German folklore and that it may have been too gruesome for children, the Grimms removed it from later editions.[8] In its place they wrote their own variant, "Fitchervogel," or "Fitcher's Bird," a no less violent tale about an evil sorcerer who dresses like a beggar to trap unsuspecting girls and bring them to his house deep in the forest. This Bluebeard-like figure kidnaps three sisters one by one, prohibiting them from entering one room "which this small key here opens." To test their honesty, he gives each girl an egg with a warning to guard it closely. On opening the door, the first two sisters drop their eggs in horror and are soon murdered. The third, however, has the wisdom and presence of mind to put her egg down in a safe location, and once inside the chamber she calmly sets about reassembling the chopped-up bodies of her sisters, which, in the manner of fairy tales, soon spring back to life. The girls all escape.

Folklorists place "Bluebeard" and "Fitchervogel" in a category known as "forbidden chamber" stories, a type of narrative common to many cultures in which characters, either male or female, struggle between their desire to gain knowledge of hidden secrets and the certainty of danger or swift punishment should they do so.[9] In Greek mythology, Jupiter keeps his thunderbolts in such a chamber, the keys to which are known only to Minerva. The twelfth-century Indian hero Saktivega, confronted with three pavilions he is forbidden to approach, cannot resist the temptation of entering; in each pavilion he finds the body of a dead maiden. "Bluebeard," perhaps the most familiar of these stories to Western readers, has assumed the status of archetype. Like its counterparts, it derives its effectiveness from what Maria Tatar refers to as the "prohibition/violation plot sequence," a narrative design that throws into relief the human trait of curiosity and its consequences.[10] It plays upon a very human response to the forbidden: the prohibition of something often acts to increase its desirability, perversely driving humans to do the very thing from which rationality dictates we should refrain. When Bluebeard forbids his wife from opening one particular door in the castle, his interdiction ignites a gnawing fascination in her mind that smolders, unresolved, until she takes steps to satisfy her curiosity.

The Bluebeard Story prior to the Twentieth Century

Over the centuries every conceivable authorial point of view has been given voice through this story, ranging from the comic to the serious. Bluebeard has been portrayed as hen-pecked fool and glowering madman; his wives as twittering socialites and fearless heroines. Humorous adaptations were plentiful in earlier eras. "Of wives I've had at least a score," Bluebeard burbles in one American theatrical spectacle,

> The lot of some of them I deplore;
> But they my orders disobeyed
> And so a penalty painful paid.
> Despite their shrieks of wild despair
> I grabbed them tightly by their long black hair,
> And altho' they prayed and begged and pled,
> Since I'd lost mine, each lost her head.[11]

Proper names were adjoined to the Bluebeard epithet, personalizing the man. The number of wives was set anywhere from two to seven, with seven being the general rule in French- and English-speaking countries.[12] Folk variants arose, too, as in the Estonian legend mentioned by Vizetelly in which a cruel husband who has already murdered eleven wives nearly murders the twelfth for opening a secret chamber with a golden key. A friend of her childhood rescues her at the last minute.[13] In Hungary the ballad of Anna Molnár tells the story of a knight who lures Anna Molnár from her home and family with promises of riches. The amorous couple stops to rest under a tree on their journey. Anna, at this moment, happens to look up: the bodies of six women lie hanging from the tree's branches. She escapes from the murderous knight, avoiding a similar fate, and returns home. This ballad was well known to Bartók from his ethnomusicological field work. In the years immediately prior to composing *Bluebeard's Castle* he included three variant forms in his published collections of folk songs.[14]

By the mid-nineteenth century, if not earlier, the tale became sufficiently familiar to theater audiences that it developed into a cliché for the stage. Earlier adaptations, such as those by Ludwig Tieck and opera composers Grétry, Mayr, Morlacchi, and Dalayrac, hewed more closely to the tone and message of the original story, though new characters and plot situations were freely added in order to make the tale more suitable to stage presentation.[15] In Tieck's *Ritter Blaubart* (1797), the earliest known theater adaptation, Agnes, Bluebeard's new wife, is rescued at the end by her three brothers (not two), one of whom had earlier anticipated this conclusion in a stirring dream scene. Agnes's psychological devastation upon seeing the chamber of horrors is masterfully portrayed: we don't witness the moment of actual entrance, but must wait until several days later when she breaks down and tearfully recounts to her sister Anne the visions of bloody walls, eery cries, and dangling skeletons, each labeled with the name of a former wife, which had greeted her entry. In Tieck's hands Bluebeard becomes a self-deprecating knight who can heroically vanquish enemies in battle and then proclaim, as he hands the keys to Agnes in Act 4, that life is a "silly puppet play." At the end, no one mourns his death.

While not without moments of comic relief, Tieck's retelling explores the story's potential as serious drama, in much the same way as André Grétry, in his *Raoul Barbe-bleue* (1789), crafted the last-minute escape into a rescue opera of the type then fashionable in France. Half-a-century later, comic and burlesque elements had begun to take an upper hand, if we may judge from the surprisingly large numbers of Bluebeard retellings written for popular theater in the decades after 1850. Jacques Offenbach's operetta *Barbe-bleue*, set to a libretto by Meilhac and Halévy (Paris, 1866), is only the most well known of these. In this lighthearted parody, Bluebeard becomes an amiable knight who sings graceful airs while scouring rustic villages for attractive women. At the end his six wives, each thought to be a victim of poisoning, are revived suddenly by a clever alchemist in order to marry the king's courtiers. In a grand wedding scene reminiscent of *A Midsummer Night's Dream*, Bluebeard graciously yields the hand of his would- be seventh bride, a princess disguised for much of the

drama as a rustic peasant girl, to the king's son, while the other men and women sort out mistaken identities to their mutual satisfaction, leaving all happily
paired. The chorus rejoices "He is Bluebeard . . . never widower was so gay!"
as Bluebeard takes back his sixth wife Boulotte. Offenbach's librettists dis-
pense with the story's darker elements, fully aware of the limited potential
these plot devices offered for an evening of entertaining theater. Curiosity and
its consequences have no place here. Bluebeard instead rids himself of wives,
as a contemporary synopsis explains, "from a half-crazy desire to be married
often."[16]

British audiences exhibited a particular fondness for farcical treatment of
the Bluebeard tale. Playwrights churned out popular entertainments that poked
fun at Bluebeard's womanizing and his wife's notorious curiosity. Representative
theater productions from this time include *Bluebeard, or, Harlequin and Freedom in
Her Island Home*, London, 1869; *Bluebeard! From a New Point of Hue: A Burlesque Extravaganza*, London, no date; *Blue Beard, or, Hints to the Curious: A Burlesque Burletta*,
London, no date; *The Grand Comic Christmas Pantomime Entitled Blue Beard*, Birm-
ingham, no date; *Bluebeard Re-paired: A Worn Out Subject Done-Up Anew: An Operatic
Extravaganza in One Act . . . the Music by J. Offenbach, Arranged by J. H. Tully*, London, [1866?].[17] The subtitle of the latter, "A Worn Out Subject Done-Up Anew,"
speaks volumes about the familiarity of the Bluebeard story in nineteenth-
century England. We may surmise that continental audiences were equally well
versed, especially given the rampant popularity of Offenbach's operetta, a work
that was widely performed after its Paris premiere in 1866 and that even made it
to American shores, with performances in New York and Boston in the late
1860s.

Burlesque was also the intent behind William Makepeace Thackeray's
"Bluebeard's Ghost" (1843), probably the most gracefully written Bluebeard
short story of the nineteenth century. Thackeray, author of *Vanity Fair* and a
shrewd observer of English manners, begins his story after Bluebeard's death
during the long mourning period of his wife Fatima, who rejects all solace as she
cherishes the memory of a man she refers to as her "blessed husband." Fatima ab-
hors her brothers as wild, vulgar men who ruthlessly cut down this "best of hus-
bands." Suitors soon gather to compete for the favor of her hand and her now-
considerable fortune. To honor her former spouse, whose reputation she vigorously
defends, she erects over his tomb a splendid monument, replete with a bust of
Virtue. With her sister Anne she moves from the rural confines of Bluebeard Hall
to his elegant townhouse, where this comedy of manners then unfolds. An episode in which the feckless parson's son dresses as Bluebeard's ghost to gain her
affection convinces her that the hard-drinking Captain Blackbeard instead is to
be her future husband.[18]

Starting in the 1870s, the Bluebeard subject appears to have recaptured
some of its former gravity, perhaps a result of renewed interest in the fairy tale itself or a growing weariness with the prevailing comic mode of presentation. In
1875, Walter Crane published one of his handsome toy books in which Perrault's
original story was retold, accompanied by elaborate color illustrations. Crane's

picture books found enthusiastic reception in northern Europe, including Belgium and France, where they had some influence on the late-nineteenth-century symbolist movement.[19] By 1891, when the subject resurfaced in J.-K. Huysmans's novel of satanism and the occult, *Là-Bas*, an extended rumination on the life of Gilles de Rais, the story of Bluebeard had been divested of its comic remnants. Versions for children continued to be written and produced on stage, but for many authors after Huysmans, the landscape was forever changed by revelations of the historic Bluebeard's ferocious cruelty.

The Historic Bluebeard: Gilles de Rais

In 1440 a young French nobleman, Gilles de Laval, Baron of Rais, was put on trial by the French Inquisition to face charges that he had knowingly practiced magic, committed repeated sacrilege against the Church, engaged in heretical behavior, and over the preceding years caused many children to be murdered in the most cruel, horrible manner.[20] Gilles came from a wealthy and distinguished family whose extensive landholdings in western France, dotted with castles, stretched along the Loire Valley from the Atlantic coast inland to the regions of Poitou and Anjou. The Barony of Rais, or Retz, as it was also spelled, lay to the immediate south of the Duchy of Brittany, in a region now referred to as the Pays Nantais, after its capital city, Nantes. The oldest of two sons, Gilles had inherited this estate and, with it, access to the French court of Charles VII, whose military campaigns during the Hundred Years' War he supported with troops drawn from his personal army, most notably at the side of Joan of Arc during the liberation of Orléans in 1429. He was known for his interest in music and theater; he maintained a large boys' choir and was given to staging extravagant spectacles for his townspeople to enjoy.

This public image of an honorable, distinguished aristocrat, however, concealed a private life of increasing dissolution and vice. The baron's lavish tastes forced him to begin selling off properties from his estate. Members of his family convinced the king to issue an injunction in 1435 banning further losses of this nature, but the indebtedness he incurred eventually closed in upon him, leading a frustrated Gilles in 1440 to threaten a cleric in the service of a creditor, which led to his arrest and subsequent trial. During the 1430s the baron experimented with alchemy and black magic and began to slaughter children for pleasure within the walls of his castles. As court documents would later demonstrate, he raped, fondled, hanged, and dismembered the children, laughing as he did so and sometimes sitting on his dying victims, predominantly boys between the ages of seven and twelve, to watch them expire. Their body parts and blood were then used in satanic rituals to evoke demons. Prosecutors estimated the number of his victims at about 140, although informal counts by the local populace ran higher. Witnesses came forth to testify against him. At the trial, Gilles was excommunicated and convicted of heresy, sacrilege, sodomy, and violating the immunity of the Church. He was burned alive for his crimes in Nantes on October 26, 1440. He was thirty-six.

Gilles de Rais's reputation as a brutal child murderer developed legendary status among the people of Brittany and Rais after his death, and when Perrault's fairy-tale Bluebeard appeared in the seventeenth century, oral tradition gradually folded Gilles and his crimes into the fictional Bluebeard character. As with most folk traditions, it is difficult to retrace exactly how and when the names of Bluebeard and Gilles de Rais became entwined. There is no historical evidence to suggest, as some writers have done, that "Bluebeard" was a nickname for Gilles de Rais during his lifetime.[21] Folklore enthusiasts in France in the later nineteenth century reported that certain crumbling castles at Pornic, Chéméré, and Mâchecoul, at one time part of Gilles's estates, had been known locally as "Châteaux de Barbe-Bleue" since the early nineteenth century, if not earlier. A travelogue published in Nantes in 1823 by one Édouard Richer added fuel to this legend.[22] On the banks of the Erdre River, near Nantes, Richer had observed seven ancient trees clustered in the shadow of a castle formerly owned by Gilles, and he imagined them to be memorials to Bluebeard's seven wives planted years earlier by unknown persons.

In 1885 it was reported that in Tiffauges, another of Gilles's redoubts, he was commonly referred to as Bluebeard by older inhabitants, an observation confirmed seventeen years later by Vizetelly.[23] For people in Brittany, Bluebeard was not merely the cruel man who kills his wives but, as Eugène Bossard noted, "more generally, a wicked lord, a menace to his people, in a word: Gilles de Rais."[24] Differences in the nature of the crimes committed by the two Bluebeards were not held to be significant when measured against the larger memory of their legendary cruelty. Denizens of rural western France, it appears, accepted as fact the notion that Perrault's Bluebeard had at one time lived among them. When biographers began to take note of the legend in the 1880s, this folkloric custom quickly became a truism that spread from France to other countries where the Bluebeard story was known.

Of the approximately half-dozen books on Gilles de Rais in existence by 1910, few, if any, fail to mention his role as the possible inspiration for the familiar Bluebeard from children's literature. Thus, Thomas Wilson's *Blue-Beard: A Contribution to History and Folk-Lore* (1899) proclaims on its title page that the reader will encounter in its pages "the history of Gilles de Retz of Brittany, France, who was executed at Nantes in 1440 A.D. and who was the original of Blue-Beard in the tales of Mother Goose." Vizetelly's engaging *Bluebeard: An Account of Comorre the Cursed and Gilles de Rais* (1902) investigates folk legends relating to two possible historic Bluebeards. From these authors and their counterparts in France and Germany, notably the influential scholar Bossard, descended the "Gilles de Raiz–Bluebeard mélange," in the words of one, which pervades most historical Bluebeard accounts to the present day.[25]

The confusion of these two figures transformed the centuries-old image of Bluebeard. To adults, it was no longer possible to perceive Bluebeard merely as the vivid but somewhat distant villain of childhood memory. Scholarly research on Gilles de Rais, and the fictional accounts that ensued, gave Bluebeard a more concrete identity as a real man from the fifteenth century whose horrible crimes spoke through the ages and whose ruined castles stood as testimony to his one-time existence. Paradoxically, then, Bluebeard began to assume a more human form, in the sense that the one-dimensional fairy-tale figure was invested with the psychological complexity of a genuine human being. From here it would be a short but significant step to the suffering Bluebeard image soon found in litera-ture of the time, including Bartók's opera.

The Emergence of a Sympathetic Bluebeard in Turn-of-the-Century Literature

A French abbot named Eugène Bossard published portions of the extensive court documents for the first time in a massive study of Gilles de Rais that ap-peared in 1885 (a second edition followed in 1886). Such was the authority of Bossard's book that it became the point of departure for all subsequent debate on the Baron of Rais, a status earned in part due to its exhaustive coverage of the relevant fifteenth-century source material. From archives in Paris, Nantes, and across the Loire Valley, Bossard gathered the surviving historical records and, with impressive scholarship, used them to build a case, surprisingly, for Gilles's spiritual salvation. At the 1440 trial, shortly after he was excommunicated, Gilles had confessed to his sins and asked to receive forgiveness. The ecclesiastical judges in charge of the proceedings looked favorably upon the confession, for they saw it as proof that this man who had sinned so deeply had renounced his past and now sought reconciliation with God. The Bishop of Nantes reversed the sentence of excommunication, and Gilles was welcomed back into the fold of the church as a repentant sinner. His conviction on other charges, however, still stood, and he was remanded to civil authorities for prosecution and sentencing.

The notion of Christian forgiveness for such a vicious individual deeply en-gaged Bossard in his review of the trial documents more than four centuries later. He glories in the Church's compassion toward one who had fallen so far. His por-trayal of the execution reads like a biblical martyrdom scene. Before the flames are lit, Gilles prays on his knees for God's grace and nobly insists on dying prior to his two accomplices, who had been condemned to the same fate. As an im-mense crowds watches, he recalls the words of his confessor (Bossard is not above inventing dialogue to enliven dry facts), and, crying "Miserere," all the while imploring his fellows to repent, he remits his soul to the Judge supreme, flames crackling at his heels. "Here was a spectacle," Bossard concludes appre-ciatively, "which has scarcely been equaled in history."[26] As a man of the cloth himself, Bossard might be expected to find a positive message in Gilles's repen-tance, even though he condemned the baron's crimes with an appropriate sense of moral indignation. What is of interest to us is that Bossard, in his description of the trial, chooses to emphasize the defendant's humility and contrition, thereby giving him sympathetic qualities that might not otherwise be suspected in such a cruel individual. Bossard humanizes Gilles and, through him, Bluebeard.

Historical studies like Bossard's played a significant role in modifying the Bluebeard image around 1900. Ongoing debate in France over the fairness of the original legal case brought against Gilles de Rais kept the name of the purported original Bluebeard in the public eye at this time. Oddly enough, his star was entwined with that of Joan of Arc, who, like Gilles, had fallen prey to the French Inquisition's prosecutorial zeal. An actual historic connection linked the two figures. Joan, the celebrated Maid of Orléans who drew praise for her role in rallying French forces against the English at a critical juncture in the Hundred Years' War, rose from humble origins to shape the course of French history in the fifteenth century before being burned at the stake in 1431 for the heresy of believing herself to be an instrument of God's will. Gilles, along with many other French citizens, had been swept up by her sudden appearance. He was one of the commanders of her troops at Orléans and other engagements in 1429. Some historians ascribe to him a more important role as her personal protector.[27]

A movement was under way in the late nineteenth century to make Joan a Catholic saint. She had been found innocent of her supposed crimes in 1456, when Pope Calixtus III reopened her case at the behest of Charles VII. But sainthood eluded this cherished figurehead of French national pride until in 1909 she was beatified by the Church and in 1920 formally declared a saint. Joan's case received considerable public attention in the decades prior to her canonization. Parisian journals were filled with essays debating subtler points about her life and trial. One result was the magisterial two-volume biography, twenty years in the making, by Anatole France, published in 1908. The scrutiny accorded Joan had the effect of rekindling interest in another fifteenth-century person who, it was felt, also may have been the innocent victim of political intrigue during the Inquisition, Gilles de Rais. The name Bluebeard, therefore, surfaces often in writings about Joan of Arc at this time.

Two literary works from the 1920s exemplify this trend, Georg Kaiser's *Gilles und Jean* (Potsdam, 1923) and George Bernard Shaw's play-cum-manifesto *Saint Joan* (London, 1923), in which a certain "Bluebeard" hovers in the background as a minor character. It was not a coincidence that Anatole France turned to the story of Bluebeard immediately following his Joan of Arc biography, with *The Seven Wives of Bluebeard (from Authentic Documents)* of 1909 (discussed in more detail below). Another French writer, Charles Lemire, published studies of both Gilles de Rais (1886) and Joan of Arc (1891). Writers used comparison with Joan to leverage arguments for and against the reputation of Gilles de Rais, depending on their point of view. Frances Winwar, in his historical novel of Joan's life, spoke for the majority when he juxtaposed the two as case studies in evil and saintly behavior. On the other hand, some historians invoked Joan's rehabilitation as a prominent instance of posthumous justice; the implication was that Gilles, too, might merit such consideration. Doubts about the validity of the baron's original trial were widespread in the wake of Bossard's book, which led to at least one improbable result: Gilles de Rais was briefly considered for sainthood by the Catholic Church in the early twentieth century.[28]

This was the time of the Dreyfus affair in France, and the fiercely partisan public debate touched off by Alfred Dreyfus's conviction on charges of espionage spilled over to the two most important French criminal trials of the fifteenth century, which were seen by some as similar cases of justice gone awry. In the heated atmosphere created by France's notorious scandal, it was not long before scholarly opinion polarized around Gilles de Rais and, to a lesser extent, Joan of Arc, whose case had not involved murder. Proponents stepped forth to argue that Gilles was innocent of his crimes, that the whole trial process had been corrupted by the political agenda of the powerful Duke of Brittany, Jean V, who was bent on annexing his neighbor's landholdings and therefore seized on the opportunity to destroy him by capitalizing on rumors of disappearing children. Howland, Reinach, and Monod, all writing in the early twentieth century, came to see the trial as a miscarriage of justice and vigorously denounced the verdict based on their reading of the trial documents.[29] Noting that torture was frequently used in those days to extract confessions of dubious veracity, they expressed doubt that Gilles had even committed the murders to which he confessed.

The issue of Gilles's guilt or innocence lies well beyond the scope of this study, for its ambiguous points are numerous and by no means easy to resolve. It is noteworthy, however, that the controversy has simmered up to the present day. In 1992 the *New York Times* reported that a panel of experts had gathered in the French Senate to rehear evidence of Gilles de Rais's crimes.[30] A jury of politicians, historians, and former ministers acquitted the baron after hearing arguments for his rehabilitation from biographers and scholars. (The verdict carried no legal weight.) "To say Gilles de Rais is guilty is just as scandalous as denying the innocence of Dreyfus," the chair of the honorary jury was quoted as saying. The Nantes tourist board disputed the finding, fearing an economic loss should travelers no longer visit their region in search of Bluebeard's past. The Roman Catholic Church, reluctant to review a ruling by the Inquisition, alleged that the proceeding was the work of Freemasons.

Though advocates for Gilles's canonization were ultimately unsuccessful (it has not been determined who was behind the nomination), the fact that such a claim could even be put forth indicates the extent to which turn-of-the-century interpreters saw Gilles/Bluebeard in an ambivalent light, as a man whose rapacious behavior was mitigated—and complicated—by the mental and physical anguish he later suffered on account of his crimes and by his reputation as a model of chivalry and intellectual attainment in the Middle Ages. Were it not for his darker side, the reasoning went, he would have been recorded by history as a companion-in-arms to Joan of Arc, an eager student of occult sciences, and a well-known, if somewhat spendthrift, patron of the arts. Biographers aggrandized the baron's virtuous qualities. "This extraordinary man had a taste for all forms of literature and art," Vizetelly enthused.[31] "He seems the model of a gentleman of his time," writes Putnam.[32] They even fabricated accomplishments: Gabory fancied that Machaut's *Mass* had been performed by the baron's choir, at the request of their "artistic and sensitive" lord.[33] No one went further in this direction than Huysmans, whose fictional account of Gilles's life perversely glorifies the murderer's intellectual refinement. "In an age when his peers were simple brutes," he writes in *Là-Bas*, "he sought the delicate delirium of art, dreamed of a literature soul-searching and profound; he even composed a treatise on the art of evoking demons; he gloried in the music of the Church, and would have nothing about him that was not rare and difficult to obtain. He was an erudite Latinist, a brilliant conversationalist, a sure and generous friend."[34] Even among those eager to castigate him for his cruelty, the baron was seen as a pensive, melancholy man whose conscience was tormented by guilt. In this they were guided by the ancient Latin scribes who had duly noted the "copious shedding of tears" that accompanied his final confession.

The Gilles de Rais furor, although largely forgotten today, was very much a part of the Bluebeard topos in the early part of the twentieth century. The translator of the first English edition of Maeterlinck's *Ariane et Barbe-Bleue*, Bernard Miall, devotes several pages of his preface to possible historic precedents for Perrault's Bluebeard.[35] Anatole France's "Les sept femmes de la Barbe-bleue," a clever parody of Perrault's tale, took inspiration in the current contretemps, as its content and subtitle—"from Original Documents"—indicate. Both he and Miall take care to point out the improbability of any actual connection between the historic and fictional Bluebeards, a distinction that we, many decades later, might do well to remember. But their writings are symptomatic of a larger phenomenon, observable in many literary reworkings of the Bluebeard story from the time, in which the psychological portrait of Gilles de Rais began to filter into, and alter, the premises of the traditional tale.

Bluebeard Interpretations from the Turn of the Century

Some indication of the number and diversity of Bluebeard retellings dating from the decades prior to Bartók's opera can be gained from the list presented in table 6.1. Several of these works are already familiar to Bartók scholars. One in particular, Maeterlinck's *Ariane et Barbe-bleue*, has long been recognized as a spiritual cousin to Bartók's opera and a major work in its own right. But the majority attracted little attention in their day. They are resurrected here in order to convey the full extent of the Bluebeard story's international appeal at the turn of the century. Naturally, the literary merit of these poems, plays, short stories, and children's productions varied considerably. Their sheer number, however, stands as testimony to a high level of general cultural interest in the Bluebeard story, a level perhaps unmatched at any point in the story's long history.

Among the works listed here, E. Oueslay Gilbert's 1897 operetta and adaptations of Perrault's tale by Laura Richards (1916) and Edgar Browne (1919) serve as reminders that one core constituency had not changed—children continued to be transfixed, as they had in earlier ages, by the dramatic rescue of Bluebeard's wife. A deft pen could also create entertaining versions for adults. Alongside the earnest dramatic efforts of Maeterlinck, Eulenberg, and Balázs, each of which would be turned into an opera, we find works like Kate Wiggin's clever satire of Wagnerian drama (1914) and a musical comedy produced in New York with the irreverent title *Little Miss Bluebeard* (1923). Wiggin, known to American audiences for her novel *Rebecca of Sunnybrook Farm*, retells the Bluebeard tale in

TABLE 6.1 Retellings of the Bluebeard story in European and North American literature and music, ca. 1880 to ca. 1920. Publishers are included where known. For musical works, the place of first performance is given.

Musical works

1879?	*Bluebeard / written by the Brothers Grinn* [*sic*], music by Ferdinand Wallerstein (London)
1894	*Barbe-Bleue*, lyric representation with music and dance by Charles Lemire (Paris)
1896	*Blaubart*, ballet with music by Pyotr Schenck (St. Petersburg)
1897	*Bluebeard*, children's operetta by E. Oueslay Gilbert, text by L. B. Tisdale (London)
1898	*Barbe-Bleue*, ballet-pantomime by Charles A. Lecocq (Paris)
1907	*Ariane et Barbe-bleue*, opera by Paul Dukas, text by Maeterlinck (Paris)
1911	*A kékszakállú herceg vára*, opera by Béla Bartók, text by Balázs (Budapest)
1920	*Ritter Blaubart*, opera by Emil N. von Reznicek, text by Eulenberg (Darmstadt)
1923	*Little Miss Bluebeard*, musical comedy by George Gershwin and others (New York)

Theatrical works

1882	*Bluebeard, or, The Key of the Cellar*, anonymous play in three acts (London: R. Washbourne)
1886	*Blaubart. Lustspiel in einem Akt* by Max Bernstein (Munich)
189-?	*Bluebeard: A Melodramatic Travesty*, play by Sarah Annie Frost (New York: Dick & Fitzgerald)
1894	*L'Épisode de Barbe-Bleue (le maréchal Gilles de Rais) au théâtre*, by Charles Lemire, 2d ed. (Angers: Germain et G. Grassin; reprint, Paris: Trebse et Stock, 1898)
1896	*The Tragedy of Blue Beard; a Greek Play* by Mary G. Duckworth (London: J. S. Forsaith)
1899	*Ariane et Barbe-bleue; ou, la délivrance inutile*, play by Maurice Maeterlinck (Paris and Vienna)
1903	*Mr. Bluebeard . . . the Great Drury Lane Spectacular Entertainment . . . Adapted for the American Stage by J. J. McNally, Music by Frederic Solomon* (New York and Chicago: Sol Bloom, 1903)
1905	*Ritter Blaubart*, play by Herbert Eulenberg (Berlin: Egon Fleischel)
1910	*A kékszakállú herceg vára*, play by Béla Balázs (Budapest: *Magyar Színpad*)
1921	*La huitième femme de Barbe-bleue*, play by Alfred Savoir (*La Petite Illustration* 39)
1923	*Gilles und Jeanne. Bühnenspiel in drei Teilen*, by Georg Kaiser (Potsdam: Gustav Kiepenheuer)

Short stories, novels, and other works (selected)[b]

1888	"Bluebeard's Closet," poem by Rose Terry Cooke in *Poems* (New York)
1891	*Là-Bas*, novel by J.-K. Huysmans (Paris: Plon-Nourrit)
1899	*The Black Douglas*, novel by Samuel Rutherford Crockett (New York: Doubleday and McClure)
1909	"Les sept femmes de la Barbe-bleue; d'après des documents authentiques," short story by Anatole France (Paris: Calmann-Lévy)
1910	*Chevalier Blaubarts Liebesgarten*, by Joseph Lux (Berlin/Leipzig)
1911	"Ritter Blaubart," short story by Alfred Döblin (*Der Sturm* 85/86)
1911	"Der Ritter Blaubart," poem by Reinhard Koester (*Pan* 1/16)
1913	"Ritter Blaubart," short story by El Hor (pseud.) (*Saturn* 3/7)

TABLE 6.1 (*continued*)

1914	*Bluebeard; a musical fantasy. Herein lies the story of the miraculous discovery in a hat box of an un-published opera by the late Richard Wagner, dealing in the most unique and climactic manner with feminism, trial marriage, bigamy and polygamy;* [etc]. Novella by Kate Douglas Wiggin (New York: Harper & Bros.)
1917	"Bluebeard," poem by Edna St. Vincent Millay in *Renaissance and Other Poems* (New York)

Adaptations for children of Perrault's fairy tale

1875	*The Bluebeard Picture Book*, ill. Walter Crane (London: George Routledge and Sons)
1916	"Bluebeard" in *Fairy Operettas*, by Laura Richards, ill. Mary R. Bassett (Boston: Little, Brown)
1919	*Bluebeard*, a children's play by Edgar A. Browne
1920	*Ritter Blaubart. Nach Perrault*, fairy tale by Joachim Zimmerman (Berlin)

Biographical studies of Gilles de Rais (selected)

1885	*Gilles de Rais, maréchal de France, dit Barbe-bleue (1404–1440). D'après les documents inédits*, by L'Abbé Eugène Bossard (Paris: H. Champion; 2d ed., 1886)
1886	*Un maréchal et un connétable de France; le Barbe-bleue de la légende et de l'histoire*, by Charles Lemire (Paris: E. Leroux)
1897	*Bluebeard: A Contribution to History and Folk-lore, Being the History of Gilles de Retz of Brittany*, by Thomas Wilson (New York: G. Putnam's Sons)
1899	*La magie en Poitou; Gilles de Rais*, by J.-K. Huysmans (Ligugé, France: M. Bluté)
1902	*Bluebeard: An Account of Comorre the Cursed and Gilles de Rais*, by Ernest Alfred Vizetelly (London: Chatto & Windus)
1909	*Das Urbild des Blaubart. Lebensgeschichte des Barons Gilles de Rais, Marschalls von Frankreich*, by Otto Krack (Berlin: Richard Eckstein)
1926	*La vie et la mort de Gilles de Raiz, dit à tort Barbe-bleue*, by Emile Gabory (Paris: Perrin)

Notes

a. Maeterlinck's play was first published, in German translation, in *Wiener Rundschau*, July 15, 1899. In its original French it was published in Paris two years later, in 1901. Suhrbier (*Blaubarts Geheimnis*, 214) lists the early editions.

b. A more complete listing can be found in the bibliography in Suhrbier, *Blaubarts Geheimnis*.

the style of a pompous lecture-recital at the Metropolitan Opera House in New York City. She brilliantly skewers this lecture format with demonstrations — musically notated — of an imaginary Wagnerian Bluebeard opera's *Immer-wieder-heirathen Motiv, Hochzeits Reise und Flitter Wochen Motiv*, and other fictitious leitmotifs. And, in what may be the earliest critique leveled at the Bluebeard story's misogynist underpinnings, Wiggin remarks that the fate of her heroine incites women who are members of "the Feminist party . . . to boycott any opera-house in which this drama is given." The *Little Miss Bluebeard* actually produced in New York nine years later starred Irene Bordoni as the comely object of Bluebeard's desire; one of her songs, bearing the flippant, Broadway-style title "I Won't Say I Will, But I Won't Say I Won't," was contributed by the young George Gershwin. The show ran for a respectable 175 performances.

Duke Bluebeard's Castle appears to have been the only eastern European version of the Bluebeard story dating from the turn of the century. While it stands within the larger tradition of Bluebeard retellings from this time, it also represents a geographical exception that lies outside the normal perimeters of the story's dissemination. Use of the Bluebeard legend as a basis for literary work seems to have prevailed in northern and western Europe—chiefly France and England and, to a lesser degree, Germany. Patterns of migration and, more important, cultural influence brought the tale to a wider international audience. In Hungary, Balázs reportedly studied Perrault's "Bluebeard" in a folklore class at the Eötvös Kollégium around 1905.[36] Both he and Bartók traveled to Paris as young men and took an avid interest in the latest cultural and artistic trends emanating from the French capital. Balázs knew and appreciated *Ariane et Barbe-bleue*, as discussed in chapter 2. He was therefore familiar with at least two versions of the tale, both French. Bartók knew the Hungarian ballad of Anna Molnár, a Bluebeard-like story, and undoubtedly had some awareness, through Kodály, of Dukas's operatic version of *Ariane*.

Generally speaking, we can observe in turn-of-the-century interpretations a tendency to offer some justification for the relationship between Bluebeard and his wives by emphasizing the mystery and power of human love. In Perrault's original story, personal sentiment is glossed over: little is revealed of the reasons why Bluebeard sought out new wives, or why he felt compelled to murder them. By the later nineteenth century, however, nothing interested writers more than the psychological dimension of this familiar and disturbing tale. The story of Bluebeard and his wives came to be seen as one of mutual unhappiness between the lonely man who yearned for the enriching presence of a woman in his life but could not tolerate the spiritual closeness love demands, and the woman, or newest wife, who felt a mysterious attraction to this darkly violent man but could not—or would not—break down the emotional walls he had erected around his soul. A short poem by Reinhard Koester titled "Ritter Blaubart," published in 1911, epitomizes the new direction.

> Er liebte mehr als irgend einer,
> denn seine Sehnsucht war ein Meer.
> Er liebte viele—aber keiner
> gab er die ganze Seele her.
>
> Und sah er sich im Lustgeniessen,
> nach dem sein Blut verzweifelnd schrie,
> in eine Frau hinüberfliessen—
> erschlug er sie.[37]

[He loved more than anyone, for his longing was an ocean. He loved many—but not a one surrendered to him her entire soul. And he saw that the joys of life, for which his blood cried out in despair, in a woman overflowed—He killed her.]

Images of "longing," "soul," and "blood crying out in despair" in Koester's poem reflect the inner passion of this man whose need to love and be loved was so extreme that, if it were not reciprocated fully, he could be driven to murder. Here is a sad Bluebeard, fated by the demanding nature of his love to find women wanting in their commitment to him. The cold brutality of the poem's final line is unexpected, a frank reminder that violence directed against women remained at the heart of the Bluebeard story for many interpreters. "For each man kills the thing he loves," Oscar Wilde famously pronounced in the "Ballad of Reading Gaol."[38] This morbid sentiment finds an unmistakable echo in Bluebeard stories from the turn of the century.

In the first two decades of this century, a number of music-dramatic works were written that attempted to dramatize internal psychological states. Like Schoenberg's *Erwartung* (1909), *Die glückliche Hand* (1910–13), and Oskar Kokoschka's *Mörder, Hoffnung der Frauen* (1909, set to music by Hindemith in 1921), Bartók's opera steps back from the world of action and traditional dramatic dialogue into the recessed realm of the imagination, where dreamlike sequences of events enfold characters who are never defined as individuals and who speak to each other in the halting, portentous phrases of those unaware of the passing of time. In this atmosphere, Bartók presents one of the period's great themes, the difficulty of complete and total love between man and woman. His opera is very much a piece of its era, written when the Freudian investigation of human relationships had moved into the sphere of art, instilling there a willingness to portray the unknown, and sometimes darker, undercurrents of the human mind. In developing the theme of man's thirst for redemption through the agency of a woman and in emphasizing the basic humanity of the two characters, Bartók's symbolic tale of spiritual isolation finds striking analogues in other, contemporary retellings of the same story.

Maeterlinck's *Ariane et Barbe-bleue* signals a new tone in its treatment of the complicated love relationship between Bluebeard and his wives, one that found an echo in Balázs and Bartók's Hungarian opera and other contemporary European settings. In its operatic version by Paul Dukas, premiered in Paris in 1907, it set out to reinterpret the story along symbolist lines by emphasizing the imponderable depth and mystery of the bond linking Bluebeard to his wives, all of whom are now still living. In Dukas's operatic version the former wives, entombed alive by their husband, hesitate at the prospect of leaving the man who has so cruelly mistreated them. Ignoring Ariane's entreaties to follow her to freedom, they instead remain by their husband's side when he comes on stage, wounded after his escape from hordes of vengeful peasants outside. Maeterlinck's Bluebeard is a stony individual who speaks little and wields power ineffectively; he is no match for Ariane's forceful personality. The other women, meek, forgiving, and nurturing, appear incapable of abandoning him, however, and kneel in a silent circle around the helpless man. "Oh, how pale he is. . . . See how he suffers!" Mélisande exclaims to Bellangère, Sélysette, and the other wives (all named for women in Maeterlinck's earlier plays). "He is no longer so monstrous," she sighs, in words that could stand as a motto for the turn-of-the-century perception of the Bluebeard figure.

Anatole France tames Bluebeard's fearsome reputation still further in "The Seven Wives of Bluebeard" (1909), a tongue-in-cheek attempt to rehabilitate Perrault's Bluebeard, whose good name, France alleges, had been unjustly slandered by history.[39] If Maeterlinck's Bluebeard still retained some of the fearsome, gruff demeanor of his fairy-tale namesake, France now fundamentally alters the character into a bashful, simple man—an orphan, no less—whose timidity led him to seek out unsuitable marriages that foundered when his wives deceived or abandoned him. A strong emotional desire for female companionship left him intimidated by the women he loved. "Women exercised an invincible attraction for him, and at the same time inspired him with an insuperable fear," France explains.[40] Shades of other Bluebeards, including Bartók's, can be seen in this man who "trusted when he loved" and with whom we are openly encouraged to sympathize.[41] (Maeterlinck's Bluebeard, closer to the tyrant image, invites less pity.) The incorporation of fear into Bluebeard's psychological profile helped moderate his image among European intellectuals and creative artists, who saw in Bluebeard's approach toward love a lens through which to project their own contemporary concerns. Why Bluebeard began to be portrayed with increasing sympathy can explained in part by observing how violent aspects of his character were reduced, trivialized, or parodied in their interpretations.

Ever since Perrault, the conflicting emotions of fear and desire have formed part of the Bluebeard story. Formerly, though, these sentiments were generally ascribed to the women who stood, hesitant, before the forbidden door. Transferred to the man, they invert, or at least confound, the accepted male-female roles in this story. The classic Bluebeard fairy tale plainly differentiates its male and female roles. Bluebeard is fierce, dominant, martial, decisive, and aggressive. His wife is demure, beautiful, scared, and emotional. Writers at the turn of the last century demonstrated a willingness to dismantle these stereotypes: the women became confident and more assured (Ariane and Judith are good examples), while their husband became less physically threatening. One contemporary depiction of Bluebeard graphically illustrates the diminishment of his fearsome reputation (fig. 6.1). Shown here as an effete dandy, hand poised on a gracefully tapered cane, Bluebeard holds out a key chain to his wife in silent accusation. Keys dangle from slender fingers against a ruffled cuff, and his coat descends around a narrow waist, flaring outward to imitate the cut of his wife's petticoat. As if to confirm this Bluebeard's sexual ambiguity, or, at least, the exposure of his latent feminine side, in the trees overhead lurks an androgynous nude.

Anatole France's Bluebeard is a far cry from his fairy-tale ancestor. Self-conscious, unassertive, and emotionally needy, he finds himself completely at the mercy of his final wife, the scheming and hard-hearted Jeanne de Lespoisse. Neither character acts in a way that readers of the time would have recognized as typically masculine or feminine. Bluebeard thus steps easily into the traditional female role (in this story) of victim, his wife into the male role of murderer. From such fractured gender distinctions emerged new possibilities for interpretation for France and other writers of the time. One result is that the pity formerly re-

"'WHAT, IS NOT THE KEY OF MY CLOSET AMONG THE REST?'"

FIGURE 6.1   *"Bluebeard." Illustration by Harry Clarke for a 1920 collection of Perrault's fairy tales.*

served for the wives was no longer theirs alone but was extended, in some cases, to Bluebeard as well.

Bartók's Bluebeard

It is evident from the start of Bartók's opera that both characters are caught in their own struggle between fear and desire. As the drama proceeds and the doors open, internal conflicts intensify until, in the fifth door scene, Judith's growing fears harden into a curiosity both self-destructive and implacable, and Bluebeard begins to resign himself to the eventual outcome. Judith, by demanding keys and penetrating farther into the castle, initiates the activity that propels the drama forward. She possesses a mixture of what might be called traditionally masculine and feminine traits. At times determined, assertive, and impassive (masculine), she can also appear hesitant, emotionally expressive, and alluring (feminine). Bluebeard, Judit Frigyesi notes, shares many of these same traits.[42] Lawrence Kramer, writing about *Tristan und Isolde*, describes a similar instance of gender leveling in which Wagner's two lovers speak to and about each other using language that conveys desire in a general sense, without articulating what Kramer terms "the polarity of masculine and feminine," wherein sexual identity is constructed and reinforced by operatic convention—male voices for male roles, female voices for female roles, costuming decisions, and social expectations governing our perceptions of the characters on stage.[43] Wagner, seeking to portray a state of idealized love, mitigates gender distinctions by creating in Tristan a passive, wounded hero and, in Isolde, a decisive, altogether more active character who assumes the dominant role in their love relationship. The parallels with *Bluebeard's Castle* are apparent.

Bartók's Bluebeard, in the face of his wife's passionate devotion to her mission, can merely watch and hope. Like Tristan, he is essentially a passive participant in the drama of his own unfolding love. His most decisive step in the opera, Frigyesi has observed, is closing the outer door through which Judith was initially admitted. Once he has brought her to the castle, Frigyesi writes, he is powerless; "he can only wait, in fear, hoping that Judith will be able to see and understand."[44] The dynamics of their relationship are reflected in their dialogue: in the operatic text, Judith's lines outnumber Bluebeard's by approximately two to one.

The softening, or blurring, of gender contours in the opera's two characters has the effect, as it does in *Tristan und Isolde*, of elevating their love to a higher, spiritual plane, where the perfectibility of human love gleams as an ascetic ideal. Judith and Bluebeard's love transcends the physical. As human beings, they are attracted to the idea of love as much as, or more than, the object of this love. This is why Bartók's two lovers refer infrequently to each other's physically attractive qualities and why their few onstage embraces seem to arise out of thirst for emotional reassurance rather than sensual desire. In lines Bartók cut from the play's introduction, Judith tells Bluebeard how she had been transfixed by the image of his dark castle:

> Bluebeard, by day I always
> Stood in my latticed window
> Because your castle was so black
> By night I always wept
> Because your castle was so black.[45]

Like Senta looking at the Dutchman's picture on the wall, Judith's longing for Bluebeard arose before she knew him. It welled up in abstract form, from a distance and, significantly, in the absence of her future beloved. When she arrives in Bluebeard's castle, she continues to express her love for him through the medium of the castle. Bluebeard and Judith, it must be remembered, stand apart for most of the opera. An air of repressed sensuality surrounds them, as if they were channeling their desires inward out of fear of discovery. Their eyes meet, their hands touch—gestures that say much but cannot be expressed in words. Erotic allusions, when they occur, are directed not at each other but, again, at the castle. "I'll warm its cold stone," Judith cries, "with my body I'll warm it." The castle moans and sighs in response to her actions, but Bluebeard stands apart, observing.

In an essay entitled "My Socratic Mask," Georg Lukács, Balázs's close friend and muse, explains in philosophical terms something close to what Balázs and Bartók expressed artistically through *Duke Bluebeard's Castle*.[46] Writing in 1909 to a woman from whose overture of love he had fled, Lukács uses the metaphor of a mask to express why he felt compelled to retreat into the loneliness of his intellect rather than submit to his longings for physical intimacy with a woman. With the "cold, plaster mask" of intellect in place, man can remain in control of his passions. But he yearns to tear this mask away and reveal his true self, his elemental aliveness. "Why," he asks, "do I long for someone who would recognize and love what she sees, and why do I dread that she glimpse what is behind the mask?" Invoking Socrates, Lukács argues that the most profound human love exists in a state of longing for something we do not have. Erotic love cannot fulfill this need. In his view, a truly great man, one who is cursed with the knowledge that love cannot exist unless it is channeled inward, necessarily renounces love to idealize it, as the ancient troubadours did.[47] The warm human being in him wants to tear aside his mask, but the rational being inside hesitates. "My own mask lies at my feet shattered in pieces," Lukács confides at the end of his essay. His confession sounds as if torn from Bluebeard's soul:

> My longings and desires reach forth like tear-stained emaciated arms. Spread wide, they are waiting. And yet, were anything to approach, my arms would withdraw for fear of opening up old wounds, aware that if love turned to flesh it would become one with it. The lover and beloved must part. The one who departs carries away part of the beloved's flesh, only to increase his loneliness and deepen his wounds.[48]

And thus Lukács suffers. He is driven to his suffering by his pessimistic view of love's redeeming powers. And when his "old wounds" are reopened, like Bluebeard, he retreats into the castle of his sorrow and solitude, immured in the existential loneliness of the human soul. Lukács's expressed belief that lover and beloved are forever alien to each other articulates the fundamental tragedy of Bartók's opera.

That Bartók's Bluebeard deeply loves Judith is evident throughout the opera. He idealizes her. She brings light and warmth to his heavy soul. She is beautiful. And she loves him deeply in return, even to the point of ignoring the rumors about previous wives. Out of some barely understood, inchoate need, she has sought him out, as Balázs wrote, because Bluebeard's "suffering withdrawal into seclusion . . . attracted the woman with strange power." For such a woman he allows the doors to his soul to be opened—wants them to be opened—affording her glimpses of his real, human self behind the cold mask of intellect.

One of the opera's curious features, almost never commented upon, is the gesture with which Bluebeard greets his former wives when they step forward from behind the seventh door: he kneels. He falls on his knees and addresses them reverentially. "Beautiful, beautiful, one hundred times beautiful. They always were, they always lived," he sings in a hushed voice. As memories, he adores them, but as flesh-and-blood women who sought to uncover his mask, he feared their attempts to gain knowledge of his true self. Susan McClary's assertion that Bluebeard cannot live with someone who understands that beneath everything he is merely human, rather than transcendental, points to what is probably the real, if unspoken, reason behind his odd renunciation of a woman whose love he craves.[49] This, too, may have been the root of Lukács's fear: that without his intellect in place he would appear to the woman as just a man like any other, yearning for physical intimacy out of some deep and barely understood animal passion incompatible with his own self-image. To preserve control, Bluebeard kills his wives, metaphorically, by imprisoning them behind the seventh door, even as he glorifies them. Lukács writes an essay, retreating behind words. The object of their affection, once physically removed, can be worshiped from a distance.

Here, then, we begin to get close to the opera's elusive meaning. Human love cannot survive expectations of perfection, even when sustained by the ardent hopes of two lovers. Bluebeard's idealized vision of a love so warm and complete it will redeem him from his melancholic state is doomed from the start, for he places unrealistic expectations on the women he marries, hoping that they will love him unconditionally while he maintains his essential reserve—symbolized by the closed doors in his castle. (He would gladly keep them all closed, one senses, but has learned from past experience that he must open at least several to give love a chance to blossom.) Bluebeard's essential tragedy is that, fearing disappointment in love, he plants the seeds for its eventual destruction. His behavior is self-fulfilling. The closer he gets to being released from his loneliness, the more he recognizes the inevitability of his retreat into its embrace. Hence, in the opera, his increasing reluctance to open the doors that divulge his secrets. The darkness enveloping his soul at the end is a darkness he has anticipated all along. "My castle shall not glitter," he declares at the opera's outset, rebuffing Judith's vow to brighten his castle walls.

Judith, in turn, sees her illusions begin to crumble when the focus of her love retreats before her advances, even as he encourages her love. She succeeds in piercing the veil of his reserve. But the more she lifts the veil, the further his soul shrinks from her. This is symbolized by Bluebeard's increasing reluctance to give her the keys to his doors. Like Bluebeard, she is a lonely individual. She has turned her back on the sunny outside world to pursue a life at Bluebeard's side. "I don't need roses, I don't need sunlight," she proclaims as she enters the castle. She recognizes that marrying Bluebeard is fraught with peril. Inside the castle, her decision to press forward, to overcome her fears, is motivated by the knowledge that her love for this mysterious man cannot flourish in an environment where secrets lurk around every corner. She wants to bring healing light to his castle. He demands more.

Bartók's Bluebeard, as Kroó has noted, yearns for the affirmative power of one woman whose faith and trust can redeem his darkened soul, a distinctly Wagnerian theme when presented in the context of opera.[50] Other, now-forgotten Bluebeard retellings contemporary with Bartók's opera develop this theme extensively and may thus be considered spiritual forebears to their more renowned Hungarian counterpart. Neither Alfred Döblin's "Ritter Blaubart" (1911) nor Herbert Eulenberg's *Ritter Blaubart* (1905) have received their proper due from Bartók scholars as exemplars of the same themes presented in *Bluebeard's Castle*. In the case of the former, not even its existence has been acknowledged in studies of the opera. Döblin gives the story a modern setting, with policemen and coroners investigating the women's mysterious deaths.[51] A certain Baron Paolo, on a long sea voyage, disembarks from his ship at a swampy northern seaport and builds a castle high on the cliffs overlooking the sea. Each of his three wives dies of inexplicable causes within days or months, inciting fear among the local populace. The last, however, wept for the plight of this "monster," as Döblin describes him. And when the vivacious Miss Ilsebill appears one day, she, too, takes pity on the town's pariah. The power of her love invigorates his soul; they laugh and sing as he has never done. When she discovers and survives his secret chamber one night, however, a bond of trust is broken. Her death, when the castle goes up in flames, provides closure to the saddened knight's quest for love. Mounting his horse the following morning, he rides silently away.

The Dutchman legend, so evident here in the northern seaside setting and the darkly mysterious man who inspires women to a combination of pity and love, also inspired Eulenberg to place redemption at the center of his play *Ritter Blaubart* (1905). His Bluebeard, who bears the name Raul, marries two sisters, Judith and Agnes, in succession. The first falls victim to her curiosity by entering the forbidden chamber. She had anticipated her own death at the hands of this ferocious man, however, and, before she wed, asked her sister to take her place at his side. Agnes accedes to this unusual request. Unlike her sister, however, she survives the test to which he puts her, having seen through his brutal exterior to recognize his need to be loved unconditionally, without the intrusion of fear or doubt. When a fire sweeps through the castle (this idea, also encountered in Döblin, originated with the Grimms), she attempts to flee rather than perish at his side, as he demands. She dies among the burning ruins, and Bluebeard is killed by her vengeful brother. Emil von Rezniček's "Märchenoper," based on Eulenberg's drama, was produced in Berlin (at the Staatsoper) and Karlsruhe following its premiere in Darmstadt in January 1920. It was published by Universal Edition in 1920. In what must have appeared at the time as a remarkable coincidence, the same publishing house, when it brought out Bartók's opera one year later, had two Bluebeard operas in its catalog, both featuring a wife named Judith.

At the end of Eulenberg's play, Bluebeard confesses his previous murders in the vain hope that Agnes will forgive his past and his secrets in order to love him. This Bluebeard differs from Bartók's only in the exterior details of their personality. Inwardly, he aches for the same redeeming power of a woman's love to lift him from his misery. But the kiss that, moments before, had confirmed her love for him ("Ah! Behind your kisses burns paradise," she sighs) also induces him to reveal his darkest secret, knowledge of which instantly inspires her fear and distrust. He pleads with her, but it is too late: "I sought you like a vessel, heavily weighed down, to bear my melancholy burden. You should have brought peace to my heart, you should have seen me weak like a child, you alone! . . . Stay with me, Agnes! You can save me. I mixed my own poison; take it away from me! I have waited for you a million nights, for one whose love is stronger than me."[52] Unfortunately, Agnes's love, like Judith's in *Bluebeard's Castle,* cannot sustain itself once suspicion of Bluebeard's past has been confirmed. She flees, and meets her death out of Bluebeard's sight. Even before she is gone, Bluebeard senses that the peace and comfort he had hoped for are no longer hers to give. He dies, in the words of an onlooker, "a lamentable man," without having found the woman who can release his darkened soul from its agony. In the flesh, standing almost within his grasp, his beloved cannot fulfill the exalted role he has dreamed of during those million nights of loneliness.

7

JUDITH
The Significance of a Name

In a drama imbued with symbolism at every turn, it can hardly be an accident that Balázs chose as the name of Bluebeard's newest wife the name of the well-known biblical woman who kills a man to save her people. In the early twentieth century, at the time Bartók and Balázs were writing *Bluebeard's Castle*, the name Judith was strongly identified in artistic circles with the image of a fatally seductive woman. Like Salome, whose popularity as the subject of artistic representations far surpassed that of Judith's, Judith was often depicted as a young woman of considerable sexual allure. In paintings of the time she is shown semi-clothed or naked, holding in her hand a sword or the head of a man. The foundation for this image lay in the biblical tale of Judith and Holofernes, where Judith is the Jewish heroine who decapitates the Assyrian general Holofernes with a sword in order to save her people. In the embroidered versions of their stories popular at the turn of the twentieth century, Judith and Salome became symbols of the women men feared and desired, women whose physical attractiveness enabled them to wield enormous power over men. To love them, or to lust for them, was to court violent death.

Over the years, a great deal of analytical attention has been devoted to the figure of Bluebeard, its historical origins, and its implications for the opera's dramatic situation. But Bartók scholars, even the otherwise thorough Kroó, have never drawn attention to the significance of Judith's name. She has endured a long critical tradition of being treated as a generalized representative of the female sex, as a character whose female identity constitutes her only noteworthy feature. This should change. Like the name Bluebeard (as we saw in the previous chapter), the name Judith descends from an extended lineage in European art and literature. Consequently, it bears considerable symbolic meaning in the context of this opera, particularly when we realize just who it is that Bluebeard has invited into his castle.

It is unusual, in the historical context of the Bluebeard story, to find a wife with this name. Only one other retelling, Eulenberg's *Ritter Blaubart* (1905), features a wife named Judith. In adding the figure of Judith to his Bluebeard drama, Balázs places on stage a striking combination of characters: the fairy-tale character of a man who kills women, and the biblical character of a woman who kills a man. Given this theoretical antagonism between the two principal figures, it seems unlikely that the symbolism of her name was intended to be overlooked, though surely not all people would catch the reference while listening to the opera or reading the play. Judith's name adds an edge of uncertainty to the *Bluebeard* opera's tale of spiritual alienation. It instantly suggests that Bluebeard's newest wife will prove to be a formidable individual, a prediction actually fulfilled in the course of the dramatic action. It also introduces the expectation, slow to dwindle away, that this version of the Bluebeard tale may turn out quite differently: his wife could have the last word. The name is more than a witty dramatic touch, though, or a bit of philological trivia for the cognoscenti to savor. Knowing how the figure of Judith was perceived in turn-of-the-century European culture enables an audience to recognize more clearly what she represents to Bluebeard as she steps into his castle and begins to open its doors. The desire and trepidation Bluebeard feels for her are the same feelings she had engendered in other men and in other settings—where still more disastrous results ensued.

The general perception of Judith's story and its meaning has evolved with time. In the Apocrypha of the Old Testament, Judith is the Jewish heroine who saves her city from destruction at the hands of Holofernes, the proud, powerful commander of Nebuchadnezzar's army. The biblical Judith is a rich widow and a deeply religious woman. She receives divine inspiration and realizes that she alone can save the city from the siege placed upon it by Holofernes's army. She goes to Holofernes in his camp outside the city walls. She is received by Holofernes, and they dine together. After dinner, he attempts to seduce her. The liquor he has drunk, however, causes him to fall asleep. Judith seizes this opportunity and, with his own sword, beheads him. She and her maidservant carry the bloody head back to the city as a sign of victory. Holofernes's army scatters, and the city is saved. The message of her story is clear: trust and faith in God will lead to victory over the most adverse circumstances.

Visual depictions of Judith and Holofernes are frequently encountered in the history of art. Since the Middle Ages the story has been used to illustrate the moral belief that virtue will triumph over vice. The moment of actual beheading, not surprisingly, was a favored scene. Perhaps the most familiar early Judith is that of Donatello, dating from the mid–fifteenth century. This sculptural figure captures the moment just prior to decapitation. A robed, confident Judith stands over the slumped body of Holofernes at her knees, her upraised arm clasping a

wickedly curved saber about to fall upon the outstretched neck of the uncon-
scious man beneath her. An inscription on the sculpture's original underlying column, now lost, testified to the story's moral interpretation for contemporary
viewers: "Kingdoms fall through luxury, cities rise through virtues: behold the
neck of pride severed by the hand of humility."[1] Canvases showing the bloody decapitation or other distinct moments from the story were created by, among others, Caravaggio, Botticelli, Correggio, Giorgone, Gentileschi, and Rubens. The
subject's popularity waned from the Baroque period forward, only to be resurrected with vigor later in the nineteenth century.[2] In music history, relatively few
dramatizations of the Judith story have been composed during the past three
centuries, suggesting that the subject held less appeal for composers than for visual artists. Vivaldi wrote an opera in 1716, *Juditha Triomphans*, and Thomas
Arne composed an oratorio, *Judith*, in 1761. New England composer George W.
Chadwick wrote a lyric drama on the subject for performance at the Worcester
Festival in Massachusetts in 1901. Arthur Honegger and Max Ettinger both
wrote *Judith* operas in the 1920s. Emil von Reznicek followed his *Ritter Blaubart*
with an opera entitled *Holofernes* in 1923.

A different conception of Judith began to emerge in the nineteenth century
as interest arose in her psychological motivations for decapitating Holofernes.
Whereas earlier centuries had viewed Judith as a righteous instrument of God's
will, beginning in the nineteenth century she became transformed into a young,
sexually attractive woman determined to seek vengeance against men. Friedrich
Hebbel's 1840 drama *Judith* was in many ways the source for this new image,
which soon spread to all the arts. In transferring the familiar story to the stage,
Hebbel dramatized for the first time the psychological battle of wills between the
two antagonists, making several important changes. As Sigmund Freud would
later note, Hebbel "sexualized" the patriotic Old Testament tale.[3] Unsatisfied in
her earlier marriage to a weak, effeminate man, Hebbel's Judith, in a marked departure from the story's biblical outlines, now finds herself perversely attracted
to Holofernes's masculinity at the same time that she is pursuing her mission to
destroy him. "God of my fathers," she whispers to herself while in Holofernes's
tent, "protect me against myself lest I have to admire what I abhor! He is a
man!"[4] The subsequent act of decapitation is given a new, personal twist: Judith
swings the sword not to save her people but to seek vengeance against Holofernes, for in Hebbel's version, Judith was sexually assaulted by Holofernes before he fell asleep. A cruel twist of fate brings this tragedy to a bitter and uncertain end when Judith, in the play's final moments, realizes that as a result of her
one encounter with Holofernes she may bear the child of the man she has just
killed, an enemy of her people.

Hebbel's portrayal of Judith set the tone for subsequent interpretations of
the story by focusing on the internal struggle in Judith's mind as she carried out
her divine mission inside Holofernes's tent. Visual artists at the turn of the century elevated this aspect—the solitary confrontation between Judith and Holofernes, overlaid with elements of physical desire on both sides—into a symbolic
struggle between contemporary man and woman, in effect stripping away the

story's external details to concentrate on the central issue burning forth from this ancient story. In this regard the story of Judith and Holofernes bears a curious resemblance to the story of Judith and Bluebeard in Bartók's opera. Both men are figures of legendary cruelty. Holofernes, in Hebbel's play, tells stories of the people he has killed or put to death, and even kills an officer for frivolous reasons in the course of the drama. Inside the tent, Judith, like her namesake in *Bluebeard's Castle*, struggles with conflicting emotions of desire and fear as she stands before this man. And both Judiths enter the man's territory motivated by a mission which guides their actions and from which they do not deviate, regardless of the consequences. Such parallels suggest that the dramatic situation in Bartók's opera owes something to the Judith story in addition to its more obvious connections with the Bluebeard theme.

The decades around 1900 witnessed a tremendous upsurge of interest in the figure of Judith in central Europe, in part due to the vogue female mythological, biblical, and historical subjects then enjoyed in artistic circles.[5] Paintings by Gustav Klimt, Albert von Keller, Carl Strathmann, and other artists show a marked similarity in their approach to the story's iconography. An 1895 painting by the Swiss-born Keller clearly demonstrates the shift of emphasis toward a more erotic portrayal of events.[6] Keller paints Judith as a full-length nude turning slightly away from the viewer, her elegantly coiffed head, earrings dangling, retreating into the shadows while a sword dangles easily against her thigh. A young maidservant stands directly behind her, equally naked, her slender body arched seductively against the wall in a moment of intimate consultation prior to the murder. Though Holofernes is not visible, the sexual undercurrents latent in Judith's imminent encounter come to the fore quite openly.

Two paintings of Judith and Holofernes by the celebrated Viennese artist Gustav Klimt exemplify fin-de-siècle man's perception of Judith. Klimt's canvases date from the first decade of the twentieth century. The 1901 Judith has become one of his more familiar images (fig. 7.1). Genteel and sensual, Judith is portrayed from the waist up, grasping to her side the barely visible head of a man and looking directly at the viewer with an expression of mingled pleasure and confidence. Diaphanous raiment loosely draped over her shoulders does not conceal, but rather emphasizes, her nudity. This is a woman completely unruffled by the violent murder she has committed. Keller's subject had been described at the time of its creation as a "modern Judith" to distinguish it from the Judith of previous eras.[7] Klimt's 1901 Judith was equally modern in the eyes of Viennese critic Felix Salten, to whom

> she is a beautiful Jewish society hostess . . . who, her silk petticoats rustling, attracts the eyes of men at every première. A slim, lithe, and supple woman with a sultry fire in her dark glances, with a cruel mouth and nostrils trembling with passion. Mysterious forces seem to slumber in this seductive female, energies and a violence which for the moment are suppressed, kept down to a slight, bourgeois flicker, but which, once ignited, could never be put out. Then an artist . . . presents her to us adorned in her timeless naked-

FIGURE 7.1   *Gustav Klimt*, Judith and Holofernes *(1901)*

ness and—ecce Judith—the heroic women of days gone by rise up before
our eyes, are given life and move among us.[8]

Salten's description perfectly captures the sense that Judith is a woman that man
cannot control: the flame of her hidden passion and violence can burst forth suddenly, he writes, and never be put out. Yet his sexual attraction to this mysterious, seductive woman with the "slim, lithe, and supple" body is unmistakable. To
him, Judith had cast off her biblical identity. She now represented modern woman, and Holofernes represented modern man. Klimt's second Judith (1909)

clutches the head of Holofernes with clawlike hands, her face reflecting an uncertain, disturbed mental state. She is no longer an alluring woman. Instead, this
Judith exudes the coldness and cruelty of a predator. Both paintings are covered
with Klimt's customary decorative surface designs. It is indicative of how viewers
understood these two works that they also circulated under the alternate title *Salome* during Klimt's lifetime.[9] The second Judith painting can still be found labeled *Salome* in art books today.[10] Such confusion is understandable. With Judith
now portrayed as a young, attractive woman holding the head of a man, the
iconography of her story differed little from that of the pagan princess.

The story of Salome was ubiquitous in European art and literature at the
turn of the century. Her notoriety stemmed from works like Oscar Wilde's drama
Salome (1893) and Gustave Flaubert's short story *Hérodias* (1877), both of which
render the steamy sensuality of the young princess in evocative detail. In Wilde's
version, the young princess is given a new psychological motivation for demanding the head of John the Baptist: sexual rejection. By making this request
of Herod, she gains revenge and, in the play's climactic final scene, appears to
receive sexual gratification from the bloody head. Wilde's play garnered wide
publicity due to its perceived depravity. Censorship difficulties only increased
its appeal. Strauss's operatic version, which Gustav Mahler could not mount
in Vienna due to official opposition, received performances in over fifty European cities between 1905 and 1907. A series of Salome paintings by the
French artist Gustave Moreau in the 1870s and 1880s stirred the imagination
of many writers and artists, including J.-K. Huysmans, the Parisian writer
whose discussion of one of Moreau's Salome paintings in his novel *A Rebours*
(1884) firmly linked Salome with the fashionable decadence movement in turn-
of-the-century literature.

Against the backdrop of cultural fascination with the figure of Salome, the
story of Judith and Holofernes came to be perceived as a similar tale of man's
misfortunes at the hands of woman. Just how readily the iconography of Judith
and Salome overlapped for artists of this time can be seen in an illustration that
German artist Thomas Theodor Heine made in 1908 for a limited-edition print-
ing of Friedrich Hebbel's complete works.[11] Heine prepared a series of line draw-
ings for the *Judith* volume that included the decapitation scene reproduced here
in fig. 7.2. In this carefully composed scene, a lithe, partially robed Judith looks
indifferently over her shoulder at the head of Holofernes lying on the floor a
short distance away. Rivulets of blood or hair (it is hard to say which) stream toward her feet from the grotesquely misshapen head, and at her back springs an
oddly shaped tree whose teardrop leaves readily evoke the image of blood spurt-
ing from a punctured vein. Her sword is nowhere in sight. A cool, rational feel
emanates from the illustration, created by the background of simple geometric
lines and the presence of a self-absorbed cluster of robed men conversing in the
distance, completely unaware of the violent murder just committed in their presence. Divorced from its context among the pages of Hebbel's play, Heine's illustration could easily pass for one of the many depictions of Salome and the head of
John the Baptist created in the early years of this century. The robed men, in
that case, might represent the arguing crowd of Jews so familiar from Strauss's

FIGURE 7.2   *Thomas Theodor Heine, illustration for act 5 of Hebbel's* Judith *(1908).*
By permission of the Houghton Library, Harvard University.

opera. The Judith/Salome complex as it appeared in the visual arts has been the
subject of a study by Nadine Sine. These two biblical women, she explains, one
a pagan princess, one a Jewish heroine, came to symbolize a single female type:
"The sexual awakening and lust for revenge experienced by both virgins forced
the images of these two seemingly opposite types to merge."[12] Additional Judith
paintings from the turn of the century corroborate this overlapping identity. A
costume design created by Léon Bakst in 1922 for performances of a *Judith* ballet by Diaghilev's Ballets Russes finds Judith swathed in billowy, multicolored
silks tied tightly at the ankles, delicate slippers on her feet, with a scarf muffling
the lower half of her face (fig. 7.3). Holofernes's head, eyes closed in death and
bloated tongue purpling with decay, hangs by the hair from her muscular raised

FIGURE 7.3   *Léon Bakst. Costume design for the ballet* Judith *(1922). Robert L. B. Tobin Collection, McNay Art Museum, San Antonio, Texas.*

arms. Judith's garb gives her an oriental appearance, a look commonly associated with the princess from the exotic East, Salome.[13] In spite of the head's grotesque appearance, she seems fascinated by it, her pose—somewhere between sitting and standing, as if she were about to sit down and cradle the head in her lap—suggesting an erotic attraction to this repugnant object. Holofernes's face bears an unmistakable resemblance to the devil.

Outside the visual arts, the very name Judith was often enough to evoke the image of an attractive, potentially dangerous young woman. In early-twentieth-century literature, women with this name surfaced in plays by Georg Kaiser, Herbert Eulenberg, George Bernard Shaw, August Strindberg, and others.[14] Naturally these writers portrayed Judith in different manners; in Shaw's *The Devil's Disciple* (1897), for example, she is a minister's wife. But the symbolism of her name was available to be drawn upon if needed. In Part 2 of Strindberg's drama of marital misery, *The Dance of Death* (1900, first performed in 1905), a new character is introduced: Judith, the adolescent daughter of Edgar and Alice, the play's two antagonists. Judith is presented as "a flirtatious little vixen with a braid down her back and with skirts that could be a little longer."[15] She innocently yet cruelly manipulates the men around her. "You already have me as your slave," laments her young admirer, "but you are not satisfied with that. The slave has to be tortured and thrown to the wild beasts." The powerful symbolism of Judith's name forms an important subtext to the plot of this play. Twice she is explicitly connected with the Judith of the Old Testament, only now it is clear that this reference alludes not to the biblical Judith but to that particular fin-de-siècle Judith with whom Strindberg's audiences (largely German) would have been familiar. In the end, however, this Judith does not destroy the men around her, but instead falls genuinely in love with the youth to whom she had been so cruel.

Most of the painters or sculptors who depicted the figure of Judith were German or Austrian. Few French or English artists were attracted to the subject. Hungarian painters seem to have avoided it entirely.[16] How it was presented, moreover, depended to an extent on geography. Outside of Germany and Austria, Judith's encounter with Holofernes was still interpreted more or less as it had been for centuries, as a parable for faith in God in the face of adversity. Honegger's opera *Judith*, for example, is largely a retelling of the story in its biblical form, with a concluding chorus glorifying God's power and wisdom. G. W. Chadwick adopts a similar tone in his *Judith* oratorio. The Judith portrayed in Hebbel's play and popularized by later German-speaking artists, however, became the dominant image of Judith found in central Europe at this time.

Hungarian Views of the Judith Figure

We have no way of knowing whether Bartók was familiar with any of the specific Judiths mentioned here. There is no reason to assume that he would have been, for most of the images were not widely disseminated. Nonetheless, some general inkling of Judith's fin-de-siècle interpretation had apparently begun to trickle down the Danube toward Budapest by the early decades of this century. Balázs, not Bartók, proves to be the principal point of contact with the Judith tradition. Balázs was deeply interested in Hebbel's plays at the very time he was working on the *Bluebeard* play. A Hebbel scholar as well as a writer and hopeful young dramatist, in 1908, at the outset of his literary career, he completed his doctoral studies at the University of Budapest with a dissertation on Hebbel's dramatic theories. (Balázs's interest in Hebbel is discussed in chapter 2.) It was during this time that he began to develop and work on sketches for the play that in June 1910 would be published as *Duke Bluebeard's Castle*. Shortly afterward, several prominent productions of *Judith* were mounted in Budapest, reacquainting the public at large with Hebbel's tragic heroine. It was through Hebbel's play that the figure of Judith gained wider recognition among Hungarians.

At the turn of the century, a lively cult of interest had formed around the German dramatist's writings and plays. Young dramatists keen on creating modern tragedies looked to their great forebears of the romantic era, Goethe, Hebbel, and Schiller, for insights into the art of writing for the theater. Numerous dissertations on Hebbel were written at German universities during the decades before World War I. The plays were revived, and his diaries and letters earnestly combed for ideas. In Hungary, Georg Lukács wrote extensively on Hebbel in his 1907 study *The Modern Drama*, a book his friend Balázs later helped prepare for publication. Lukács anointed the German playwright "the founder of modern drama," a title

Balázs echoed when he praised Hebbel as "the last great theoretician of drama."[17] Both men played the role of ardent Hebbel enthusiasts in a country whose political and cultural orientation leaned far more toward France than Germany. Balázs, whose cultural outlook was strongly defined by his upbringing as the son of Jewish German immigrants, found in German literature and philosophy a congenial home for his roving intellect and gravitated naturally in that direction during his formative years as a writer. It would be a decisive step.[18]

Occasional performances of Hebbel's plays in Hungary during the first decade of the century confirm that these works appealed theatrically as well as intellectually. Thália, the small independent theater group established in 1904 whose members included, in their student years, Lukács, Balázs, and Kodály, produced *Maria Magdalena* twenty-two times between 1905 and 1908, to considerable critical and popular success.[19] Budapest's professional theaters scheduled Hebbel plays alongside the naturalistic dramas of Sándor Bródy and Western classics in translation. Two separate productions of *Judith* were introduced between 1910 and 1912, one by famed German stage director Max Reinhardt and his Berlin-based Deutsches Theater, the other by Budapest's own National Theater, under the direction of Sándor Hevesi. Visits to the Hungarian capital by the Deutsches Theater were a staple of Budapest's cultural life in the years before World War I. At the end of every season, the famous German theater company would travel to Budapest for an intensive two-week residency at the Vígszínház during which performances of plays from their repertory were given daily. Their May 1910 residency offered two performances of *Judith*, a play just coming off a tremendously successful run in Berlin, where, that spring, thirty-five performances had been given, more than any production except Goethe's *Faust* and Shakespeare's *The Taming of the Shrew*.[20]

Reinhardt's *Judith* attracted considerable attention among Budapest's intellectual and cultural elite. It featured one of the finest actors on the German stage, Paul Wegener, as Holofernes. *Nyugat*'s editor-in-chief, Ignotus, had seen the play in Berlin and enthusiastically announced its impending arrival to his readers.[21] A longer postperformance review was also published in *Nyugat*. The writer of this review took for granted the quality of the Deutsches Theater's production and instead used his column as a forum for analyzing Hebbel's play.[22] Reinhardt's guest performances in Hungary exerted a strong influence on the repertory and acting style of Hungarian theaters in the first two decades of the twentieth century. The success of his *Judith* galvanized Hungarian theater professionals into mounting their own production the following season. The National Theater's *Judith* premiered in January 1912. Unfortunately, it met with little of the enthusiasm accorded its precursor. Budapest's leading literary weekly, *A Hét* (The Week), severely criticized the performances, expressing deep disappointment in the actors and in the imagination of the stage direction. As if that were not bad enough, lamented the reviewer, "the National Theater simply copied Reinhardt's scenery and entire production."[23]

From 1910 to 1912, no fewer than four reviews of *Judith* were published in *Nyugat*, to mention nothing of Budapest's other journals or newspapers.[24] The language of these reviews reveals how Hungarians, too, perceived the conflict between Judith and Holofernes as an expression of man's and woman's essential differences. Dezső Kosztolányi, likening Judith to female characters in other Hebbel plays, finds her simultaneously erotic and exotic: "The eroticism of Hebbel's women is modern and new today as well. He saw something unique in women. . . . There, on their faces, one finds sphinx-like features, the smile and pearls of idols. The temperature of their eroticism is incredible. The eastern air brings the women's stylized beauty to a boil."[25] To Menyhért Lengyel, future author of the *Miraculous Mandarin* ballet scenario that Bartók set to music in 1918–19, Hebbel's *Judith* was an imposing precedent for a modern dramatist to contend with. He, too, reviewed the 1912 performances of *Judith*. And for Lengyel, "the dramatist of today beholds *Judith* with the same giddiness and amazement that a modern architect feels when confronted with the pyramids. . . . Never has a drama of greater simplicity been performed than Hebbel's story of Judith and Holofernes."[26] The clue to this simplicity, he argues, may be found in the new psychological interpretation of the drama in fashion at the turn of the century. Strongly sexual motives underlie Judith's decision to seek out Holofernes, he explains. Extremes of masculinity and femininity come into conflict. Holofernes is the "mighty, strong, bloody, and savage pagan," while Judith, perversely, becomes a creature who "seeks nothing other than her sexual satisfaction." (This is a recurrent theme in male attitudes toward women at the time.) Lengyel reduces the entire play to a psychological conflict between one man and one woman. "This universal and overpowering sexual battle is the foundation of Hebbel's play," he proclaims.[27]

The nineteenth century had witnessed, partly in response to the rising tide of women's social advances, the promulgation of numerous theories designed to bolster claims of men's physical and mental superiority to women. The notion that women's role in humanity was to be beautiful and to reproduce, while to men belonged the higher realms of the intellect, held widespread acceptance among men during this period—not just uneducated men, but also those in the intellectual and artistic elite. In this view, women were essentially passive human beings who needed the intellectual and physical vitality of men to give their life meaning.[28] Balázs, in his doctoral thesis, expresses a viewpoint similar to Lengyel's in its focus on Judith's inchoate need, as a woman, to seek out Holofernes. Judith, he writes, echoing Hebbel, represents an instrument of God's will caught in the larger conflict between the individual and the whole, or what Hebbel identified in his writings as the individual and universal wills that govern human existence as opposing forces.[29] Tellingly, Balázs also comments on Judith's motive for seeking out Holofernes. He quotes a passage from act 2 as evidence of what he calls the drama's "fundamental motive." "A woman is nothing," Judith laments, "she can only develop into something through the man; she can become a mother through him. The child she bears is the expression of thanks she can give to Nature for her own life." Judith, he explains, acts out of a need to realize, or fulfill, her own sexuality. Like Lengyel and Kosztolányi, however, he perceives larger meanings behind their actions than Hebbel perhaps had intended. Holofernes becomes, in his view, something of a masculine ideal. "It is interesting," he further notes, "how in Hebbel's Holofernes we can see an enlarged form of the

Übermensch idea."[30] Judith's response to this man is one of irrepressible physical attraction: "Confronted with Holofernes's greatness and arrogance, the individual in her, the woman, at once begins to appear."[31]

An attitude like this could easily be taken as a reflection of Balázs's own wishful thinking about women; Balázs had the reputation among his peers in Budapest as something of a Don Juan figure, forever in pursuit of women.[32] But here he describes what, to him, seemed a higher truth about the relationship between men and women. For Balázs, even a woman as heroic as the biblical Judith, a woman ennobled by the divine force behind her actions, proves, in the end, unable to remain focused on her lofty goals in the presence of a man to whom she is physically attracted. In light of the *Bluebeard* drama he would soon write, it is of more than passing interest to see Balázs thus reducing the complexities of a play like *Judith* to an elemental conflict between a man and a woman who, despite their nominal identities as biblical characters, each act out their larger sexual identities as constructed in turn-of-the-century male thought. The lofty but intimidating man and the sensuous, beautiful woman, placed in close contact for the first time—what are these but the characters in *Bluebeard's Castle*? The names would change, and the sexuality would be suppressed, but the underlying theme—the "fundamental motive"— remained constant.

It is surely a coincidence that the performance history of the *Judith* play in Budapest so neatly overlaps with the composition history of the *Bluebeard* opera. But at the same time, such confluences should not be overlooked, for the attention given to Hebbel's play helped fix both Judith's name and, perhaps to a lesser extent, its general connotation in the minds of those who were actively involved in the city's cultural life. The presence, during the Opera House's 1913–14 season, of a one-act "choreographed drama" entitled *The Jewish Woman from Bethulia*, with music by Hans Knauer-Halen, attests still further to the subject's sudden popularity. The *Bluebeard* play appeared in print one month before the first Budapest performances of *Judith*. Just over a year later, in January 1912, as Bartók prepared to submit his opera to the Rózsavölgyi opera competition, performances of *Judith* began at the National Theater. Balázs's closer friends and acquaintances—among them Zoltán and Emma Kodály, Lukács, and Bartók—knew how deeply he was inspired by the works of this nineteenth-century German playwright and may well have observed shades of resemblance between Bluebeard's new wife and her spiritual forebear in Hebbel's own drama. In 1918, when the opera received its belated premiere, the allusion would not have been as fresh, but it was still present.

Bartók's Judith

In describing the opera *Bluebeard's Castle*, some writers paint Judith in terms that evoke women of the Salome type, apparently without recognizing that Judith is, in fact, closely bound up in that tradition. To György Kroó, for example, Judith symbolically represents "passion with all its destructive power." She is a woman who possesses what he calls "the monomania of an almost insane woman."[33] Kroó describes Judith as an irrational, passionate woman beyond the control of the man who loves her. His choice of words reveals the extent to which he identifies with Bluebeard and sees Judith as the force that destroys love in this opera. Interpretations like this raise several important questions with regard to Judith. How does the image of a young, attractive, and dangerous Judith come into play in the story of *Bluebeard's Castle*? And if that image does come into play, can awareness of it deepen our understanding of the opera?

A close reading of the *Bluebeard* libretto reveals a Judith who is similar in several important, but not immediately obvious ways to the Judith portrayed in turn-of-the-century paintings. Bartók's Judith is a strong female character whose actions largely determine the outcome of the drama. She is young, of marriageable age. She is attractive: "You were my most beautiful wife," Bluebeard sings at the end. Once inside the castle, she is the one who propels the drama forward to its conclusion through her persistent requests for keys. Her character has a hard, unyielding core over which Bluebeard exerts little control. Bluebeard feels a strong emotional desire for Judith's presence in his life but also fears her entry into his castle because she may seek to discover his deepest secrets. That Judith can generate mixed feelings of desire and trepidation in Bluebeard gives her, in a very general sense, one of her namesake's most basic characteristics.

What is missing from this portrait, of course, is the element of human sexuality. Bluebeard and Judith kiss and embrace on stage, it is true, but in the strained atmosphere of the castle these gestures are more acts of comfort and emotional consolation than expressions of physical attraction. Bluebeard's imploring requests for kisses after the sixth door ("Kiss me, kiss me, ask me nothing") may be read as diversions intended to keep Judith away from the seventh door instead of expressions of desire for physical intimacy. He does not speak to Judith with the thinly veiled lust of Wilde's Herod speaking to Salome. His impassive, concealing personality does not permit him to openly express sexual desires, even to his new wife. The erotic attraction between man and woman, in this opera, has little direct impact on the dramatic situation. It is more important to Bartók's conception, as discussed in the previous chapter, for the love between Bluebeard and Judith to occupy a profoundly spiritual, and hence transcendent, dimension. This does not mean that eroticism is absent, only that it has been muted to the point where it is not immediately noticeable to outside observers. To Bluebeard's query, "Why did you come to me, Judith?" Judith responds passionately

> I shall dry off its [the castle's] dank walls,
> with my lips I will dry it!
> I shall warm its cold stone,
> With my body I will warm it!

Such imagery carries strong erotic overtones, particularly when we recall that, for Balázs, the castle was a symbol for man himself. Within the drama as a whole, however, no other lines such as these are spoken by Judith that reinforce the image of her as a sexual woman. The overall effect is to minimize an aspect of her character that, while undoubtedly present, quickly recedes into the background as the drama progresses.

The operatic Judith thus is not entirely consistent with the qualities observed in other Judiths from the turn of the century; however, we must recognize that Balázs had to adapt the Judith image to fit the context of a different story and dramatic situation. In effect, he places her in his drama as a symbol for a particular female type, then he proceeds to draw limits around the associations her name is bound to evoke. Other literary Judiths from the same period demonstrate a similar tendency to downplay sexual references in the text itself, their authors preferring, like Hebbel and Balázs, to introduce sexual tension in more suggestive, restrained ways. What the name symbolizes, most important, is that Judith is a formidable woman, capable of articulating a mission and manipulating a man to achieve her goal, even if she is destroyed in the process. Attributes both physical (appearance) and intellectual (focused on goal) come together in the operatic Judith, enabling her to consistently maneuver Bluebeard into giving her keys to the seven doors. Moral certitude gives her the strength to continue deeper into the castle even when confronted with unspeakable horrors about his past. What is different about this Judith, however, is that she engages the man through his emotional love for her, not his physical desire.

The dramatic situation in *Bluebeard's Castle* gives Bluebeard's newest wife many opportunities to exert the forceful personality that lies, concealed, within the hesitant, nervous woman who first appears on stage. Unlike most other versions of the Bluebeard tale, going back to the Perrault original, Judith is not handed a key ring at the beginning of the tale and then told she can open all the doors except one. She is not left alone to struggle with her curiosity—the usual scenario—and then yield to temptation in the absence of her husband. Bartók's Judith must wrest keys, one by one, from a reluctant husband. This places the drama's conflict directly between the two characters and their opposing wills, rather than within the character of the wife herself as she struggles with the conflicting emotions of prudence and curiosity. Bartók's opera may well be the first version of the Bluebeard tale where Bluebeard never leaves his wife's side. He shepherds her through the castle, observing and commenting on her attempts to open the forbidden doors.

In the end, it seems likely that the Judith found in *Bluebeard's Castle* was never intended to conform in all regards to the modern Judith image found in the visual arts. Neither she nor Bluebeard brings the full symbolism of their names into this new dramatic situation. Judith leaves her sword—her basic identifying feature—behind. Bluebeard himself is hardly the cruel, violent character found in most versions of the fairy tale; he is a commanding presence but is also more tender toward Judith than the grim Bluebeards of earlier times would have been. It is important to the meaning of the opera that this biblical woman and this fairy-tale man exist on stage in their more fundamental identities as *a* woman and *a* man. This way, as intended by the opera's creators, the audience can perceive the drama as a metaphor relevant (perhaps) to their own lives. The dramatic tension inherent in their names helps carry this message forth from the stage.

Balázs, we know, had no intention of making Judith a female demon. At the time of the opera's premiere in 1918, he recorded his thoughts about the production in his diary. He took exception to the manner in which the stage director Dezső Zádor was encouraging Olga Haselbeck to play the role of Judith. "[Zádor] would make Judith a hysterical little beast if the text would permit it," he lamented; "he hasn't the least idea what the work is about."[34]

Bartók's music indirectly confirms that he, too, was aware of Judith's larger symbolic identity. At Judith's first vocal entrance, after Bluebeard has asked, "Judith, are you still following me?" she responds, "Yes, Bluebeard, I'm coming, I'm coming" (fig. 3 in the score). On the word *Kékszakállú*, Bartók has Judith sing a descending melodic line to the four syllables of Bluebeard's name, using a series of pitches — F–Db–A–Gb — that together outline an enharmonically spelled F♯-minor seventh chord (in reverse order, F♯–A–C♯–E♯). The minor seventh chord in its various permutations held strong symbolic meaning for the Bartók of these years. It is none other, of course, than the much-commented-upon Stefi motif that is found in many of Bartók's early compositions from the years 1907–10 and has not been thought to play a very large role in his compositions after that time frame. By linking Judith with this particular motif at the outset of the opera, Bartók immediately draws the operatic character into his own personal and emotional world, where she becomes another manifestation of the complex welter of feeling that he experienced toward Geyer and that surfaced programmatically in works such as the *Two Portraits* and the *First String Quartet*.

Late-twentieth-century audiences listening to Bartók's opera have lost the thread of allusion inserted into this drama with the figure of Judith. The story of Bluebeard is more familiar to us. We think of *Bluebeard's Castle* as a drama containing many symbols, but we ignore one of the most important — the name of Bluebeard's newest wife. In the end, the meaning of this symbol, like that of other symbols in the opera, remains veiled in ambiguity. Audiences at the time the play and opera were written, however, could not have failed to connect this Judith at some level with the biblical Judith who stirred the imagination of artists and intellectuals in Germany, Austria, and also, it appears, Hungary.

ᴄᴏ Appendix

DUKE BLUEBEARD'S CASTLE

Notes on the Text by
Béla Balázs, circa 1915

At some point after 1913 Josef Kalmer, a Viennese theater producer, asked Balázs to provide notes for a possible German-language production of the Misztériumok *in that city. Kalmer's typewritten translations of the three plays are preserved in the Balázs estate at the Hungarian Academy of Sciences (Ms. 5012/2). They are accompanied by the following explanation of the* Bluebeard *play, prepared by Balázs for performances that apparently never took place. The original is in German.[1]*

Is it permissible to "explain" verse? Let us suppose that, perhaps, not all its parts are entirely clear; isn't it just then that the essence—music—does its work in sleeping shadows? All explanations are Roentgen pictures: they break up the shape, the form. Prefaces are all in vain. True poetry is: *seduction*!

But if the poetry is available to us only in translation, then there is some need of explanation. Because just where the work's sense and meaning do not come to light in logical, clearly formulated matters—no doubt this happens with all true poetry—these dual essences are comprehensible only in the linguistic shape and the text's musical irradiation of the words' music. This, however, is lost in translation.

In such a case it is perhaps not superfluous to say a few words about what the original poetry actually wanted to say, since it was Béla Bartók's wonderful music that gave musical form to the spirit of the original Hungarian verse, and the translated text cannot always bring this out convincingly. So we need to say a little about the original poetry *to be able to explain the music.*

201

I did not write the Hungarian original of *Duke Bluebeard's Castle* as a libretto, but simply as poetry, as one is used to writing verse in general. It appeared separately, and was also given as a dramatic scene, even before Bartók had set it to music.[2] I created this ballad of mine in the language and rhythms of old Hungarian Székely folk ballads. In character these folk ballads closely resemble old Scottish folk ballads, but they are, perhaps, more acerbic, more simple, their melodic quality more mysterious, more naive, and more songlike. Thus, there is no "literature" or rhetoric within them: they are constructed from dark, weighty, uncarved blocks of words. In this manner I wrote my Hungarian language *Bluebeard* ballad, and Bartók's music also conforms to this.

I called my *Bluebeard* a ballad for the stage because the stage here occupies not only the necessary space for the unfolding of the dialogue. The stage itself takes part in the dialogue. In the Hungarian dramatis personae I identified the play's three participants: Bluebeard, Judith, and the castle.

My ballad is the "ballad of inner life." Bluebeard's castle is not a real castle of stone. The castle is his soul. It is lonely, dark, and secretive: the castle of closed doors.

It is precisely this tragic obscurity, this suffering withdrawal into seclusion, that attracted the woman with strange power, even though she had heard frightful rumors about murdered women. Into this castle, into his own soul, Bluebeard admits his beloved. And the castle (the stage) shudders, weeps, and bleeds. When the woman walks in it, she walks in a living being.

And the woman wants to throw open all the doors. Her love and compassion lead her to this. She would like to bring light, and warmth, into the dark, closed castle. "Your poor castle won't be dark, There will be windows, There will be balconies!"—she speaks in this manner, and thinks only of the castle, of it alone!

When the castle's doors open forth, labored and painfully at first, she, however, has no fear of the dangerous and, until then, hidden secrets that spring forth from the depths of the rooms; after all, more light enters the poor, dark castle. But she sees traces of blood everywhere. Where will they lead? Do they not mark the path of her own fate?

She opens the doors one after the other, each with increasing restlessness and impatience. She searches for the cause of the traces of blood. She demands: From whence does the blood come? And when, through the fifth door, a flood of light and warmth engulfs the castle, and Bluebeard—liberated, redeemed, luminous, grateful in his happiness—wants to embrace the woman in his arms, already the daylight is no longer visible to the woman who brought it to him. She sees only the bloody shadows.

Nevertheless, she searches further; she wants to throw open the last door, too. "What do you want, then?"—Bluebeard asks her. "Look, my castle now gleams, Your blessed hands did this." "I don't want you to have any doors closed to me"—answers the woman. She left everything behind, and came to him, because she loves him. Not a single door should be locked before her if he wants his home to become her home. She says this, and inquires about the women whom the man loved before her.

Her every flattery useless, the man does not give her the seventh key. "You are my castle's radiant splendor. Kiss me, kiss me, ask me nothing."

The woman then cries out in the man's face: "I know, Bluebeard, I know what the seventh door conceals. All your former wives are there! Slaughtered, frozen in blood. Ah, the rumors were true, the horrible rumors!"

The man now hands her the key. "Open it, Judith. You shall see them. There are all my former wives." And when the woman looks inside, she staggers back in alarm: not as if she had seen the dead women, no! The women are *alive*! From behind the seventh door the wives—who had been loved at one time by the man—rise to their feet, dreamlike, from the deep recesses of slumbering memory. And wreathed with diadems and halos, they are more beautiful than all women presently living. Oh, how plain, how miserable Judith feels when Bluebeard sings in dreaming ecstasy of his past loves.

But she doesn't shudder in horror until he begins to beautify her, to adorn her with jewels. "Ah, Bluebeard, you are not dreaming, I am your poor, living wife." But the man covers her with glittering ornaments, and Judith gradually grows numb with death. The man's dream kills her, the very dream she herself has conjured up in him. And the dreaming man remains alone once more, his castle again locked and dark.

This is the meaning of the Hungarian ballad about Duke Bluebeard's castle.

NOTES

Abbreviations Used in the Notes

BBChron Béla Bartók Jr. *Apám életének krónikája* (Chronicle of my father's life). Budapest: Zeneműkiadó, 1981.

BBFamLet *Bartók Béla családi levelei* (Béla Bartók family letters). Edited by Béla Bartók Jr. and Adrienne Gombocz. Budapest: Zeneműkiadó, 1981.

Essays *Béla Bartók Essays*. Edited by Benjamin Suchoff. New York: St. Martin's Press. Reprint, Lincoln: University of Nebraska Press, 1992.

Letters *Béla Bartók Letters*. Edited by János Demény. New York: St. Martin's Press, 1971.

Introduction

1. Which pieces Bartók played on this occasion have not, to my knowledge, been identified.

2. Balázs recorded the details of this fiasco in his diary several months later, in July 1913 (*Balázs Béla: Napló* [Béla Balázs: Diary], ed. Anna Fabri [Budapest: Magvető Könyvkiadó, 1981]: 1:603–5). References to these diaries (hereafter *Napló*) will be found frequently in the following pages. In most cases translations will be my own, although many of the more prominent entries concerning Bartók have already been translated into English by other authors. This passage is taken from Joseph Zsuffa, *Béla Balázs: The Man and the Artist* (Berkeley and Los Angeles: University of California Press, 1987): 45–46.

3. Zoltán Kodály, "Bartók Béla első operája" (Béla Bartók's first opera), *Nyugat* 9,

no. 1 (1918): 938–39. This English translation is taken from the Bartók issue of *Books from Hungary: Quarterly of the Hungarian Publishers and Book Distributors*, ed. Imre Kőműves, vol. 3, nos. 3–4 (1961): 1–2.

    4. Kodály, "Bartók Béla első operája," 939.

    5. An exception to this trend may be found in the early work of György Króo ("Duke Bluebeard's Castle," *Studia Musicologica* 1 [1961]: 251–340) and in Judit Frigyesi's *Béla Bartók and Turn-of-the-Century Budapest* (Berkeley: University of California Press, 1998), two chapters of which are devoted to *Bluebeard's Castle* as an expression of Hungarian modernism (pp. 192–294).

    6. Béla Balázs, "A kékszakállú herceg vára: Megjegyzések a szöveghez" (Duke Bluebeard's Castle: Notes on the text), in *Balázs Béla: Válogatott cikkek és tanulmányok*, edited by Magda Nagy, 34–37 (Budapest: Kossuth Könyvkiadó, 1968). See the appendix.

    7. Carl Dahlhaus, *Nineteenth-Century Music*, trans. J. B. Robinson (Berkeley: University of California Press, 1989), 347.

Chapter One

    1. Bartók, "On Bluebeard's Castle," in *Essays*, 407. Originally published as "A kékszakállu herceg vára: I. Szerzők a darabjukról [Duke Bluebeard's Castle: I. Authors about their piece]," *Magyar Színpad* 21/143 (May 24, 1918): 1.

    2. See *Essays*, 412–13 and 416.

    3. László Somfai discusses the challenges to musicologists posed by Bartók's lifelong reserve in *Béla Bartók: Composition, Concepts, and Autograph Sources* (Berkeley, CA: University of California Press, 1996): 9–24.

    4. Bartók, "About *The Wooden Prince*," in *Essays*, 406. Originally published as "A fából faragott királyfi: II. A zeneszerző a darabjáról" [The Wooden Prince: II. The composer about his piece], *Magyar Színpad* 20/105 (May 12, 1917): 2.

    5. Peter Bartók, letter to the author, September 1992.

    6. Bartók to Ernest Latzko, 15 May 1925. Translated in *Bartók Letters: The Musical Mind*, ed. Malcolm Gillies and Adrienne Gombocz (Oxford: Clarendon Press, forthcoming).

    7. Balázs's diaries and personal papers are preserved in the Library of the Hungarian Academy of Sciences, Manuscript Department. A catalogue of the library's Balázs collection was published as Dóra F. Csanak, ed. *Balázs Béla hagyatéka az akadémiai könyvtár kézirattárban (Ms 5009–Ms 5024)* [Béla Balázs's estate in the manuscript department of the academy library] (Budapest: Magyar Tudományos Akadémia Könyvtára, 1966). Selections from the diaries have been published as Anna Fabri, ed., *Balázs Béla: Napló* [Béla Balázs: Diary], 2 vols. (Budapest: Magvető Könyvkiadó, 1982). For more on Balázs in English, see Joseph Zsuffa, *Béla Balázs: The Man and the Artist* (Berkeley, CA: University of California Press, 1987); Mary Gluck, *Georg Lukács and his Generation, 1918–1918* (Cambridge, MA: Harvard University Press, 1985); and Arpad Kadarkay, *Georg Lukács: Life, Thought, and Politics* (Cambridge, MA, and Oxford: Basil Blackwell, 1991). In the Bartók literature, Judit Frigyesi (*Béla Bartók and Turn-of-the-Century Budapest* [Berkeley, CA: University of California Press, 1998]) offers the most detailed explanation of the artistic beliefs shared by Bartók and Balázs. See also Króo, "Duke Bluebeard's Castle." A dictionary entry on Balázs and chronological list of works can be found in Albert Tezla, *Hungarian Authors: A Bibliographical Handbook* (Cambridge, MA: The Belknap Press of Harvard University Press, 1970): 74–79. Excerpts from Balázs's diaries are translated into English in István Gál, "Béla Balázs, Bartók's First Librettist," *The New Hungarian Quarterly* 55 (Au-

tumn 1974): 204–8. The undated quotation at the head of this chapter is taken from Gál's translations.

8. All the Balázs books in Bartók's personal library, for example, are inscribed to Bartók by "Herbert." In 1913 Balázs formally changed his name from Herbert Bauer to Béla Balázs.

9. Kodály and Bartók both had attended the Liszt Academy of Music since 1900 (Bartók entered in 1899, Kodály in 1900), yet they did not meet until 1905. Prior to that time, the two budding ethnologists nurtured separate interests in Hungarian folk music. On the meeting between Bartók and Kodály, see Denijs Dille, "La rencontre de Bartók et de Kodály," in *Béla Bartók: Regard sur le passé*, ed. Yves Lenoir (Louvain-la-Neuve, Belgium: Institut Supérieur d'Archéologie et d'Histoire de l'Art, Collège Érasme, 1990): 199–212.

10. Balázs, diary entry, 5 September 1906, *Napló* 1: 339.

11. Quoted in Zsuffa, *Béla Balázs*, 66.

12. Balázs, diary entry, 5 September 1906. This translation is adapted from the one found in Mary Gluck, *Georg Lukács and his Generation*, 35. Gluck mistakenly places this encounter between Bartók and Balázs a year earlier, in 1905.

13. Bartók to his mother, 10 September 1905, *Letters*, 53. Bartók was writing from Paris, where he had been competing as a pianist and composer in the Rubinstein competition.

14. Bartók to Delius, 7 June 1910. In Lionel Carley, ed., *Delius: A Life in Letters*, vol. 2, 1909–1934 (London: Scolar Press, in association with The Delius Trust, 1988): 48.

15. Balázs, diary entry, 5 September 1906, *Napló* 1: 339.

16. I have copied this text from a photocopy of the manuscript's last page, kindly sent to me by Peter Bartók.

17. Denijs Dille, "Angaben zum Violinkonzert 1907 . . .," in *Dokumenta Bartókiana* 2 (Budapest: Akadémiai Kiadó; Mainz: B. Schotts Söhne, 1965): 93–94.

18. Frigyesi, *Béla Bartók and Turn-of-the-Century Budapest*, 199–200. See also pages 203–11 on "Loneliness in the Hungarian Modernist Experience."

19. Balázs, diary entry, December 18, 1907, *Napló* 1:458.

20. Balázs, diary entry, August 4, 1908, *Napló* 1:477.

21. Describing his brief encounters with Lena Grabenko in February 1912, Balázs likens them to "Don Juan's last adventure, out of which I want to write a serious short story" (*Napló* 1:548). A project of this name, "Don Juan utolsó kalandja," was included on a list of future projects Balázs drew up in April 1912 (*Napló* 1:561–62). Arpad Kadarkay, author of a recent biography of Georg Lukács, titles his chapter on Balázs "Don Juan in Budapest" (*Georg Lukács*, 118–42).

22. Edith Hajós to Lukács, December 26, 1909, cited in Kadarkay, *Georg Lukács*, 143. In the published selections of Balázs's diaries, no entries are reproduced for a period of over two years, from February 16, 1909, to July 1911. Assuming that Balázs maintained his diary during these years, this omission precludes access to his thoughts during the very time when he was writing *Bluebeard* and Bartók was beginning to compose the opera.

23. A note accompanying the publication of the prologue indicates that the play from which this was taken would appear in a future issue of the journal. The prologue was reprinted at the head of the entire work in the June 13 issue.

24. Balázs, *Az én utam* (Budapest: Atheneum, 1945): 11.

25. Balázs, "Balázs Béla: Napló" (Béla Balázs: Diary), *Bécsi Magyar Újság* (Vienna Hungarian news), May 21, 1922, p. 7. Translated in part in Kroó, "Duke Bluebeard's Castle," 277–78.

26. This is a reference to the rules of the Rózsavölgyi competition, which stipulated

that rights for prizewinning works belonged exclusively to the Rózsavölgyi firm (see chapter 5).

27. Balázs to Bartók, July 13, [1911]. Published in Hungarian, with a German translation, in *Dokumenta Bartókiana* 3, 83–85, where the date is given incorrectly as 1914. Balázs's year-long leave of absence from his teaching job began in summer 1911. In June 1911 he left for Bern, Switzerland, to visit Edith (Zsuffa, *Béla Balázs*, 37). The address Balázs gives at the end of this letter agrees with this information: "Until the 24th: Bern, Gesellschafts Str. 16 parterre."

28. Balázs, diary entry, September 7, 1911. This translation is by Gál ("Béla Balázs," 205). I have made several small changes in order to transmit Balázs's expressions more precisely. Gál inexplicably leaves off the first sentence of Balázs's recollection.

29. On February 28, 1912, Balázs noted in his diary, "I wrote to Fenyő on account of the Mysteries, set to appear around Easter" (*Napló* 1:551). Each of the plays had appeared previously in literary journals.

30. Swedish playwright August Strindberg also gave opus numbers to some of his late chamber plays, written starting in 1907. Balázs could not have known these works—they remained unpublished until later in the 1910s.

31. Balázs, diary entry, February 28, 1912, *Napló* 1:550.

32. Balázs, "Remembering Béla Bartók," cited in Zsuffa, *Béla Balázs*, [photo caption, after p. 402].

33. Balázs, "Béla Balázs: Napló," 7. This quotation is from earlier in the article. Translated in Kroó, "Duke Bluebeard's Castle," 277, with modifications by the author.

34. This incident is recorded in Zsuffa, *Béla Balázs*, 35.

35. Balázs, "From a Distant Land, to a Distant Land: On the Occasion of Béla Bartók's Sixtieth Birthday," trans. Balázs Dibuz, in *Bartók and His World*, ed. Peter Laki (Princeton, N.J.: Princeton University Press, 1995), 270–71. The same story was told, details consistent with its later version, in Balázs's 1922 article for *Bécsi Magyar Újság* ("Balázs Béla: Napló," 7–8).

36. On the history of *The Wooden Prince*, see György Kroó, "On the Origin of The Wooden Prince," in *IMC in Commemoration of Béla Bartók 1971*, ed. Josef Ujfalussy and János Breuer (Budapest: Editio Musica; New York: Belwin Mills, 1972), 97–101.

37. Balázs, "From a Distant Land," 271.

38. Balázs, diary entry, May 28, 1917, *Napló* 2:222. Balázs devotes many pages in his diary to the discussion of *The Wooden Prince* premiere (*Napló* 2:220–23).

39. Balázs, diary entry, May 28, 1917, cited in Gál, "Béla Balázs," 206.

40. Béla Balázs, *Játékok* (Plays) (Gyoma: Kner Izidor, 1917). Béla Bartók Jr. recalls the events of May 12, 1917, in *Apám életének krónikája* (Chronicle of my father's life, hereafter cited as *BBChron*) (Budapest: Zeneműkiadó, 1981), 156.

41. Bartók to Ion Buşiţia, [August 1917], *Letters*, 136.

42. Balázs, diary entry, May 16, 1918, *Napló* 2:309.

43. Balázs, diary entry, May 25, 1918, *Napló* 2:312–13. This translation is by István Gál ("Béla Balázs," 208). I have made some minor emendations. The entire passage occupies several paragraphs in Balázs's diary.

44. Balázs, diary entry, May 25, 1918, *Napló* 2:312.

45. Balázs, diary entry, October 17, 1917, *Napló* 2:283.

46. Bartók to Ion Buşiţia, [August 1917], *Letters*, 136.

47. Gyula Wlassics to Bartók, October 1923, *Letters*, 163.

48. Balázs, "Béla Balázs: Napló," 7.

49. Bartók and Balázs met after a performance Bartók gave of his First Piano Concerto at the Berlin Kroll Opera in April 1928. As it turned out, this would be the last time

they saw each other. A description of the meeting may be found in Zsuffa, *Béla Balázs*, 158–59.

50. See Christopher Hailey, *Franz Schreker, 1878–1934: A Cultural Biography* (Cambridge: Cambridge University Press, 1993), 237. In 1925 Schreker had approached Balázs about preparing a ballet scenario based on Wilde's *Der Geburtstag der Infantin*.

51. Egon and Emmy Wellesz, *Egon Wellesz: Leben und Werk*, ed. Franz Edler (Vienna and Hamburg: Paul Zsolnay Verlag, 1989), 73.

52. Ferenc Bonis, ed. *Bartók Béla Táncs-Szvitje*. Facsimile edition. Score and critical notes. (Budapest: Balassi Kiadó, 1998): 18.

53. These letters have been republished in Balázs, *Balázs Béla: Válogatott cikkek*.

Chapter Two

1. Aladár Kuncz, *Black Monastery* (Fekete Kolostor), trans. Ralph Murray (New York: Harcourt, Brace, 1934): 1.

2. Buda had historically been German, Pest much less so. By 1900, eight out of ten Budapesters counted Hungarian as their first language; only one out of seven claimed German. Many were bilingual. See John Lukacs, *Budapest 1900: A Historical Portrait of a City and Its Culture* (New York: Grove Weidenfeld, 1988), 101.

3. Judit Frigyesi discusses the political development of nationalism in the early years of the twentieth century and its effects on the Hungarian outlook in "Béla Bartók and Hungarian Nationalism" (Ph.D. diss., University of Pennsylvania, 1989), especially chapters 1, 2, and 3.

4. The events of Balázs's year abroad are described in Zsuffa, *Béla Balázs*, 29–31. Kodály was able to go along because Balázs shared his thousand-crown grant with him.

5. I have always felt that shades of Ibsen's Nora, a woman whose strong will toward independence is stifled and misread by an outwardly adoring husband, can be seen in the interaction between Balázs's Judith and Bluebeard.

6. Balázs, "A kékszakállú herceg vára: Megjegyzések a szöveghez," 35. See the appendix.

7. Judit Frigyesi offers an alternative interpretation of the stage lighting in *Béla Bartók and Turn-of-the-Century Budapest*, chapter 8.

8. Small stage props sometimes provide visual confirmation of a door's contents. In the third door scene, Judith digs into the hidden treasure (which we cannot see) and steps back to place a crown, a mantle, and some jewels on the threshold before the audience. In the fourth door scene, green boughs push inward from the door when Judith opens it.

9. Kandinsky's *Der gelbe Klang* is translated as *The Yellow Sound: A Stage Composition* in *The Blue Rider Almanac*, ed. Wassily Kandinsky and Franz Marc, new documentary edition, ed. Klaus Lankheit (New York: Viking Press, 1974; reprint, New York: Da Capo Press, 1989), 207–25.

10. Emil Haraszti, *Béla Bartók: His Life and Works* (Paris: L'Oiseau-Lyre, 1938): 71–75; Halsey Stevens, *The Life and Music of Béla Bartók* (New York: Oxford University Press, 1953): 285–94.

11. Simon Broughton, "Bartók and World Music," in *The Stage Works of Béla Bartók*, ed. Nicholas John, English National Opera Guides, vol. 44 (New York: Riverrun Press, 1991), 19.

12. Haraszti, *Béla Bartók*, 72.

13. Maeterlinck, *Le Trésor des Humbles* (1896), published in English as *The Treasure of the Humble*, trans. Alfred Sutro (New York: Dodd, Mead & Co., 1916), 106–7. One essay

from this volume, "The Tragical in Daily Life," is particularly relevant to the study of Maeterlinck's philosophy.

14. Maeterlinck, "Silence," *Treasure of the Humble*, 4.

15. Balázs, "Maeterlinck," *Nyugat* 1, no. 1 (January 1908): 446–54. This essay is a major document of Balázs's intellectual affinities in the years before he wrote *Bluebeard's Castle*. Unless otherwise stated, quotations from Balázs's writings in this chapter are drawn from his Maeterlinck essay. A complete English translation, by Adam Tolnay, may be found in Leafstedt, "Music and Drama in Béla Bartók's Opera *Duke Bluebeard's Castle*" (Ph.D. diss., Harvard University, 1994), 332–39.

16. Balázs, "Maeterlinck," 448.

17. Ibid., 449.

18. Ivan Sanders, "Symbolist and Decadent Elements in Early-Twentieth-Century Hungarian Drama," *Canadian-American Review of Hungarian Studies* 4, no. 1 (Spring 1977): 27.

19. Balázs, "Maeterlinck," 450.

20. Ibid.

21. "Strindberg paradoxonok" (Strindberg paradoxes), *Nyugat* 1, no. 1 (1908): 517–19. The English translation is by Adam Tolnay.

22. Ibid., 518, 519.

23. Ibid., 519. Two years earlier, in 1906, Balázs had mused in his diary about the possibilities of "a new dramatic form: showing internal pictures, too. The struggles which lie within dialogue" (*Napló* 1:357).

24. Interest in mysticism was widespread in Europe at the turn of the century, and it is not unusual to find a dramatic work thus identified. Gabriele d'Annunzio labeled his *Le Martyre de Saint Sébastien* (1911) a "mystére," and Frank Wedekind subtitled his *Franziska* (1912) a "modern mystery." Alexander Scriabin, a man thoroughly steeped in the spirit of mysticism, worked for years, until his death in 1915, on a grandiose composition entitled *Mysterium* that would engage all the arts and human senses in a profound synaesthetic experience.

25. A good general discussion of the history of *Ariane et Barbe-bleue* and its place in Maeterlinck's dramatic output may be found in W. D. Halls, "Les débuts du Théâtre nouveau chez Maeterlinck," *Annales du Fondation Maurice Maeterlinck* 3 (1957): 45–58.

26. Sanders, "Symbolist and Decadent Elements," 30.

27. According to W. D. Halls, the years from 1890 to 1895 represented Maeterlinck's "symbolist period" (*Maurice Maeterlinck: A Study of His Life and Thought* [Oxford: Oxford University Press, 1960]: 43). Elsewhere, Halls describes *Ariane* as an "intermediary between the symbolist theater and the works of 'the second style' ("Les débuts," 53). Some of Maeterlinck's earliest biographers also recognize the plays from this era (roughly 1890–95) as distinct from his later plays, though the term "symbolist" is not used. See Edward Thomas, *Maurice Maeterlinck* (New York: Dodd, Mead and Co., 1911), 95.

28. Maurice Maeterlinck, "The Modern Drama," in *The Double Garden*, trans. Alexander Teixeira De Mattos (New York: Dodd, Mead & Co., 1911), 126.

29. Ibid., 126–27.

30. Sanders, "Symbolist and Decadent Elements," 30.

31. Gustave Flaubert, *Salammbô* (New York: Modern Library, 1929), 127.

32. Miklós Szabolcsi, "On the Spread of Symbolism," in *The Symbolist Movement in the Literature of European Languages*, ed. Anna Balakian (Budapest: Akadémiai Kiadó, 1984), 188.

33. Balázs, "Maeterlinck," 419. Balázs prefers to overlook the stylistic differences between *Ariane* and the earlier plays. He sees them as all part of a unified dramatic aesthetic.

34. Judit Frigyesi, personal communication to the author, June 1997.

35. Sanders, "Symbolist and Decadent Elements," 26.

36. Balázs, "Parizs-e vagy Weimar?" *Nyugat* 7, no. 2 (1914): 200. Zsuffa briefly summarizes this article in his biography (Zsuffa, *Béla Balázs*, 53). This is the source of my description.

37. Balázs, "Maeterlinck," 452. Anselma Heine's recent German-language biography of Maeterlinck forms a point of departure for Balázs's essay.

38. Balázs, "A tragédiának metafizikus teóriája a német romantikában és Hebbel Frigyes" (Friedrich Hebbel and the metaphysical theory of tragedy in the German romantics), *Nyugat* 1, no. 1 (1908): 87–90.

39. Ibid., 88. This translation was prepared by Adam Tolnay.

40. Ibid., 90.

41. Gluck, *Georg Lukács and His Generation*, 138. Gluck describes the reactions of Lukács, Balázs, and others to what she labels "the crisis of aestheticism" that gripped many young Hungarians in the decade from 1900 to 1910. She provides penetrating insight into a topic that is far too complex to cover here. Lukács's rejection of symbolism based on its lack of spiritual content resembles the position taken around 1910 by some German intellectuals who rejected impressionist art and literature because its beautiful external surface was not matched by inner substance. (See Richard Sheppard, "German Expressionism," in *Modernism: A Guide to European Literature, 1890–1930*, ed. Malcolm Bradbury and James McFarlane [New York and London: Pelican Books, 1976; reprint, New York and London: Penguin Books, 1991]: 277.)

42. Gluck, *Lukács and His Generation*, 131.

43. Balázs, "A tragédiának metafizikus teóriája," 80. Frigyesi (*Béla Bartók and Turn-of-the-Century Budapest*, chapters 1 and 4) explores this topic in greater depth.

44. Sanders, "Symbolist and Decadent Elements," 26. Balázs and Lukács both came from German Jewish families who had settled in Hungary during the great influx of German settlers in the nineteenth century. The social history of Jews and Germans within Hungary, which sometimes resulted in a retention of German cultural affinities, is discussed in Lukács, *Budapest 1900*, 84–107.

45. Mihály Babits, "Dráma," *Nyugat* 1, no. 1 (1913): 166. It has been suggested to me that Babits's choice of the word "German" here was probably meant as a euphemism for "Jewish." Undercurrents of anti-Semitism may therefore be present in Babits's review.

46. Ibid., 166–67.

47. Ibid., 166.

48. The ideas summarized here are taken freely from two sources: Hebbel's own 1843 essay, "My Word Concerning Drama," in *Three Plays by Hebbel*, ed. and trans. Marion Sonnenfeld (Lewisburg, Pa.: Bucknell University Press, 1974); and "Conception of Tragedy," in Edna Purdie, *Friedrich Hebbel: A Study of His Life and Work*, 2d ed. (Oxford: Oxford University Press, 1969), 255–69.

49. This passage is often mistranslated due to the difficulty of rendering Balázs's truncated Hungarian phrase "Életemet, halálomat, Kékszakállú," into appropriate English.

50. György Kroó is especially forceful in his negative comments about the character of Judith. He sees her as a blindly passionate, instinctive woman who brings about her own ruin ("Duke Bluebeard's Castle," 302–3, 307).

51. Szabolcsi, "On the Spread of Symbolism," 184.

Chapter Three

1. Charles Perrault, *The Fairy Tales of Charles Perrault*, illus. Harry Clarke, ed. Thomas Bodkin (New York: Dodge Publishing Co., 1920).

2. Emil Haraszti, *Bartók Béla élete és művei* (Béla Bartók's life and works). Cited in Sanders, "Symbolist and Decadent Elements," 30.

3. The principal studies of *Bluebeard* mentioned here are: Kroó, "Duke Bluebeard's Castle," 251–340; Sándor Veress, *"Bluebeard's Castle," Tempo* 13 (1949): 32–38 (Part 1); and 14 (1949–50): 25–35 (Part 2); Ernő Lendvai, "Bluebeard's Castle," in *The Workshop of Bartók and Kodály* (Budapest: Editio Musica Budapest, 1983): 219–45; Elliott Antokoletz, "Bartók's *Bluebeard*: The Sources of Its Modernism," *College Music Symposium* 30, no. 1 (1990): 75–95; and Frigyesi, *Béla Bartók and Turn-of-the-Century Budapest*, chaps. 7, 8. Two additional articles by Kroó focus attention on particular aspects of the opera: "Monothematik und Dramaturgie in Bartóks Bühnenwerken," *Studia Musicologica* 5, nos. 1–4 (1963): 449–67; and "Data on the Genesis of *Duke Bluebeard's Castle*," *Studia Musicologica* 23 (1981): 79–123. See also Siegfried Mauser, "Die musikdramatische Konzeption in 'Herzog Blaubarts Burg,'" *Musik-Konzepte* 22, ed. Heinz-Klaus Metzger and Rainer Riehn (Munich: Edition Text and Kritik, 1981): 66–82; and Carl Leafstedt, "Structure in the Fifth Door Scene of Bartók's *Duke Bluebeard's Castle*: An Alternative Viewpoint," in *College Music Symposium* 30, no. 1 (1990): 96–102. Further studies by Rhodes, Oláh, and others are cited in the bibliography.

4. Lendvai's 1964 study of the opera in his book on Bartók's stage works, *Bartók dramaturgiája* (Budapest: Zeneműkiadó Vállalat), for example, was revised and condensed for the chapter on *Bluebeard* in *The Workshop of Bartók and Kodály*. Left out, among other things, were his analyses of individual scenes.

5. See Kroó, "Opera: Duke Bluebeard's Castle," in *The Bartók Companion*, ed. Malcolm Gillies (Portland, Ore.: Amadeus Press, 1994): 356.

6. Bartók to Márta Ziegler, February 4, 1909, cited in Somfai, *Béla Bartók: Composition, Concepts, and Autograph Sources*, 11.

7. Veress, *"Bluebeard's Castle,"* 44.

8. Lendvai, *Workshop*, 221.

9. Bartók, "Harvard Lectures," *Essays*, 362.

10. Ábrányi's *Monna Vanna*, an opera in three acts after Maeterlinck's drama of the same name, was published in Budapest in 1906.

11. Bartók, "Harvard Lectures," 362.

12. Bartók explained the features of authentic Hungarian folk music in numerous writings throughout his life. A comprehensive review of their essential characteristics can be found in his *The Hungarian Folk Song*, ed. Benjamin Suchoff (Albany: State University of New York Press, 1981), 12–23. See also his essay "Hungarian Folk Music" (1921) in *Essays*, 58–70. The following pages will refer frequently to a "pentatonic" mode. By "pentatonic," I mean the particular mode Bartók discovered in Hungarian folk song, with an interval content m3–2–2–m3 (i.e., A–C–D–E–G). No other modes are implied in my discussion.

13. Antokoletz, "Bartók's *Bluebeard*," 81.

14. Antokoletz (ibid., 78–79) discusses the resemblances between these two operas.

15. Antokoletz provides a slightly different analysis of these opening measures in ibid., 79–81.

16. Lendvai, *Workshop*, 220.

17. In Bartók's autograph full score (FS1, p. 2), he draws an arrow from the stage direction *Hirtelen kinyílik fent a kis vasajtó* (suddenly the small iron door above opens) to the sforzando third beat of figure 2 in such a way as to make clear the precise moment at which the door was to open. Published versions of the opera do not retain his exact correlation of music and stage action at this point, but the sforzando designation remains.

18. Lendvai, *Workshop*, 222.

19. In the Budapest Bartók Archive are preserved two manuscript copies of the libretto for *The Wooden Prince*. One is a manuscript copy of the text in Balázs's hand showing numerous textual revisions by Balázs and another, unidentified individual (not Bartók). The other is a forty-two-page manuscript of the German translation prepared by Balázs, again largely in his own hand, showing minor corrections throughout.

20. Bartók to Frederick Delius, March 27?, 1911. In Carley, *Delius*, 2:70.

21. See the appendix.

22. Bartók's article includes texts and tunes for fifteen songs. "Székely balladák," *Ethnographia* 9 (January 1908; March 1908), reprinted in *Bartók Béla: Összegyűjtött írásai*, ed. András Szőllősy (Budapest: Zeneműkiadó, 1966), 15–50.

23. See Bartók, "Hungarian Peasant Music" (1933), *Essays*, 80–102.

24. Bartók, "Ungarische Bauernmusik," *Melos* 11, nos. 11–12 (June 1920). Translated into English as "Hungarian Peasant Music," *Essays*, 305.

25. Bartók, "Harvard Lectures," *Essays*, 386.

26. Zsigmond László, *Költészet és zeneiség: Prozódiai tanulmányok* (Poetry and musicality: Prosody studies) (Budapest: Akadémiai Kiadó, 1985), 115. In a separate chapter devoted to *Bluebeard's Castle* in this book, László examines the characteristics of Bartók's text declamation.

27. "These eight musicians should be lined up in two groups behind the scenes so that the four trumpeters are near the fifth door, and the four trombonists on the other side of the stage, near one of the other doors. They should hold their instruments horizontally, bells in the direction of the open door (toward the auditorium)" (FS1, p. 63; FS2, p. 77). For undetermined reasons these instructions are not retained in the modern Universal Edition full score.

28. Bartók to Márta Bartók, March 31, 1917, *BBChron*, 155.

29. Judit Frigyesi feels that, ultimately, the entire opera is built upon the two themes with which it opens. Continuous transformation of the motivic and gestural features of these ideas, she suggests, generates all the themes of the opera (*Béla Bartók and Turn-of-the-Century Budapest*, 255).

30. See Ann Besser Scott, "Thematic Transmutation in the Music of Brahms: A Matter of Musical Alchemy," *Journal of Musicological Research* 15 (1995): 177–206.

31. Antokoletz, "Bartók's *Bluebeard*," 85–87.

32. Judith's approach to the sixth door generates another sigh when she turns the lock after fig. 90. Here Bartók employs a different sound, a low F in the strings glissandoing down a major seventh to G♭, to create a groaning effect. (He borrowed this idea from Strauss's *Salome*, where an identical orchestral effect is heard at fig. 303 to the word "seufzend.") The sigh motif can also be found at fig. 24/10 and in the second version of the opera's ending, eventually discarded. See p. 49 in VS1 and pp. 116–17 in FS1. Bartók adds the motif as a decorative contrapuntal line beneath the first statement of the F♯-pentatonic melody, giving it to the violas and the English horn.

33. Bartók to Ernst Latzko, December 16, 1924, *Letters*. Latzko was the conductor of the National Theater in Weimar from 1913 to 1927.

34. On Bartók's relationship to Stravinsky see David E. Schneider, "Bartók and Stravinsky: Respect, Competition, Influence and the Hungarian Reaction to Modernism in the 1920s," in Laki, *Bartók and His World*, 172–99.

35. Bartók, "Harvard Lectures," *Essays*, 370–71.

36. Bartók, "The Folk Songs of Hungary," lecture given in Portland, Oregon, in 1928, reprinted in *Essays*, 338.

37. Ibid.

38. Bartók to Frederick Delius, ca. September 1910, in Carley, *Delius*, 2:58. This letter is also translated in János Demény's collection of Bartók's letters, where it reads "since writing them, I have regained some inner 'harmony'" (*Letters*, 105).

39. Bartók explains how he came to view the flat seventh degree as consonant in "The Folk Songs of Hungary," *Essays*, 335.

40. Bartók to Stefi Geyer, ca. September 1907, *Letters*, 87.

41. Cited in Tibor Tallián, *Béla Bartók: The Man and His Work* (Budapest: Corvina, [1988?]), 66.

42. Jozsef Ujfalussy, *Béla Bartók* (Budapest: Corvina Press, 1971), 88.

Chapter Four

1. Kodály, "Béla Bartók's Opera," 1.

2. An excellent discussion of the opera's introduction can be found in Frigyesi, *Béla Bartók and Turn-of-the Century Budapest*, 253–76.

3. Bartók, *The Hungarian Folk Song*, 12–13. Bartók does not treat regős songs in his book. He only mentions them for the sake of completeness.

4. Kodály, *Folk Music of Hungary*, 3d ed., rev. Lajos Vargas, trans. Ronald Tempest and Cynthia Jolly (Budapest: Corvina, 1960), 77.

5. An example cited by Kodály (ibid., 185) is "Agyon az Úristen ennek a házigazdának," which reads, in English, "May God grant this husbandman / Two little oxen / *Haj, regö, rejtë,* even that has been granted by the great God."

6. On secular monophony in Hungary during the medieval and Renaissance eras, a repertoire largely of biblical, historical, and satirical songs sung by poet-musicians who accompanied themselves on the lute or violin, see Otto Gombosi, "Music in Hungary," in *Music in the Renaissance*, rev. ed., Gustave Reese (New York: W. W. Norton, 1954), 718–19.

7. I am indebted to Judit Frigyesi for bringing this discrepancy to my attention.

8. Béla Bartók, "Székely Balladák," reprinted in Szőllősy, *Bartók Béla*, 15–50.

9. Veress, "*Bluebeard's Castle,*" reprinted in *Béla Bartók: A Memorial Review* (New York and London: Boosey & Hawkes, 1950), 49. Antokoletz proposes an alternate reading of the first door scene's structure based on his belief that the form of some scenes in the opera reflects, on a large scale, the formal properties of Hungarian folk song ("Bartók's *Bluebeard,*" 87–88).

10. Bartók would later employ orchestral techniques similar to these in *The Miraculous Mandarin*, at the moment when the young girl and the three tramps see the weird figure of the Mandarin for the first time. As the girl and tramps see the Mandarin in the street and he starts to climb up the stairs to them (offstage, unseen by the audience), half-step trills and tremolos undulate over a tritone-based series of chords that represent the Mandarin. Shrieking gestures appear in the upper winds. (See figs. 34–36 in the *Mandarin* score.) As in *Bluebeard*, the cause of the characters' anxiety has not yet been revealed to the audience.

11. By asserting the pitch C$\sharp$ as an arrival point, Bartók gives the music a sense of tonality that, in retrospect, can be seen to govern much of the preceding music. Emphasis on G$\sharp$ occurs earlier in the scene, where it alternates with C$\sharp$ as important structural pitches in the chord progressions from fig. 36 to fig. 37. Veress has stated that the first door scene is "maintained in the tonalities C$\sharp$–G$\sharp$, but with sharp harmonic deviations" ("*Bluebeard's Castle,*" Part 2, p. 31).

12. Lendvai, *Workshop*, 219–45.

13. Further prominence is given to C♯ at the opening, when it (with its lower fifth F♯) sustains measure after measure while the underlying trumpet theme shifts among the sharp keys.

14. Veress, *"Bluebeard's Castle,"* Part 2, p. 32.

15. The omitted stage directions are *(nem felel)* (he doesn't respond) and *szünet mulva* (after a pause).

16. In performance, the practical question of how three trumpets can sustain an unbroken D-major triad for several minutes must be addressed. Bartók recognized that this would present difficulties, and in a note at the bottom of page 48 in his 1911 manuscript full score he suggests a solution: the offstage group of four C trumpets waiting for the opening of the fifth door can step in and relieve their orchestral comrades by alternating every six to eight measures. One group fades out to *pp* as the next group enters, and so on to the end. A small accompanying diagram illustrates how this is to be done.

17. Lendvai, *Workshop*, 223. Veress anticipated Lendvai's theory in 1949 by referring to "an effect of imaginary harmonics" caused by the C/C♯ and D/D♯ clashes in the opening moments of the scene (*"Bluebeard's Castle,"* Part 2, p. 32). Kroó refers to the "overtone-series chord" that acts as the "nucleus of the treasure chamber scene" (Kroó, "Duke Bluebeard's Castle," 335).

18. One could quibble, therefore, about whether the scene is "in" or "on" D major. I have adopted the former.

19. Seventh chords and pentatonic chords built on two pitches a fifth apart, such as the A and D here, will share a majority of their pitches. Combined, A pentatonic (A–C–D–*E*–G) and D pentatonic (D–*F*–G–A–C) differ only on two pitches, E and F (italicized). Their other pitches are common to both modes.

20. Judith's D♮'s at fig. 59 in the score represent a printer's error. As indicated by Bartók in all his manuscript scores, including the one sent to Universal for the preparation of the published piano-vocal score, the correct pitch should be a D♭. Bartók did not catch this mistake until after the score had been printed. He entered the D♭ correction in his Handexemplar, now in the possession of the Bartók Archívum in Budapest. This is but one of the many small textual or musical errors that plague the published *Bluebeard* score.

21. Antokoletz, "Bartók's *Bluebeard*," 78; Veress, *"Bluebeard's Castle,"* 38–41.

22. Balázs, "Duke Bluebeard's Castle." See the appendix.

23. Antokoletz, "Bartók's *Bluebeard*," 92–94.

24. Antokoletz (ibid., 91–94) suggests an alternative analysis for this scene.

25. The sentence "Idejöttem, mert szeretlek" is first spoken by Judith in the second door scene; its essential phrase *mert szeretlek* (because I love you) recurs in various guises throughout the drama, most often as a means by which Judith obtains keys from Bluebeard. See Judith's words before the opening of the first, second, and third doors. The other sentence, *Egy életem, egy halálom* (I have one life, one death), is a more specific evocation of Judith's line moments earlier, at the end of the fifth door scene: *Életemet, halálomat, Kékszakállú* (Be it my life or my death, Bluebeard). Repetitions such as these take place across the broader span of the entire drama. Most verbal repetitions are more local in nature, coming in quick succession separated by only a few lines.

26. Used at the first performances of *Bluebeard* in 1918 and 1919, this score is now in the possession of the Budapest Bartók Archívum. See the list of manuscript sources for the opera in chapter 5, where it is identified as the Opera House Score. The pencil annotation referred to here may have been written by Egisto Tango at the premiere.

27. Lendvai, in *Bartók dramaturgiája*, 100–101, discusses the bimodal qualities of the lament.

28. Siegfried Mauser ("Die musikdramatische Konzeption in 'Herzog Blaubarts Burg,'" 77) notes a resemblance between the opera's dramatic form—one act articulated around two distinct dramatic peaks—and general tendencies in early modern and expressionist theater.

29. Balázs, "Duke Bluebeard's Castle." See the appendix.

30. Benjamin Suchoff, *Bartók: Concerto for Orchestra. Understanding Bartók's World* (New York: Schirmer, 1995), 66–67.

Chapter Five

1. Bartók to János Buşiţia, June 6, 1918, *Letters*. Bartók's experiences with his publishers are detailed in Adrienne Gombocz, "With His Publishers," in *The Bartók Companion*, ed. Malcolm Gillies (Portland, Ore.: Amadeus Press, 1994), 89–98.

2. Kroó, "Data on the Genesis." Unless otherwise stated, all references in the present chapter to Kroó's research are taken from this 1981 study. Kroó's research was originally published in Hungarian in 1969. His findings have begun to reach the musical community at large through biographers such as Kenneth Chalmers, who describes the opera's history in *Béla Bartók* (London: Phaidon Press, 1995), 93–95.

3. Kroó, "Data on the Genesis," 109.

4. Kroó, "Duke Bluebeard's Castle," in *A Guide to Bartók* (Budapest: Corvina Press, 1974), 60.

5. The collection of Peter Bartók represents what was formerly known as the New York Bartók Archive and the Bartók Estate, both of which devolved upon Peter Bartók in the early 1980s following the death of Bartók's second wife, Ditta. The majority of the *Bluebeard* sources are preserved in the United States; only one major source (VS1) is found in the collection of the Budapest Bartók Archívum. Bartók brought most of his manuscripts, *Bluebeard* scores included, to America when he moved to this country in 1940. Following his death, these manuscripts became part of the Bartók Estate. Brief descriptions of the manuscript sources not examined in the present chapter can be found in Kroó, "Data on the Genesis," 71.

6. The fate of Bartók's early sketches is discussed in Somfai, *Béla Bartók: Composition, Concepts, and Autograph Sources*, 35.

7. See László Somfai, ed., *Béla Bartók: Black Pocket-Book. Sketches 1907–1922* (Budapest: Editio Musica Budapest, 1987). No secure dating can be made for this sketch, even though the proximity to the *Two Pictures* suggests that Bartók might have jotted the tune down in the summer of 1910, when Bartók was actively working on the *Two Pictures*.

8. Somfai reproduces Bartók's entire 1938 list of missing manuscripts in "Manuscript versus Urtext: The Primary Sources of Bartók's Works," *Studia Musicologica* 23 (1981): 40–41. Bartók's reference to the missing *Bluebeard* manuscript reads, in Hungarian, "Kékszakállú 2-soros skicce." The fact that Bartók refers to the missing *Bluebeard* item as a sketch, instead of sketch*es*, suggests that he was thinking of this score he had given away, not a collection of miscellaneous sketch pages.

9. Somfai summarizes Márta's career as a copyist in *Béla Bartók: Composition, Concepts, and Autograph Sources*, 213.

10. Béla Bartók, letter to Frederick Delius, [mid-July 1911], in Carley, *Delius*, 2:76.

11. Márta Bartók to Béla Bartók, July 15, 1911, cited in *BBChron*, 119.

12. Márta Bartók to Béla Bartók, July 18, 1911, cited in *BBChron*, 119. See also her letter of July 19, ibid.

13. Bartók to Márta Bartók, July 22, 1911, *Bartók Béla családi levelei* (Béla Bartók family letters, hereafter cited as *BBFamLet*), ed. Béla Bartók Jr. and Adrienne Gombocz (Budapest: Zeneműkiadó, 1981), 208–9.

14. His description of these pages corresponds exactly to the first eight pages of the surviving FS1 manuscript. The misplaced gran cassa Márta is urged to correct can be seen clearly on p. 3, where Bartók forgot to leave space in his score for that percussion instrument and wrote its part in the top margin; he places a little star down lower in the system indicating the proper location for the missing instrumental line. Also, Bartók's references to "six-line" and "twelve-line" systems at the beginning of the score match the page layout found in FS1.

15. Bartók's movements and activities during the months of July and August are outlined in *BBChron*, 118–21.

16. Balázs describes this week in his diary. See chapter 1.

17. Bartók to Márta Bartók, August 14, 1911, *BBFamLet*, 214.

18. Bartók to Etelka Freund, August 19, 1911, cited in *BBChron*, 121.

19. Somfai, "Manuscript versus Urtext," 42.

20. The original ending is preserved in two manuscripts, in Bartók's autograph scores from 1911, and (incompletely) in Márta's two copies, where it once existed in toto before being removed or pasted over by Bartók to make way for the 1917 version of the ending. See VS1: 48–49–50 (*not* 48bis and 49bis); FS1: 111–112–119–118; VS2: [65?]–66; FS2: 142 (remainder removed).

21. Scholars have not yet reached a consensus on when Bartók made this first layer of revisions. Kroó estimates that the second ending followed after "an interval of one or two years," probably in 1912 (p. 116). Katalin Szerző Szőnyiné ("'A Kékszakállú herceg vára' szöveges forrásai," 22), after examining the text sources preserved in the Budapest Bartók Archive, concludes that it dates from the fall of 1911—from before or after the competition, however, she doesn't specify.

22. Three manuscripts preserve all or part of the ending's second version: VS1: 48bis–49bis–50; FS1: 111–112–113–114 (also 114A)–115–116–117–118 (*not* 119); Márta Fragment: all six pages. Additional changes to the seventh door scene, mostly of minor importance, are listed in Kroó, "Data on the Genesis," 102–3.

23. Ibid., 104.

24. Kroó, "Duke Bluebeard's Castle," in *A Guide to Bartók*, 62.

25. John Lukacs, letter to the author, January 24, 1992. Regarding this institution, Lukacs explains that the National Casino was the club of the high aristocracy, the Country Casino of the gentry, while the Leopoldstadt ("Lipótvárosi" in Hungarian) was third in rank as well as in chronological origin. Its building still stands in Budapest's Fifth District, at Nádor utca 10—Zrinyi utca 5.

26. Gombocz, "With His Publishers," 92–93.

27. *A Zene* 2, no. 6 (June 1910): 107; *Zeneközlöny* 8, no. 20 (June 1, 1910): 265–66. Information about the two competitions was gleaned chiefly from *A Zene* and *Zeneközlöny*, two prominent music journals in early-twentieth-century Hungary. The latter was the house publication of Rózsavölgyi, at whose firm its editorial offices were located.

28. A search through all issues of *A Zene*, *Zeneközlöny*, and *Zenelap* from the years 1909 to 1912 uncovered no mention of the Lipótvárosi Kaszinó competition. Investigation of other journals and dailies devoted to Budapest's cultural life may yield additional information, however.

29. Balázs, unpublished letter to Bartók, [mid- to late October 1911], Budapest Bartók Archive, BH-N 52. According to his diary, Balázs arrived in Paris on October 11, 1911, and stayed until early 1912. In an undated entry prior to November 1 he mentions assembling the mystery plays for publication (*Napló* 1:529). His letter to Bartók evidently dates from this time.

30. Balázs's revised ending remains unpublished (Budapest Bartók Archive, BH-N-xx). The text begins with the line "Melléjük a negyedik állt."

31. Frigyesi incorrectly attributes this line to Bartók (*Béla Bartók and Turn-of-the-Century Budapest*, 228).

32. The libretto is thirty-six pages long and written in black ink. Its red leather binding dates from the 1960s (Budapest Bartók Archive, BH-IV-400).

33. Márta Bartók to Béla Bartók's mother, February 15, 1912, *BBFamLet*, 217.

34. After the other copyist had prepared his or her portion of the score, to Márta fell the task of assembling the completed product. The entire score is paginated continuously in Márta's characteristic manner, with the page numbers in the upper outer corner of each page followed by a period and a single parenthesis, like this: "102)." Much later, in 1917, Bartók removed the final pages of this manuscript and replaced them with another version of the ending written in his own hand. In the surviving state of FS2, therefore, the copyist's hand appears to break off in the middle of the seventh door scene, after page 142. The last seven pages of the 149-page manuscript are written in Bartók's own hand.

35. The existence of page 142 is a fortunate happenstance caused by its being a verso side to a page (141) that Bartók changed little from 1911–21.

36. Later, before this score was sent to Universal Edition (1920?), Balázs's name was erased and Bartók's own name reinstated on the title page.

37. The unusually high page numbers of the Márta Fragment suggest that at one time these pages were attached to a score of extraordinary dimensions. Only a copyist, paid by the page and writing in a spacious, legible script, could extend a score of *Bluebeard's* scale to 200 pages in length.

38. *Zeneközlöny* 11, no. 4 (November 1912): 153.

39. This is a reference to the simultaneous competition, also sponsored by Rózsavölgyi, for a Hungarian-style orchestral work of fifteen to twenty minutes' duration, first prize for which would be awarded 600 crowns.

40. A capsule summary of Hevesi's career can be found in the editor's notes to Laki, *Bartók and His World*, 274.

41. Information on Opera House production is taken from Zsuzsa Mátyus, "Az Operaház előadásai, 1909–1913," typed manuscript in the possession of the Institute for Musicology of the Hungarian Academy of Sciences. Courtesy Tibor Tallián.

42. Balázs, undated diary entry [between June 2 and July 21, 1912], *Napló* 1:582–83.

43. Balázs, "From a Distant Land," 264–75. Balázs wrote an open letter to Bartók from Moscow to America on this occasion, remembering the spirit of their earlier collaborations. The manuscript is preserved in the Balázs Estate at the Hungarian Academy of Sciences, MTA Ms 5014/55.

44. Balázs, "Béla Balázs: Napló," 7. Similarities between this account and what he later wrote—the stories reuse many of the same words and phrases—suggest that Balázs referred back to his 1922 article when composing "From a Distant Land" in 1941.

45. Bartók to Géza Zágon, August 22, 1913, *Letters*, 124.

46. Bartók to Márta Bartók, [1915], *BBFamLet*, 235–36. Translated in Tallián, *Béla Bartók*, 91.

47. Bartók to Miklós Bánffy, June 17, 1917, cited in *BBChron*, 157.

48. Bánffy, unpublished letter to Bartók, June 21, 1917. The Opera House received the scores by July 17 (Dezső Vidor, unpublished letter to Bartók, July 17, 1917).

49. In the first door scene, Bartók altered the figuration of the shrieking woodwind figures, added a new part for keyed xylophone, and rewrote the chords heard in the pizzicato strings, making them more dissonant. Eight measures were cut from the scene, and the vocal parts were rewritten in several locations. Many of the changes Bartók made to *Bluebeard's Castle* at this time are listed in Kroó, "Data on the Genesis," 105–9.

50. Kroó has counted the number of deleted measures in the opera. I borrow this total (seventy-two) from him (ibid., 108).

51. Ibid., 79.

Chapter Six

1. Kroó, "Duke Bluebeard's Castle," 251–340.

2. See Felix Karlinger, *Das Motiv des "Blaubart" in europäischen Märchen* (Abruzzi: Edizioni Accademiche, 1973); Maria Tatar, *The Hard Facts of the Grimms' Fairy Tales* (Princeton, N.J.: Princeton University Press, 1987); and J. Herzog, "Die Märchentypen des 'Ritter Blaubart' und 'Fitchervogel'" (Ph.D. diss., University of Cologne, 1937). Emil Heckman provides an overview of what he terms "artistic and scientific arrangements of the Bluebeard material" in "Blaubart: Ein Beitrag zur vergleichenden Märchenforschung" (Ph.D. diss., Ruprecht-Karl-Universität zu Heidelberg, 1930), 165–73. See also the Bluebeard entry in Elisabeth Frenzel, *Stoffe der Weltliteratur: Ein Lexikon Dichtungsgeschichtlicher Längsschnitte*, 4th ed. (Stuttgart: Alfred Kröner Verlag, 1984), 101–5. Hartwig Suhrbier's anthology of Bluebeard stories, plays, and fairy tales (*Blaubarts Geheimnis: Märchen und Erzählungen, Gedichte und Stücke* [Cologne: Eugen Diederichs Verlag, 1984]) represents an excellent starting point for study.

3. Bernard Miall, translator's preface to Maeterlinck, *Sister Beatrice and Ariane & Barbe Bleue: Two Plays* (New York: Dodd, Mead, 1910), xiii.

4. Tatar, *Hard Facts*, 164.

5. Author unknown, London [?1860].

6. This translation is taken from *Fairy Tales or Histories of Past Times with Morals* (Haverhill, Mass.: Printed by Peter Edes, 1794). Apart from a few details, it replicates the prevailing English translation of the eighteenth century, established when Perrault's tales were first translated into English by Londoner Robert Samber in 1729. In this form, "Bluebeard" and other tales were carried to the New World, where they were reprinted in New York, Philadelphia, and other urban centers.

7. See Tatar, *Hard Facts*, 159–60; Ernest Alfred Vizetelly, *Bluebeard: An Account of Comorre the Cursed and Gilles de Rais* (London: Chatto & Windus, 1902), 14–16. Mike Ashman briefly discusses these precursors in his essay "Around the Bluebeard Myth," *Bartók Stage Works*, English National Opera guide no. 44, ed. Nicholas John (London: John Calder, 1991), 35–38.

8. Discussions of the Grimms' Bluebeard tale may be found in James M. McGlathery, *Grimms' Fairy Tales: A History of Criticism on a Popular Classic* (Columbia, S.C.: Camden House, 1993), 71–72, and Tatar, *Hard Facts*, 156–78.

9. An index of folk motifs by Antti Aarne and Stith Thompson (*The Types of the Folktale: A Classification and Bibliography* [Helsinki: Academia Scientiarum Fennica, 1981]) lists dozens of forbidden chamber variants from Irish, American Indian, Pacific, and African cultures. Tales based on this motif are the subject of E. Sidney Hartland's study "The For-

bidden Chamber," *Folk-Lore Journal* 3 (1885): 193–242. Kroó, "Duke Bluebeard's Castle," 262–63, summarizes Hartland's study.

10. Tatar, *Hard Facts*, 166.

11. From *Mr. Bluebeard [etc.]* (New York and Chicago: Sol Bloom, 1903).

12. Ernest Alfred Vizetelly, *Bluebeard: An Account of Comorre the Cursed and Gilles de Rais* (London: Chatto & Windus, 1902): 19.

13. Ibid., 19.

14. The ballad may be found in English translation in Nicholas John, ed., *The Stage Works of Béla Bartók*, 23.

15. André Grétry, *Raoul Barbe-bleue* (Paris, 1789). The name Raoul was adopted for another opera produced in Paris, Nicolas Dalayrac's three-act *Raoul, sire de Créqui* (1789). Its libretto, by Monvel, became the standard Bluebeard opera text of its time. Both Simon Mayr and Francesco Morlacchi used it, in revised form, for operas introduced outside France: Mayr's *Raùl di Créqui* was premiered in Milan's La Scala theater in 1810, and in Dresden the following year, Morlacchi's *Raoul di Créqui* (1811) inaugurated his tenure as Kapellmeister of the Italian Opera. Other early stage Bluebeards include an opera by the Czech composer Nesvabda (Prague, 1844), a ballet by Václav Pichl and Peter Winter (Monz, 1795), a pantomime with arias partly by William Reeve (London, 1791), and a dramatic romance with music by Michael Kelly (London, 1798). See Kroó 1961, 265–66. Ludwig Tieck also wrote a short story, *Die sieben Weiber des Blaubart, Eine wahre Familiengeschichte* (1797), which describes how each of the seven wives falls prey to his murdering hands. Its innovation is a leaden head, given to Bluebeard by his fairy godmother, which dispenses sound marriage advice to the lovestruck knight. Because the talking head invariably counsels against matrimony, Bluebeard disregards its words, and finally buries it (Edwin Zeydel, *Ludwig Tieck, The German Romanticist: A Critical Study*, 2nd ed. [Hildensheim and New York: Georg Olms Verlag, 1971]: 81–82). In revised form, both versions of the Bluebeard story were later included in Tieck's *Phantasus* (1828), a compendium of tales, dramas, and legends which formed one of the principal texts of German romanticism.

16. *Barbe-Bleue, composed by Offenbach, with French and English words*. Ditson & Co.'s Standard Opera Libretto. Boston: Oliver Ditson & Co., 1868.

17. The authors of these five theater productions were, respectively, John V. Bridgeman, Henry James Byron, J. H. Tully, Charles Millward, and J. H. Tully with Henri Bellingham.

18. Reprinted in Thackeray, *The Fitz-Boodle Papers, etc. etc.*, The Pocket Edition of M. Thackeray's Works (London: Smith, Elder & Co., 1887), 181–203.

19. Maeterlinck and Debussy reportedly shared a passion for these books. See Richard Smith, "The Play and the Playwright," in *Claude Debussy: Pelléas et Mélisande*, Cambridge Opera Handbooks, ed. R. Nichols and R. Smith (Cambridge: Cambridge University Press, 1989), 15–17.

20. The introduction to Reginald Hyatte, ed., *Laughter for the Devil: The Trials of Gilles de Rais, Companion-in-Arms of Joan of Arc (1440)* (Rutherford, N.J.: Fairleigh Dickinson Press, 1984) offers a concise, factual summary of Gilles's life and crimes, which I highlight here. See also Bossard, Vizetelly, Thomas Wilson (*Bluebeard: A Contribution to History and Folk-Lore, Being the History of Gilles de Retz of Brittany* [NY: G. Putnam's Sons, 1897]), and Emile Gabory (La vie et la mort de Gilles de Raiz, dit à tort babbe-bleue [Paris: Perrin, 1926]); Frances Winwar, *The Saint and the Devil: Joan of Arc and Gilles de Rais. A Biographical Study in Good and Evil* (New York and London: Harper & Bros., 1948); and Leonard Wolf, *Bluebeard: The Life and Crimes of Gilles de Rais* (New York: Clarkson N. Potter, 1980).

21. See, for example, Manfred Frank, ed., *Ludwig Tiecks Schriften* 6, 1347.

22. "Voyage pittoresque dan le Département de la Loire Inférieure" (Nantes, 1823), cited in Vizetelly, *Bluebeard*, 390.

23. Vizetelly, *Bluebeard*, 393, quoting Bossard.

24. Bossard, *Gilles de Rais*, 395.

25. Gabory, *Alias Bluebeard*, 295. Vizetelly, surveying the field of Bluebeard writings in 1902, confirms that "it is only in modern [books] that this appellation is conferred on the Marshal" (*Bluebeard*, 390).

26. Bossard, *Gilles de Rais*, 325–29.

27. Vizetelly, *Bluebeard*, 155.

28. Hyatte, *Laughter for the Devil*, 11.

29. Arthur Charles Howland, "Criminal Procedure in the Church Courts of the Fifteenth Century, as Illustrated by the Trial of Gilles de Rais," *Papers of the American Society of Church History*, 2d ser., 5 (1917): 25–45. The writings of Monod and Reinach are reviewed in Gabory, *Alias Bluebeard*, 297–310.

30. *New York Times*, November 17, 1992, p. A11. The Paris event was also covered by the *London Times* on November 7, 1992, p. 16.

31. Vizetelly, *Bluebeard*, 188.

32. Putnam, *Blue-Beard*, 27.

33. Gabory, *Alias Bluebeard*, 69.

34. Huysmans, *Down There*, 48.

35. Miall, translator's preface in Maeterlinck, *Sister Beatrice and Ariane & Barbe Bleue*, x–xii.

36. Kroó, "Duke Bluebeard's Castle," 273.

37. Reprinted in Suhrbier, *Blaubarts Geheimnis*, 160.

38. Oscar Wilde, "The Ballad of Reading Gaol," in *The Poems and Fairy Tales of Oscar Wilde* (New York: Modern Library, n.d.), 4.

39. France's story originally appeared in the European (Paris) edition of the *New York Herald*, April 12, 1908, under the title "Barbe-Bleue."

40. Ibid., 10.

41. Ibid., 25.

42. Judit Frigyesi (*Béla Bartók and Turn-of-the-Century Budapest*, 218 and 226–28) acknowledges that Judith and Bluebeard possess a blend of traditionally masculine and feminine behavioral traits. This is less significant, in her opinion, than the genderless struggle of the human soul, which desires at the same time to remain hidden and to "allow itself to be seen."

43. Lawrence Kramer, *Music as Cultural Practice, 1800–1900* (Berkeley: University of California Press, 1990), 148.

44. Frigyesi, *Béla Bartók and Turn-of-the-Century Budapest*.

45. See example 3.1 for the full extent of Bartók's cut.

46. Lukács's essay "My Socratic Mask" is translated in Arpad Kadarkay, ed., *The Lukács Reader* (Oxford, England, and Cambridge, Mass.: Blackwell, 1995), 57–62.

47. Lukács formulates this idea in another essay, "Soren Kierkegaard and Regine Olsen," in Kadarkay, *The Lukács Reader*, 17.

48. Lukács, "My Socratic Mask," 61.

49. Susan McClary, *Feminine Endings: Music, Gender, and Sexuality* (Minneapolis: University of Minnesota Press), 4.

50. Kroó, "Duke Bluebeard's Castle," 304–5.

51. Alfred Döblin, "Ritter Blaubart," in *Die Ermordung einer Butterblume und andere*

Erzählungen (Munich and Leipzig: George Müller, 1913). Döblin's story first appeared in *Der Sturm*, the Berlin periodical devoted to expressionist art, Nr. 85/86 (November 1911).

52. Eulenberg, *Ritter Blaubart*, (Berlin: Egon Fleischel, 1905) act 5.

Chapter Seven

1. H. W. Janson, *The Sculpture of Donatello* (Princeton, N.J.: Princeton University Press, 1963), 198.

2. Several studies have traced the popularity of the Judith and Holofernes tale in European literature and art. See Edna Purdie, *The Story of Judith in German and English Literature* (Paris: Librairie Ancienne Honoré Champion, 1927), and Otto Baltzer, *Judith in der deutschen Literatur*, Stoff- und Motivgeschichte der deutschen Literatur, vol. 7, ed. Paul Merker and Gerhard Lüdtke (Berlin and Leipzig: Walter de Gruyten & Co., 1930). A fine general survey of Judiths in the visual arts may be found in chapter 5 ("Judith") of Mary D. Garrard's *Artemisia Gentileschi: The Image of the Female Hero in Italian Baroque Art* (Princeton, N.J.: Princeton University Press, 1989), 278–336. No comparative study of the Judith story in music history has yet been undertaken. Mechthilde Hatz writes about nineteenth- and early-twentieth-century paintings of Judith in "Frauengestalten des Alten Testaments in der bildenden Kunst von 1850 bis 1918: Eva, Dalila, Judith, Salome" (Ph.D. diss., Ruprecht-Karl-Universität zu Heidelberg, 1972), 148–67.

3. Sigmund Freud, "Das Tabu der Virginität" (The taboo of virginity) (1917), in Sigmund Freud, *Gesammelte Werke: Chronologisch geordnet* (Frankfurt am Main: S. Fischer Verlag, 1947; reprint, S. Fischer Verlag, 1972), 12:178–79. Holofernes's decapitation, in Freud's view, represents the symbolic castration of man.

4. Act 5 of Hebbel's *Judith*, in *Three Plays by Friedrich Hebbel*, ed. and trans. Marion W. Sonnenfeld (Lewisburg, Pa.: Bucknell University Press, 1974), 81.

5. Hatz ("Frauengestalten") identifies and describes approximately fifty Judiths from the period 1850–1918. A noticeable concentration occurs in the two decades from 1890 to 1910. The artists include Eugène Aizelli, Fritz Christ, Heinrich Wirsing, Hermann Hahn, and Heinrich Günter-Gera.

6. Keller's painting is reproduced in Oskar A. Müller's catalogue raisonée of the artist's work, *Albert von Keller: 1844 Gais/Schweiz-1920 München* (Münich: Verlag Karl Thiemig, 1981), plate 181.

7. Hans Rosenhagen, *Albert von Keller*, Künstlermonographien no. 104 (Bielefeld and Leipzig: Velhagen + Klasing, 1912), 101.

8. Felix Salten, quoted in Frank Whitford, *Klimt* (London: Thames & Hudson, 1990), 168.

9. Nadine Sine, in "Cases of Mistaken Identity: Salome and Judith at the Turn of the Century," *German Studies Review* 11, no. 1 (February 1988): 9–29, explores the connection between the Judith and Salome figures at the turn of the century. Her study has been an important point of departure for this chapter.

10. This confusion originated when Klimt's first Judith was reproduced in contemporary journals without the identifying frame. See ibid., 9–21. The painting is misidentified in Edward Lucie-Smith's *Symbolist Art* (London: Thames & Hudson, 1972), 195, and Carl E. Schorske's *Fin-de-Siècle Vienna: Politics and Culture* (New York: Alfred A. Knopf, 1980), 226, where it is labeled *Salome (Judith II)*.

11. Friedrich Hebbel, *Judith, eine Tragödie in Fünf Akten* (Münich: Hans von Weber Verlag, 1908).

12. Sine, "Cases of Mistaken Identity," 14.

13. Music for the ballet was provided by Eugène Grassi (1887–1941). Bakst prepared designs for at least two other productions based on the Judith story, including a 1908 Parisian performance of the last act of Alexander Serov's opera *Judith*. See Alexander Schouvaloff, *Léon Bakst: The Theater Art* (London: Sotheby's Publications, 1991), 60–61, 222.

14. Eulenberg, *Ritter Blaubart* (1905); George Bernard Shaw, *The Devil's Disciple* (1897); Georg Kaiser, *Die jüdische Witwe* (1911). The story of Judith also featured in the early history of silent film. In 1913 American director D. W. Griffith produced the full-length film *Judith*, based on a poem by Thomas Bailey Aldrich, in which the epic story lines of the biblical tale were essentially preserved.

15. Judith's uncle, Kurt, uses these words to describe her in act 1, scene 1. August Strindberg, *The Dance of Death*, Parts I and II, trans. Arvid Paulson (New York: W. W. Norton, 1976), 85.

16. I have found no mention of any Hungarian Judith painting or sculpture in the art books I have consulted. Only one Salome was painted by a Hungarian, and then only much later: János Vaszary's 1919 *Salome*. Ilona Sármány-Parsons feels that many Hungarian artists viewed such subjects with suspicion as decadent urban themes ("Hungarian Art and Architecture, 1896–1914," in *A Golden Age: Art and Society in Hungary from 1896–1914*, ed. G. Éri and Zs. Jobbágyi [Budapest: Corvina, and London: Barbican Art Gallery, 1989], 34).

17. Balázs, "A tragédiának metafizikus teóriája," 88.

18. Balázs's interest in Hebbel, and the impact this interest had on *Bluebeard's Castle*, are discussed in my *"Bluebeard* as Theater: The Influence of Maeterlinck and Hebbel on Balázs's Bluebeard Drama," in Laki, *Bartók and His World*.

19. Ferenc Katona and Tibor Dénes, eds., *A Thália története (1904–1908)* (History of the Thália, 1904–1908) (Budapest: Művelt Nép Könyvkiadó, 1954), 49–53, 157.

20. Franz Horch, ed., *Die Spielpläne Max Reinhardts: 1905–1930* (Munich: R. Piper Verlag, 1930), 19. *Judith* received its premiere on February 25 of that year. By Horch's count, in the next season, 1910–11, *Judith*, now a repertory piece, was given twenty-eight performances, only slightly fewer than the previous season. Performances dropped sharply in the 1911–12 season, down to five; in the 1912–13 season, *Judith* was revived for three last performances. Thus, over four seasons from 1909 to 1913, one of Germany's leading theater companies gave seventy-one performances of *Judith*, with the majority of those performances concentrated in the years 1910–11. See also Géza Stand, "Max Reinhardt in Ungarn," in *Max Reinhardt in Europa*, ed. E. Leisler and G. Prossnitz, *Publikationen der Max Reinhardt Forschungsstätte* 4 (Salzburg: Otto Müller Verlag, 1973), 7–31.

21. Ignotus [pseud. Hugó Veigelsberg], "Hebbel," *Nyugat* 3, no. 1 (1910): 552.

22. László Boross, "A Juditról" (On Judith), *Nyugat* 3, no. 1 (1910): 788–90. In the next issue of *Nyugat*, another writer elaborated on points in Boross's review (Vandor Toth, "Még Néhány Szó a Juditról" [More thoughts on Judith], *Nyugat* 3, no. 2 [1910]: 850).

23. D[ezső] K[osztolányi], "Judit: A Nemzeti Színház Bemutatója" (Judith: Premiere at the National Theater), *A Hét* 24, no. 3 (January 21, 1912): 45.

24. Writing reviews for *Nyugat* were Ignotus, Boross, Toth, and Menyhért Lengyel.

25. Kosztolányi, "Judit," 45.

26. Menyhért Lengyel, "Judit: Hebbel Drámája a Nemzeti Szinházban" (Judith: Hebbel's drama at the National Theater), *Nyugat* 5, no. 1 (1912): 287.

27. Ibid., 287–88.

28. The literature on this topic is enormous. See Bram Dijkstra, *Idols of Perversity: Fantasies of Feminine Evil in Fin-de-Siècle Culture* (New York: Oxford University Press,

1986). Shearer West offers a balanced overview in chapter 6 ("Icons of Womanhood") of her *Fin de Siècle: Art and Society in an Age of Uncertainty* (Woodstock, N.Y.: Overlook Press, 1994).

29. Balázs's analysis of Hebbel's *Judith* occupies several paragraphs in "Hebbel Frigyes pantragizmusa, mint a romatikus világnézet eredménye" (Friedrich Hebbel's pantragism, as a result of the romantic worldview), *Egyetemes Philologiai Közlöny* 33, no. 2 (February 1909): 136–37.

30. Ibid., 136.

31. Ibid., 137.

32. Arpad Kadarkay, in his biography of Georg Lukács, details Balázs's obsession with women in a chapter entitled "Don Juan in Budapest" (*Georg Lukács*).

33. Kroó, "Duke Bluebeard's Castle," 303–4.

34. Balázs, diary entry, May 16, 1918, *Napló* 1:309.

Appendix

1. Balázs's notes were translated into Hungarian for inclusion in Balázs, *Balázs Béla: Válogatott cikkek*, 34–37. The present translation is my own, made from this later source. I am indebted to Peter Laki for his help in rendering some of the more ambiguous passages.

2. A reference to the April 10, 1913, staged performance of the *Bluebeard* play in Budapest.

SELECTED BIBLIOGRAPHY

To avoid unnecessary duplication, citations for the many Bluebeard retellings mentioned in chapter 6 may be found in table 6.1. Citations for literary works based on the Judith story are given in the notes to chapter 7.

Antokoletz, Elliott. "Bartók's *Bluebeard*: The Sources of Its 'Modernism.'" *College Music Symposium* 30, no. 1 (Spring 1990): 75–95.

————. *The Music of Béla Bartók: A Study of Tonality and Progression in Twentieth-Century Music*. Berkeley: University of California Press, 1984.

Balakian, Anna, ed. *The Symbolist Movement in the Literature of European Languages*. Budapest: Akadémiai Kiadó, 1984.

Balázs, Béla. "Balázs Béla: Napló." (Béla Balázs: Diary). *Bécsi Magyar Újság* (Vienna Hungarian news), May 21, 1922, 7–8.

————. *Balázs Béla: Napló* (Béla Balázs: Diary). Edited by Anna Fabri. 2 vols. Budapest: Magvető Könyvkiadó, 1982.

————. *Balázs Béla: Válogatott cikkek és tanulmányok* (Béla Balázs: Selected articles and studies). Edited by Magda Nagy. Budapest: Kossuth Könyvkiadó, 1968.

————. "Dialógus a német romantikáról" (Dialogue on the German romantics). *Nyugat* 1, no. 1 (1908): 497–506.

————. "Hebbel Frigyes pantragizmusa, mint a romatikus világnézet eredménye" (Friedrich Hebbel's pantragism, as a result of the romantic worldview). *Egyetemes Philológiai Közlöny* 33, no. 1 (January 1909): 41–55; 33, no. 2 (February 1909): 132–39.

————. "A kékszakállú herceg vára: Megjegyzések a szöveghez." (Duke Bluebeard's Castle: Notes on the text). In *Balázs Béla: Válogatott cikkek és tanulmányok*, edited by Magda Nagy, 34–37. Budapest: Kossuth Könyvkiadó, 1968.

————. "Maeterlinck." *Nyugat* 1, no. 1 (January 1908): 446–54.

————. "Strindberg paradoxonok" (Strindberg paradoxes). *Nyugat* 1, no. 1 (1908): 517–19.

————. "A tragédiának metafizikus teóriája a német romantikában és Hebbel Frigyes" (Friedrich Hebbel and the metaphysical theory of tragedy in the German romantics). *Nyugat* 1, no. 1 (1908): 87–90.

Baltzer, Otto. *Judith in der deutschen Literatur*. Stoff- und Motivgeschichte der deutschen Literatur, vol. 7. Edited by Paul Merker and Gerhard Lüdtke. Berlin and Leipzig: Walter de Gruyten & Co., 1930.

Bartók, Béla. *Béla Bartók Essays*. Edited by Benjamin Suchoff. New York: St. Martin's Press, 1976. Reprint, Lincoln: University of Nebraska Press, 1992.

————. *The Hungarian Folk Song*. Edited by Benjamin Suchoff. Albany: State University of New York Press, 1981.

————. *Bartók Béla: Összegyűjtött írásai I* (Collected writings I). Edited by András Szőllősy. Budapest: Zeneműkiadó, 1966.

Bartók, Béla, Jr., ed. *Apám életének krónikája* (Chronicle of my father's life). Budapest: Zeneműkiadó, 1981.

Bartók, Béla, Jr., and Adrienne Gombocz, eds. *Bartók Béla családi levelei* (Béla Bartók: Family letters). Budapest: Zeneműkiadó, 1981.

Bradbury, Malcolm, and James McFarlane, eds. *Modernism: A Guide to European Literature, 1890–1930*. New York and London: Pelican Books, 1976. Reprint, New York and London: Penguin Books, 1991.

Congdon, Lee. *Exile and Social Thought: Hungarian Intellectuals in Germany and Austria, 1919–1933*. Princeton, N.J.: Princeton University Press, 1991.

Dahlhaus, Carl. *Nineteenth-Century Music*. Translated by J. B. Robinson. Berkeley: University of California Press, 1989.

Dijkstra, Bram. *Idols of Perversity: Fantasies of Feminine Evil in Fin-de-Siècle Culture*. New York: Oxford University Press, 1986.

Dille, Denijs. *Béla Bartók: Regard sur le passé*. Edited by Yves Lenoir. Louvain-la-Neuve, Belgium: Institut Supérieur d'Archéologie et d'Histoire de l'Art, Collège Érasme, 1990.

Flaubert, Gustave. *Salammbô*. New York: Modern Library, 1929.

Frenzel, Elisabeth. "Blaubart." In *Stoffe der Weltliteratur: Ein Lexikon Dichtungsgeschichtlicher Längsschnitte*, 4th ed., 101–5. Stuttgart: Alfred Kröner Verlag, 1984.

Frigyesi, Judit. "Béla Bartók and Hungarian Nationalism." Ph.D. diss., University of Pennsylvania, 1989.

————. *Béla Bartók and Turn-of-the-Century Budapest*. Berkeley: University of California Press, 1998.

Gál, István. "Béla Balázs, Bartók's First Librettist." *New Hungarian Quarterly* 55 (Autumn 1974): 204–8.

Gillies, Malcolm, ed. *The Bartók Companion*. Portland, Ore.: Amadeus Press, 1994.

Gillies, Malcolm, and Adrienne Gombocz, eds. *Bartók Letters: The Musical Mind*. Oxford: Clarendon Press, forthcoming.

Gluck, Mary. *Georg Lukács and His Generation, 1900–1918*. Cambridge: Harvard University Press, 1985.

Halls, W. D. "Les débuts du Théâtre nouveau chez Maeterlinck." *Annales du Fondation Maurice Maeterlinck* 3 (1957): 45–58.

————. *Maurice Maeterlinck: A Study of His Life and Thought*. Oxford: Oxford University Press, 1960.

Haraszti, Emil. *Béla Bartók: His Life and Works*. Paris: L'Oiseau-Lyre, 1938.

Hartland, E. Sidney. "The Forbidden Chamber." *Folk-Lore Journal* 3 (1885): 193–242.

Hatz, Mechthilde. "Frauengestalten des Alten Testaments in der bildenden Kunst von 1850 bis 1918: Eva, Dalila, Judith, Salome." Ph.D. diss., Ruprecht-Karl-Universität zu Heidelberg, 1972.

Hebbel, Friedrich. *Three Plays by Friedrich Hebbel*. Edited and translated by Marion W. Sonnenfeld. Lewisburg, Pa.: Bucknell University Press, 1974.

Heckman, Emil. "Blaubart: Ein Beitrag zur vergleichenden Märchenforschung." Ph.D. diss., Ruprecht-Karl-Universität zu Heidelberg, 1930.

Herzog, J. "Die Märchentypen des 'Ritter Blaubart' und 'Fitchervogel.'" Ph.D. diss., University of Cologne, 1937.

Hyatte, Reginald, ed. *Laughter for the Devil: The Trials of Gilles de Rais, Companion-in-Arms of Joan of Arc (1440)*. Rutherford, N.J.: Fairleigh Dickinson Press, 1984.

John, Nicholas, ed. *The Stage Works of Béla Bartók*. English National Opera Guides, vol. 44. New York: Riverrun Press, 1991.

Kadarkay, Arpad. *Georg Lukács: Life, Thought, and Politics*. Cambridge, Mass., and Oxford: Basil Blackwell, 1991.

Kandinsky, Wassily. *Der gelbe Klang* (The yellow sound: A stage composition). In *The Blue Rider Almanac*, edited by Wassily Kandinsky and Franz Marc, 207–24. New documentary edition, edited by Klaus Lankheit. New York: Viking Press, 1974. Reprint, New York: Da Capo Press, 1989.

Karátson, André. "The Translation and Refraction of Symbolism: A Survey of the Hungarian Example." In *The Symbolist Movement in the Literature of European Languages*, ed. Anna Balakian, 165–82. Budapest: Akadémiai Kiadó, 1984.

Karlinger, Felix. *Das Motiv des "Blaubart" in europäischen Märchen*. Abruzzi: Edizioni Accademiche, 1973.

Katona, Ferenc, and Tibor Dénes. *A Thália története (1904–1908)* (History of the Thália, 1904–1908). Budapest: Művelt Nép Könyvkiadó, 1954.

Kodály, Zoltán. "Bartók Béla első operája" (Béla Bartók's first opera), *Nyugat* 9, no. 1 (1918): 937–39. Translated into English in the Bartók issue of *Books from Hungary: Quarterly of the Hungarian Publishers and Book Distributors*, ed. Imre Kőműves, vol. 3, nos. 3–4 (1961): 1–2. Another English translation is found in *The Selected Writings of Zoltán Kodály* (London: Boosey & Hawkes, 1974): 83–85.

Kramer, Lawrence. *Music as Cultural Practice, 1800–1900*. Berkeley: University of California Press, 1990.

Kroó, György. "Data on the Genesis of *Duke Bluebeard's Castle*." *Studia Musicologica* 23 (1981): 79–123.

———. "Duke Bluebeard's Castle." *Studia Musicologica* 1 (1961): 251–340.

———. "Monothematik und Dramaturgie in Bartóks Bühnenwerken." *Studia Musicologica* 5, nos. 1–4 (1963): 449–67.

———. "Opera: Duke Bluebeard's Castle." In *The Bartók Companion*, ed. Malcolm Gillies, 349–59. Portland, Ore.: Amadeus Press, 1994.

László, Zsigmond. "A prozódiától a dramaturgiáig" (From prosody to dramaturgy). In *Költészet és zeneiség: Prozódiai tanulmányok* (Poetry and musicality: Prosody studies). Budapest: Akadémiai Kiadó, 1985.

Leafstedt, Carl. "Music and Drama in Béla Bartók's Opera *Duke Bluebeard's Castle*." Ph.D. diss., Harvard University, 1994.

———. "Structure in the Fifth Door Scene of Bartók's *Duke Bluebeard's Castle*: An Alternative Viewpoint." *College Music Symposium* 30, no. 1 (1990): 96–102.

Lendvai, Ernő. *Bartók dramaturgiája* (Bartók's dramaturgy). Budapest: Zeneműkiadó Vállalat, 1964. Rev. ed., Budapest: Akkord Zenei Kiadó, 1993.

———. *The Workshop of Bartók and Kodály*. Budapest: Editio Musica Budapest, 1983.

Lucie-Smith, Edward. *Symbolist Art*. London: Thames & Hudson, 1972.

Lukács, György. *Béla Balázs és akiknek nem kell* (Béla Balázs and those who do not need him). Gyoma: Kner Izidor, 1918.

———. *The Lukács Reader*. Edited and translated by Arpad Kadarkay. Oxford: Blackwell Publishers, 1995.

Lukács, John. *Budapest 1900: A Historical Portrait of a City and Its Culture*. New York: Grove Weidenfeld, 1988.

Maeterlinck, Maurice. "The Modern Drama." In *The Double Garden*. Translated by Alexander Teixeira De Mattos. New York: Dodd, Mead & Co., 1911.

———. *Sister Beatrice and Ariane & Barbe Bleue: Two Plays*. Translated by Bernard Miall. New York: Dodd, Mead, 1910.

———. *The Treasure of the Humble*. Translated by Alfred Sutro. New York: Dodd, Mead & Co., 1916.

Mauser, Siegfried. "Die musikdramatische Konzeption in 'Herzog Blaubarts Burg.'" *Musik-Konzepte* 22. Edited by Heinz-Klaus Metzger and Rainer Riehn, 66–82. Munich: Edition Text and Kritik, 1981.

McClary, Susan. *Feminine Endings: Music, Gender, and Sexuality*. Minneapolis: University of Minnesota Press, 1991.

McGlathery, James M. *Grimms' Fairy Tales: A History of Criticism on a Popular Classic*. Columbia, S.C.: Camden House, 1993.

Oláh, Gustav. "Bartók and the Theatre." *Tempo* 14 (1949–50): 4–8.

Perrault, Charles. *The Fairy Tales of Charles Perrault*. Illustrated by Harry Clarke. Edited by Thomas Bodkin. New York: Dodge Publishing Co., 1920.

Purdie, Edna. *Friedrich Hebbel: A Study of His Life and Work*. 2d ed. Oxford: Oxford University Press, 1969.

———. *The Story of Judith in German and English Literature*. Paris: Librairie Ancienne Honoré Champion, 1927.

Rhodes, Sally Ann. "A Music-Dramatic Analysis of the Opera *Duke Bluebeard's Castle* by Béla Bartók." D.M.A. treatise, Eastman School of Music, Rochester, N.Y., 1974.

Sanders, Ivan. "Symbolist and Decadent Elements in Early-Twentieth-Century Hungarian Drama." *Canadian-American Review of Hungarian Studies* 4, no. 1 (Spring 1977): 23–42.

Schorske, Carl E. *Fin-de-Siècle Vienna: Politics and Culture*. New York: Alfred A. Knopf, 1980.

Sine, Nadine. "Cases of Mistaken Identity: Salome and Judith at the Turn of the Century." *German Studies Review* 11, no. 1 (February 1988): 9–29.

Somfai, László. *Béla Bartók: Composition, Concepts, and Autograph Sources*. Berkeley: University of California Press, 1996.

———. "Manuscript versus Urtext: The Primary Sources of Bartók's Works." *Studia Musicologica* 23 (1981): 17–66.

———, ed. *Béla Bartók: Black Pocket-Book. Sketches 1907–1922*. Budapest: Editio Musica Budapest, 1987.

Stevens, Halsey. *The Life and Music of Béla Bartók*. 3d ed. Edited by Malcom Gillies. New York: Oxford University Press, 1993.

Suhrbier, Hartwig, ed. *Blaubarts Geheimnis: Märchen und Erzählungen, Gedichte und Stücke*. Cologne: Eugen Diederichs Verlag, 1984.

Szabolcsi, Miklós. "On the Spread of Symbolism." In *The Symbolist Movement in the Litera-ture of European Languages*, ed. Anna Balakian, 183–89. Budapest: Akadémiai Kiadó, 1984.

Szőnyiné, Katalin Szerző. *"A kékszakállú herceg vára* szöveges forrásai—Újabb adatok a Bartók-mű keletkezéstörténetéhez" (*Bluebeard's Castle* text research—Recent data on the composition history of Bartók's work). *Zenetudományi dolgozatok* (Budapest 1979): 19–33.

Tallián, Tibor. *Béla Bartók: The Man and His Work*. Budapest: Corvina, [1988?].

Tatar, Maria. *The Hard Facts of the Grimms' Fairy Tales*. Princeton, N.J.: Princeton Univer-sity Press, 1987.

Tezla, Albert. *Hungarian Authors: A Bibliographical Handbook*. Cambridge: Belknap Press of Harvard University Press, 1970.

Thomas, Edward. *Maurice Maeterlinck*. New York: Dodd, Mead & Co., 1911.

Vasvary, Edmund, and Marion Moore Coleman. "Hungarian Drama." In *A History of Mod-ern Drama*, edited by Barrett H. Clark and George Freedley, 515–26. New York and London: D. Appleton-Century Co., 1947.

Veress, Sándor. *"Bluebeard's Castle." Tempo* 13 (1949): 32–38 (Part 1) and 14 (1949–50): 25–35 (Part 2). Reprint, *Béla Bartók: A Memorial Review*, 36–53. New York and Lon-don: Boosey & Hawkes, 1950.

Vikárius, László. "Bartók Libretti in English Translation." *New Hungarian Quarterly* 120 (Winter 1990): 158–71.

Wilde, Oscar. "The Ballad of Reading Gaol." In *The Poems and Fairy Tales of Oscar Wilde*. New York: Modern Library, n.d.

Zeydel, Edwin H. *Ludwig Tieck, The German Romanticist: A Critical Study*, 2d ed. Hildesheim and New York: Georg Olms Verlag, 1971.

Zsuffa, Joseph. *Béla Balázs: The Man and the Artist*. Berkeley and Los Angeles: University of California Press, 1987.

INDEX